Hymnwriters 3

Bernard Braley

STAINER & BELL - LONDON

©1991 Bernard Braley
First published in Great Britain by
Stainer & Bell Ltd., PO Box 110,
82 High Road, London N2 9PW

British Library Cataloguing in Publication Data

Braley, Bernard 1924 —
    Hymnwriters 3

    1. Christian Church. Public worship. Hymns.
    Words. English writers - Biographies - Collections
    I. Title

    264'.2'0922

    ISBN 0 — 85249 —789 — X
    ISBN 0 — 85249 —790 — 3 Pbk

Printed in Great Britain at the Alden Press, Oxford

Contents

Preface

This third book in the series on the lives of hymnwriters begins in 1593. It features George Herbert, whose sacred poems were taken up by later generations of Christians and sung as hymns—with alterations, the Wesleys made considerable use of them in early Methodist hymnody—although the Church of England at the time restricted itself to metrical psalms. Herbert's widowed mother entertained regularly during his childhood, with guest lists that show a wide range of acquaintances. Herbert was a skilled musician as well as poet; and would have had the chance to meet composers like John Bull and William Byrd when they visited the Charing Cross home. Two of George's brothers moved in Court circles; and he served for several years as Orator to Cambridge University. His story is interwoven with that of the poet and preacher John Donne, and the founder of the Little Gidding community, Nicholas Ferrar. George Herbert battled for much of his life against ill health; and he was cut off from his brief role as a country parson by early death. His guide book, however, setting out the duties and responsibilities of the country parson, has inspired many who served in this office through the centuries.

The Victorian, Edward Hayes Plumptre is less well-known, and this biography is the first to have been written of him. His epitath might well be, 'He was a brilliant Number 2'; and I dedicate the chapter to all Vice-Chairpersons, committee secretaries and others whose diligent and constant work affect the lives of others significantly for the better. Like the other three subjects in this book, Plumptre was a poet. His verse was widely read but very much belongs to a style which represented a passing fashion. In his quiet way, he played a significant role in the mid-Victorian battles for access to higher education through evening classes; and the opening up of academic learning to women. He was also an able theologian and wrote widely. The eduationalist Frederick Denison Maurice was his brother-in-law. When Maurice was sacked from King's College, London for views about life after death considered by the authorities as heretical, Plumptre continued at the college to provide access to liberal theological views and later wrote an excellent book on the varied views that Christians have about the after-life. Whilst his connection with Maurice almost certainly denied him preferment for many years, he finally served as Dean of Wells and wrote a biography of Bishop Thomas Ken, an author featured in *Hymnwriters 1*. He was a liberal teacher and a conciliator rather than a visionary and these are perhaps less exciting talents about which to read and write. Yet *Thy hand O God has guided*, written originally as a plea for unity of the opposing wings of the Church of England, has been taken up in the twentieth century as an ecumenical hymn.

Robert Bridges, Eton and Oxford, was poet laureate, musician, medical doctor, editor, man of leisure, eccentric, and a Victorian and Edwardian who lived on until 1930. Most of his hymnody consisted of paraphrases of Latin hymns (with additional thoughts incorporated) designed to be sung to early music, the only accompaniment that Bridges considered worthy to be used in church. *The Yattendon Hymn-Book* grew out of the worship of a Berkshire village in the 1890s. In a series of books about the writers of words of hymns, it seemed particularly appropriate to include an author who declared that the music of a hymn was much more important than the words. Robert Bridges directed that no official biography should be prepared of his life; but its varied strands make for fascinating reading.

A twentieth-century writer makes up the quartet. After retiring from a distinguished pastoral and preaching ministry in the Methodist church, poet-parson Fred Pratt Green found himself called to a ministry of hymn-writing in retirement years, leading to a widely-used corpus of texts. Perhaps the most remarkable achievement has been his ability to write hymns which cross denominational boundaries. More of his texts than those of any other living writer are to be found in the recent hymn-book of the United Methodist Church in the United States; it is equally significant that one text was sung at a Papal Mass in Tasmania. Pratt Green recorded the story of his hymnwriting in over fifty scrapbooks, which have been invaluable in writing a biography. With the exception of three late texts, the corpus of hymnody is published in *The Hymns and Ballads of Fred Pratt Green* and *Later Hymns and Ballads and Fifty Poems*. I hope the poems quoted in this biography will lead readers to Pratt Green's poetry as well as to his hymns.

As in previous volumes in the series I have noted many of the tunes which have been used with the authors' texts; and I hope that this book may be used as a starting point for many occasions of informed, lively hymn-singing. I also hope this volume will give pleasure as a dip-in book, particularly so far as marginal and other quotatons are concerned. These glimpses, not only into the work of the subject of the biography, but sometimes covering that of associates from the world of their day, reflect my personal delight in straying sometimes into byways and relishing the discoveries which may whet my appetite for a writer's work or a subject to be further explored.

I am especially indebted to earlier biographers in preparing the chapter on George Herbert. For the essay on Edward Plumptre, I am extremely grateful to the late Mr John Plumptre and his son, another Mr John Plumptre, to the Archivist of King's College, London, and to Mrs. P J Fleming, the Principal of Queen's College, London, for ready access to records and correspondence. The Reverend Dr. Frederick Pratt Green has been generous with both time and information and access to his scrapbooks has been most rewarding.

Thanks are also due to the helpful staff of the British Library, including the Music and Newspaper Libraries, the Guildhall Library of the Corporation of London, King's College Library, and the Libraries of the London Borough of Haringey.

I am indebted to Mr Keith Wakefield and Mr Roland Buggey for their expertise in the field of photography.

Thanks are due to the Archivist and Council of King's College, London, for permission to quote from material in their archives; to the Principal of Queen's College, London for similar permission, for locating and giving permission for use of a photograph from the 1880s, and for use of photographs of the College's formal portraits of Dorothea Beale and Edward Plumptre; to Stainer & Bell Limited for permission to quote from the Preface to *Partners in Praise* (co-published with the Methodist Church Division of Education and Youth), Geoffrey Ainger's *Mary's Child*, Judith Blezzard's *Borrowings in English Church Music, 1450-1950*, Sydney Carter's *The Devil wore a Crucifix* and *Lord of the Dance*, Ian Fraser's *Lord, bring the day to pass*, Fred Kaan's *For the healing of the nations*, Erik Routley's *All who love and serve your city*, Estelle White's *The People of God* (co-published with McCrimmon Ltd) and extensively from the hymns and poems of Fred Pratt Green; to Oxford University Press for permission to quote from *Correspondence of Robert Bridges and Henry Bradley, 1900-1923*, Albert Bayly's *Lord of the boundless curves of space*, Brian Wren's *Praise God for the harvest of farm and of field*; to the Society of Authors as the literary representative of the Estate of John Masefield for permission to quote from John Masefield's *The Everlasting Mercy*; to the Right Reverend Timothy Dudley-Smith for permission to quote from *Tell out, my soul, the greatness of the Lord*; to the Methodist Publishing House for use of the artwork of SUTTON TRINITY; to Mowbray, a Division of Cassells (Publishers) PLC, for permission to reprint in the margin of page 20 an extract from Mr Skipton's *The Life and Times of Nicholas Ferrar*; to the Augsberg Fortress Publishing House for permission to quote from articles by Fred Pratt Green in the *Journal of Church Music*; to Russell Schulz-Widmar for permission to quote from his review of *The Hymns and Ballads of Fred Pratt Green* and for providing a photograph of his wife and himself; to the Hymn Society of America and Canada for permission to quote from an article about John Wilson in *The Hymn;* to Canon Cyril Taylor for permission to quote from a Christmas card to Fred Pratt Green, to the Methodist Publishing House and the Hope Publishing Company for permission to quote from Fred Pratt Green's *Aldersgate Hymn*; to the Reverend Dr Fred Pratt Green for permission to quote from his father's *Verses to his Wife to be, Hannah Greenwood* and generally from his scrapbooks and unpublished notes, also for supplying a family photograph, a local postcard of Venice kept since his honeymoon and a photograph of Elizabeth Shepherd.; and for items, not needing copyright clearance in *The World* and the *Wells Journal.*

In respect of one or two brief quotations, it has not proved possible to trace copyright owners despite considerable effort.

In addition to those already mentioned, the publishers would like to thank the following for their kind permission to reproduce the photographs and line drawings in this book:

Mrs Grace Bayly: 149
Roland Buggey: 11, 20, 63, 69, 78, 82, 85
Sydney Carter: 145
Fred Kaan: 149
National Portrait Gallery, London: 14, 15, 41, 70, 76, 91, 137
Mrs Margaret Routley: 162
Bill Toop: 19
John Tydeman: 122
Keith Wakefield: 55
John Wilson: 155

Bernard Braley
East Finchley, London
February 1991

List of Illustrations

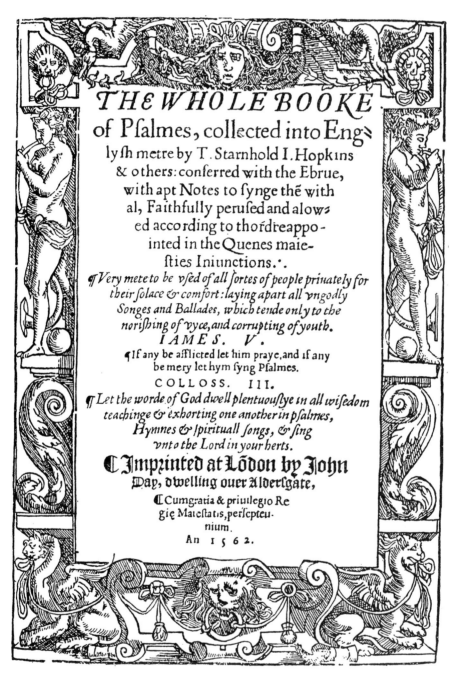

THE WHOLE BOOKE

of Pſalmes, collected into Engliſh metre by T. Starnhold I. Hopkins & others: conferred with the Ebrue, with apt Notes to ſynge thē with al, Faithfully peruſed and alowed according to thofdreappointed in the Quenes maieſties Iniunctions.

¶Very mete to be vſed of all ſortes of people priuately for their ſolace & comfort: laying apart all vngodly Songes and Ballades, which tende only to the noriſhing of vyce, and corrupting of youth.

IAMES. V.

¶If any be afflicted let him praye, and if any be mery let hym ſyng Pſalmes.

COLLOSS. III.

¶Let the worde of God dwell plentuouſlye in all wiſedom teachinge & exhorting one another in pſalmes, Hymnes & ſpirituall ſongs, & ſing vnto the Lord in your herts.

¶Imprinted at Lōdon by John Day, dwelling ouer Alderſgate,

¶Cum gratia & priuilegio Regię Maieſtatis, perſepteunium.

An 1562.

The Whole Booke of Psalmes, 1562 - *the hymnody of George Herbert's time*

George Herbert

George Herbert was born on 3rd April 1593, probably at Black-hall, *a low building, but of great capacity* built by his grandfather in the valley beneath Montgomery Castle. That year, the English Parliament passed an Act against Puritans, King Henry IV of France renounced Protestantism, and the Assembly of Uppsala made Lutheranism the state religion of Sweden.

George Herbert's great-grandfather was ruthless in putting down disturbances around the castle of Montgomery during the reign of King Henry VIII. His grandfather, a Member of Parliament, was present at the storming of St. Quentin in 1557, and later, while Deputy Constable of Aberystwyth Castle, was severe with law-breakers. And his father, Richard, who served twice as Sheriff of Montgomery, as a Member of Parliament, and regularly as a local magistrate, also enjoyed some scholarly reputation in Latin and History.

...of my father, whom I remember to have been black haired and bearded as all my ancestors of his side are said to have been, of a manly or somewhat stern look, but withall very handsome and well compact in his limbs, and of a great courage...

George 's eldest brother remembers their father in his autobiography 'The Life of Edward Lord Herbert'

On his mother's side, George descended from Wenwywyn, Prince of Upper Powys: another forebear was Lord Chief Justice of England until he allowed a prisoner too much freedom of speech in a treason trial and was dismissed by his monarch. His mother.was the daughter of Sir Richard Newport and Margaret Bromley, whose father Sir Thomas was one of the Privy Council and executor to King Henry VIII.

George was the seventh of ten children born to Magdalene: all survived to adulthood, a rare event for the times. When George was three and a half, his father died whilst his mother was pregnant with Thomas. There was no valid will, and Magdalene had to act quickly to obtain Letters of Administration and to make Edward, the eldest son, a ward of her brother and herself, so that income from her husband's estate could continue to flow into the household. As soon as this complicated business was completed and Thomas was safely delivered, she took the children, save Edward, who had returned to his studies at Oxford, to live at her mother's home at Eyton-on-Severn, not far from Shrewsbury.

The father of Mary Herbert, a member of a different line of the family, had determined that she should receive his lands in Monmouthshire and Ireland only if she married someone named Herbert. Magdalene believed that, were her eldest son Edward to marry Mary, his financial future would be secure, and consequently, the wedding was arranged at Eyton for a few days before Edward's sixteenth birthday. Subsequently, it appeared that great debts had been taken on with Mary's estate which Magdalene had to meet. Later, Edward joined the army of the Prince of Orange, served as English Ambassador in Paris, and wrote a major historical work on the reign of Henry VIII. His book, *De Veritate* (*On Truth*), published in 1624, propounded a theory of natural religion which earned him the title of Father of English Deism, as he saw the one God revealed by many faiths. Even atheists were considered by Edward only to deny the existence of God because of the misleading information conveyed by institutional religion. So, after naming several world faiths, he declared *there is a universal recognition of God*. He noted those attributes of God which all religions held as blessed, concerned with the end to which all things move, the cause of all things, at least in so far as they are good, and the means by which all things are produced, eternal, supremely good, just and wise. Edward also wrote a range of poetry, but it lacked the genius of his younger brother George.

Charles Wesley remembered the last line of the first verse of *The Pulley* **when he wrote in his incarnation hymn,** *Let earth and heaven combine:*
Our God contracted to a span
Incomprehensively made man.

When God at first made man,
Having a glass of blessings standing by,
"Let us," (said He), "pour on him all we can:
Let the world's riches, which dispersèd lie,
Contract into a span."

So strength first made a way;
Then beauty flowed, then wisdom, honour, pleasure:
When almost all was out, God made a stay,
Perceiving that alone of all His treasure,
Rest in the bottom lay.

"For if I should," (said He),
"Bestow this jewel also on my creature,
He would adore my gifts instead of me,
And rest in Nature, not the God of Nature:
So both should losers be.

"Yet let him keep the rest,
But keep them with repining restlessness:
Let him be rich and weary, that at least,
If goodness lead him not, yet weariness
May toss him to my breast."

George Herbert: 'The Pulley'

Within a year of Edward's marriage, Magdalene's mother died and her daughter moved house taking George and the other children with her to Oxford, staying there until Edward completed his studies. It seems likely that Mrs Herbert first met the poet John Donne when he visited the University city and a sustained friendship was born; he was to address sonnets to Magdalene and to preach her memorial sermon. In 1601, Mrs Herbert brought her family to London, settling in a sizeable

Come hither Womankind, and all their worth,
Give me thy kisses as I call them forth.
Give me the billing-kiss, that of the dove,
    A kiss of love;
The melting-kiss, a kiss that doth consume
    To a perfume;
The extract-kiss, of every sweet a part,
    A kiss of art;
The kiss which ever stirs some new delight,
    A kiss of might;
The twaching smacking kiss, and when you cease,
    A kiss of peace;
The music-kiss, crotchet and quaver time
    The kiss of rhyme;
The kiss of eloquence, which doth belong,
    Unto the tongue;
The kiss of all the sciences in one,
    The kiss alone.
So 'tis enough.

Edward Herbert: 'Kissing'

...and, as she ever hastened her family and her company hither with that cheerful provocation, *For God's sake let's go, for God's sake, let's be there at the Confession*; so herself, with her whole family (as a church in that elect lady's house, to whom John writ his second epistle), did, every Sabbath, shut up the day at night, with a general, with a cheerful singing of psalms. This act of cheerfulness, was still the last act of that family, united in itself and with God.

John Donne describing the family life on Sundays in a sermon in commemoration of George Herbert's mother

dwelling near Charing Cross. On Saturday 11th April, twenty eight persons joined in a house-warming, and next day, Easter Sunday, twenty-nine sat down to dinner and supper, with only a few names common to the guest lists for the two meals. Clearly, Magdalene enjoyed wide contacts for so varied a company to be present. There were fourteen servants supporting the family and the grounds were large enough for keeping pigs and poultry and for maintaining a vegetable garden.

The daily routine at Charing Cross included house prayers both morning and evening, with Mrs Herbert present at the local church for the Daily Office. On Sundays the family were regular attenders at service, and in the evening there was psalm-singing at home. Mrs Herbert entertained more extensively than might have been expected for a widow and it was rare for dinner or supper to be taken without guests being present. Musicians and dancers sometimes came to entertain: visitors included John Bull, with swan pie on the menu, and William Byrd. George's musical gifts were already in evidence and he enjoyed playing the lute and viol. Besides music, Mrs Herbert also seems to have been diverted by card-playing and once had to send her steward for funds to meet her losses. She followed her mother's practice of generosity in almsgiving: and over the years was openhanded with gifts to the Donne family.

George and his brother Richard spent part of their first London summer with Will Heather, a lay vicar of Westminster Abbey. His house was shared with William Camden, who had served

William Byrd

4

Westminster School from 1575, as Second Master and then as Headmaster. Lancelot Andrewes, who helped prepare the text of the chapters from Genesis to II Kings in the King James' Bible, was installed as Dean of the Abbey. He became a close friend of the Herbert family and went on to serve as Bishop of Chichester, later holding similar appointments at Ely and Winchester.

When Edward came of age, an arbitration award required him to provide an annuity of £30 per annum from his inheritance for George and each of his brothers: and this was to be the mainstay of George's income for many years. But first there were schooldays, initially as a day boy and then as a boarder at Westminster School. Soon after his arrival there was all the excitement of the Guy Fawkes plot to blow up Parliament, of which Edward was a member. The Westminster syllabus at that time laid special emphasis on Greek and Music. Dr Lancelot Andrewes was active in overseeing the work of the scholars, giving them personally of his time. On 3rd November 1606, there was the excitement of another family wedding when Margaret Herbert married John Vaughan in Montgomery.

The Palace of Westminster, circa 1600

In February 1609, George's mother, then in her forties, re-married. The bridegroom was Sir John Danvers, still in his twenties. Hailing from Wiltshire, Sir John was active in the Virginia Company, both as a business venture and on account of its intention to advance the Christian religion in the New World. George was to find in his young stepfather a counsellor and friend. Magdalene did not give up her Charing Cross home: the newly-weds tended to live there in the winter and to spend the summer up river at Sir John's house in Chelsea. Magdalene's new husband loved gardens, and that at Chelsea was laid out in the Italian style. George no doubt often ate dinner in the hall, with one view over the Thames to Surrey beyond and the northward vista to the garden.

George Herbert was elected as a Westminster Scholar for Trinity College, Cambridge, together with his school mate, John Hacket. Herbert was admitted to Trinity in May 1609: when he graduated as Bachelor of Arts, he was second of the 193 bachelors. There seems little doubt that it was in these years George Herbert first met his friend Nicholas Ferrar, founder of the Little Gidding community, then a student at Clare Hall. Herbert experienced indifferent health and, as early as January 1610, when he sent two sonnets to his mother, mentioned recent illness. In 1614, Herbert was appointed a minor Fellow of Trinity College: he became a major Fellow in 1616, when he gained his Master of Arts. Part of his responsibility as a Fellow would have been to oversee, as tutor, the work of a group of students, a duty which involved general oversight of their personal as well as educational needs, care for their health and, as necessary, contact with their families.

The dating of most of George Herbert's poetry is conjectural: his English verse was not published until after his death. But he was certainly writing Latin verse and, most probably, poetry in English throughout his years at Cambridge. Lectures within Trinity College were given by a principal lecturer and four sub-lectors, Herbert being appointed as one of the assistants in 1617. During these years he experienced family bereavement, first with the death of his brother-in-law, John Vaughan, then of his brother Charles, Fellow of New College, Oxford, and his soldier brother, William. Once again, in 1617, Herbert was seriously ill.

One of George Herbert's hobbies was collecting proverbs and other sayings. In his lifetime, he noted down well over a thousand; some years after his death, these were published as *Jacula Prudentum —Outlandish Proverbs, Sentences, etc.*

...You know I was sick last vacation, neither am I yet recovered; so that I am fain, ever and anon, to buy somewhat tending towards my health, for infirmities are both painful and costly. Now this Lent I am forbid utterly to eat any fish, so that I am fain to diet in my chamber at mine own cost; for in our public halls, you know, is nothing but fish and white meats; out of Lent, also twice a week, on Fridays and Saturdays, I must do so, which yet sometimes I fast. Sometimes also I ride to Newmarket, and there lie a day or two for fresh air; all which tend to avoiding of costlier matters if I should fall absolutely sick. I protest and vow I even study thrift, and yet I am scarce able with much ado to make one half-year's allowance shake hands with the other: and yet if a book of four or five shillings come in my way, I buy it, though I fast for it— yea, sometimes of ten shillings...

George Herbert: Part of a letter of 18th March 1617 to Sir John Danvers requesting money to buy books

6

John Donne's sermon at the funeral of Magdalene Herbert gives further insight into George's mother's lifestyle:

...her fortune, her estate, which was in a fair and noble proportion, derived from her first husband, and fairly and nobly dispensed by herself, with the allowance of her second, in which she was one of God's true stewards and almoners too. There are dispositions which had rather give presents than pay debts, and rather do good to strangers than to those that are nearer to them: but she always thought the care of her family a debt, and upon that for the provision, for the order, for the proportions, in a good largeness, she placed her first thoughts of that kind: for, for our families, we are God's stewards; for those without, we are his almoners. In which offfice, she gave not at some great days, or some solemn goings abroad, but as God's true almoners, the sun and moon, that pass on in a continual doing of good, as she received her daily bread from God, so daily she distributed and imparted it to others. In which office, though she never turned her face from those who, in a strict inquisition, might be called idle and vagrant beggars, yet she ever looked first upon them who laboured, and whose labours could not overcome the difficulties, nor bring in the necessities of this life; and to the sweat of their brows she contributed even her wine, and her oil, and any thing that was, and any thing that might be, if it were not, prepared for her own table...

A child's service is little, yet he is no little fool who despiseth it.

A child correct behind, and not before.

A cool mouth and warm feet live long.

A drunkard's purse is a bottle.

A dwarf on a giant's shoulder sees farther of the two.

A fat housekeeper means lean executors.

A man of a great memory, without learning, hath a rock and a spindle, and no staff to spin.

All is well with him who is beloved of his neighbours.

All truths are not to be told.

Better the feet slip than the tongue.

Better to be blind than to see ill.

Between the business of life and the day of death a space ought to be interposed.

Building and marrying of children are great wasters.

Children when they are little make parents fools, when they are great they make them mad.

Cities seldom change religion only.

Comparisons are odious.

Conversation makes one what he is.

Debtors are liars.

Deceive not thy physician, confessor, nor lawyer.

Dry bread at home is better than roast meat abroad.

Every one is a master and servant.

Every one puts his fault on the times.

Every one thinks his sack heaviest.

Everything is of use to a housekeeper.

Fair language grates not the tongue.

Give not St. Peter so much, to leave St. Paul nothing.

Giving much to the poor doth enrich a man's store.

Gluttony kills more than the sword.

Go not for every grief to the physician, nor for every quarrel to the lawyer, nor for every thirst to the pot.

God heals, and the physician hath the thanks.

God keep me from four houses, an usurer's, a tavern, a spital and a prison.

God oft hath a great share in a little house.

Good and quickly seldom meet.

Good horses make short miles.

Good words are worth much and count little.

Good words quench more than a bucket of water.

Gossips are frogs,—they drink and talk.

Half the world knows not how the other half lives.

He hath no leisure who useth it not.

He that is his own counsellor knows nothing sure but what he hath laid out.

He that is not handsome at 20, nor strong at 30, nor rich at 40, nor wise at 50, will never be handsome, strong, rich, or wise.

He that knows nothing doubts nothing.

He that will enter into Paradise must have a good key.

He that will learn to pray, let him go to sea.

He that will not have peace, God gives him war.

...And surely hyssop, valerian, mercury, adder's tongue, yarrow, melitot, and St. John's wort made into a salve, and elder, camomile, mallows, comphrey, and smallage made into a poultice, have done great and rare cures...
George Herbert: From 'The Parson's Completeness' in 'The Country Parson'

The Country Parson is a lover of old customs, if they be good and harmless; and the rather, because country people are much addicted to them, so that to favour them therein is to win their hearts, and to oppose them therein is to deject them...
George Herbert: From 'The Parson's Condescending' in 'The Country Parson'

Hell is full of good meanings and wishings.

Ill ware is never cheap.

In an hundred ells of contention there is not an inch of love.

In the house of a fiddler all fiddle.

Keep not ill men company, lest you increase the number.

Lawsuits consume time, and money, and rest, and friends.

Life is half spent before we know what it is.

Light burdens, long borne, grow heavy.

Love and a cough cannot be hid.

Love your neighbour, yet pull not down your hedge.

No sooner is a temple built to God but the devil builds a chapel hard by.

None says his garner is full.

Nothing lasts but the Church.

Of all smells, bread; of all tastes, salt.

Old wine and an old friend are good provisions.

One enemy is too much.

One father is more than a hundred schoolmasters.

One stroke fells not an oak.

Pardon all but thyself.

Pardons and pleasantness are great revenges of slander.

Poverty is no sin.

Pleasing ware is half sold.

St. Luke was a saint and a physician, yet is dead.

Service without reward is punishment.

...if any neighbouring village be overburdened with poor, and his own less charged, he finds some way of relieving it, and reducing the manna and bread of charity to some equality, representing to his people that the blessing of God to them ought to make them the more charitable, and not the less, lest He cast their neighbours' poverty on them also...
George Herbert: From 'The Parson in Reference' in 'The Country Parson'

The Country Parson is full of all knowledge...But the chief and top of his knowledge consists in the Book of books, the storehouse and magazine of life and comfort, —the Holy Scriptures...
George Herbert: From 'The Parson's Knowledge' in 'The Country Parson'

Slander is a shipwreck by a dry tempest.

Sometimes the best gain is to lose.

Step after step the ladder is ascended.

The best mirror is an old friend.

The fool asks much, but he is more fool that grants it.

The house shows the owner.

The love of money and the love of learning rarely meet.

The offender never pardons.

The shortest answer is doing.

The singing man keeps his shop in his throat.

The toothache is more ease than to deal with ill people.

There is no man, though never so little, but sometimes he can hurt.

There is more talk than trouble.

They talk of Christmas so long that it comes.

Though you see a churchman ill, yet continue in the church still.

Three helping one another bear the burden of six.

Thursday come and the week is gone.

To weep for joy is a kind of manna.

Virtue never grows old.

When you enter a house leave the anger ever at the door.

Where the drink goes in, there the wit goes out.

Who is so deaf as he that will not hear?

Wisdom hath one foot on land and other on sea.
Chosen from George Herbert's 'Jacula Prudentum'

Be covetous, then, of all good which you see in Frenchmen, whether it be in knowledge, or in fashion, or in words; for I would have you, even in speeches, to observe so much, as when you meet with a witty French speech, try to speak the like in English; so shall you play a good merchant, by transporting French commodities to your own country. Let there be no kind of excellency which it is possible for you to attain to which you seek not, and have a good conceit of your wit: mark what I say, have a good conceit of your wit; that is, be proud, not with a foolish vaunting of yourself when there is no cause, but by setting a just price of your qualities; and it is the part of a poor spirit to undervalue himself and blush...
From George Herbert's letter to his brother Henry Herbert in Paris, 1618. Henry was to purchase the office of Master of the Revels at Court in 1623 and to play a significant role in its cultural life.

On 1st January 1618, Herbert prepared on behalf of the University an official letter of congratulation to the Earl of Buckingham when he was created marquis, a duty which foreshadowed his appointment in 1619 as deputy to Sir Francis Nethersole, the University orator (and official correspondent), succeeding to the post in 1620. In 1618, he was appointed by the University as one of the four Barnaby lecturers with responsibility to lecture in English on classical authors for the benefit of first-year students. Although Herbert found life in Cambridge congenial, he seems to have suffered considerable anguish over how he should spend his future. What should his full-time employment be? Should he concentrate his efforts in the field of Divinity? A linked subject was that of money. George found it difficult to manage on the £30 annuity even when supplemented a little with income from academic appointments, the more so as recurrent illness involved the expense of special diets; and books were expensive. He particularly sought the help of his stepfather in ensuring the annuity was not too late in being paid; his sister Elizabeth paid for some of the necessary volumes. His brother Henry also sent books from Paris.

George also maintained contact with his younger sister Frances, making the effort to ride to Lincolnshire, a two-hundred mile round trip completed in a fortnight, to see her.

In 1620, the Scottish Presbyterian theologian Andrew Melville published *Anti-Tami-Cami-Categoria* and Herbert's Latin verses in reply *Musae Responsoriae* seem to have been written principally to defend both University and the Church of England from Puritan criticism. This response angered Melville. In 1622, Herbert was again gravely ill and a Cambridge correspondent wrote: *Our Orator also they say will not escape being at death's door.* He did however deliver that year an oration at the ceremony to confer degrees as Master of Arts on the Ambassadors to this country. Such speeches were far from easy to prepare; there were so many people who might be offended by a carelessly chosen word. His mother, too, was ill that year, and her son wrote to her urging good cheer, reminding her of the consolation of the Lord, and of the possibility of rejoicing even in times of affliction. Herbert particularly directed her to Psalm 55 and 1 Peter 1.7. That year, too, Magdalene lost another son and George another brother in Richard's death at the siege of Bergen-op-Zoom, to be followed in 1623 by the death of his sister Margaret, leaving three orphaned daughters.

At my last parting from you I was the better content because I was in hope I should my self carry all sickness out of your family; but since I know I did not and that your share continues, or rather increaseth, I wish earnestly that I were again with you; and would quickly make good my wish but that my employment does fix me here, being now a month to our Commencement; wherein my absence, by how much it naturally augmenteth suspicion, by so much shall make the more constant and the more earnest for you to the God of all consolation...

From George Herbert's letter to his mother on 29 May 1622

Whilst Herbert was to remain the Cambridge University Orator until 1628, and was to deliver a final oration in person in July 1626, he was from then on to delegate many duties to a deputy. But first, on 8th October 1623, Prince Charles visited Cambridge. The Prince was no stranger to the city: the Court often resided at Newmarket or Royston, neither far away, and from his undergraduate days onwards, Herbert might well have met the Prince. Herbert broke with tradition in delivering an oration which might be described as including a political dimension. The Prince had just returned from Spain, and was looking forward to further military adventures; but Herbert, already bereaved of his brothers in professional soldiering, chose to praise the Prince for having sought peace without thought for his own life. George Herbert's time at Cambridge is memorialized in Trinity College Chapel where he is one of 120 figures in the windows.

**George Herbert (2nd from right) in stained glass window,
Trinity College, Cambridge**

Richard's death in 1622 had left George as the eldest surviving son resident in England: and it was perhaps his mother's indifferent health coupled with her responsibility as co-guardian, with Edward serving in France, for her grandchildren by Margaret that induced George to leave Cambridge. Perhaps, too, he felt a family responsibility to serve for the family seat in Parliament: in November he was named for the Montgomery Borough. Parliament sat from 19th February until 29th May. Herbert served on only one committee, whose principal task was to consider charges made against school or college masters. The Parliament was especially concerned with a crisis in the affairs of the Virginia Company, following the massacre in the colony in March 1622. The business and religious interests in the affairs of the company were perhaps incompatible from the beginning: but at this time the Crown was certainly joined with other forces to destroy the company of which George's stepfather was an active supporter and his friend Nicholas Ferrar the Deputy Treasurer. The company's charter was revoked.

...But, by reason that these infections are not so frequent with us, the horror, I presume, was greater here; for the citizens fled away, as out of a house on fire, and stuffed their pockets with their best ware, and threw themselves into the highways, and were not received so much as into barns, and perished so, some of them with more money about them, than would have bought the village where they died...

From a letter, possibly to the Earl of Dorset, written by John Donne when he was staying at the Danvers' home in Chelsea during the plague of 1625.

Herbert's link with Parliament was short-lived: at the end of the session, the University Senate allowed him six months' leave, needed in part perhaps to organise care for the Vaughan nieces, and partly to determine whether his studies in Divinity should eventually lead to his becoming a parish priest. His mother possibly discouraged thoughts in this direction for fear of George's health not standing up to the task. However, he determined to be ordained deacon and secured the permission of the Archbishop of Canterbury for such ordination not to be delayed a probationary year or to depend on the consent of his own bishop. Bishop Williams of Lincoln was aware that Herbert would be in need of income to replace that from academic life and he was appointed comportioner of the rectory of Llandinam in December.

In 1625, with plague raging in London, John Donne was at the Danvers' Chelsea home recovering from illness, and it seems likely this gave the two poets opportunity for frequent contact. Sometime that year, George's brother Henry married Susan Plomer: and in the early part of 1626, Susan was anticipating the birth of their first child in the spring. Sir Henry's duties as Master of the Revels, and his service in Parliament, kept him away from the Woodford home for much of the winter when George seems likely to have been a welcome guest. George, however, was ill again at this time and prescribed his own remedy after translating a Latin text based on Ludovico Cornaro's *Trattato de la Vita sobria*, written in the author's eighty-fourth year, which urges a restricted diet, with each item carefully weighed. In June, Herbert's friend Nicholas Ferrar, freed from his duties with the defunct Virginia Company, was ordained deacon in Westminster Abbey, and the following month, almost co-incident with his oratorial duties on the installation of Cambridge University's new Chancellor, Herbert was installed by proxy as Canon of Lincoln Cathedral and Canon of Leighton Ecclesia. The church at Leighton Bromswold in Huntingdonshire was in so bad a state of repair that services were held in the Manor Hall and Herbert became dedicated to its restoration. In this he was encouraged, perhaps, by Nicholas Ferrar who, not far away at Little Gidding, had set up with his family a religious community, which emphasised the supernatural joy, even in affliction, that is the experience of the true Christian.

At this time, George Herbert was also in touch with Izaak Walton and Francis Bacon. Ironmonger Izaak Walton was much more interested in the world of books than the world of commerce and besides the classic, *The Compleat Angler*, was to leave us biographies including those of Herbert and Donne.

...and I purposed to try whether those that pleased my taste brought me commodity or discommodity; and whether that proverb, wherewith gluttons used to defend themselves, to wit, *That which savours, is good and nourisheth*, be consonant to truth. This upon trial I found most false; for strong and very cool wines pleased my taste best, as also melons and other fruit; in like manner, raw lettuce, fish, pork, sausages, pulse, and cake and piecrust, and the like: and yet all these I found hurtful. Therefore, trusting on experience, I forsook all these kind of meats and drinks...

...It is not the part of a wise man to expose himself to so many dangers of diseases and death, only upon a hope of a happy issue, which yet befalls very few. An old man of an ill constitution, but living orderly, is more sure of life than the most strong young man who lives disorderly.

But some, too much given to appetite, object that a long life is no such desirable thing, because that after one is once sixty-five years old, all the time we live after is rather death than life; but these err greatly, as I will show by myself, recounting the delights and pleasures in this age of eighty-three which now I take, and which are such as that men generally account me happy.

I am continually in health, and I am so nimble that I can easily get on horseback without the advantage of the ground, and sometimes I go up high stairs and hills on foot...

Lud Cornarus (or Ludovico Cornaro) as translated by George Herbert: From 'A Treatise of Temperance and Sobriety'

Bacon, the philosopher-politician, had just fallen from grace, having been convicted of receiving gifts from suitors who had appeared before him. Although he had been fined £40,000 by the House of Lords and sentenced to life imprisonment, he had been allowed to return to the family home at Gorhambury, near Saint Albans, after serving only a short period in the Tower of London. At this time then, George Herbert was surrounded by almost a surfeit of creative and deeply-thinking minds.

A COLLECTION OF QUOTATIONS CHOSEN FROM THE SERMONS OF JOHN DONNE

Between these two, the denying of sins, which we have done, and the bragging of sins, which we have not done, what a space, what a compass is there, for millions of millions of sins. *(1618)*

The distance from nothing to a little, is ten thousand times more, than from it to the highest degree in this life. *(1619)*

All our life is but a going out to the place of execution, to death. *(1619)*

As he that fears God fears nothing else, so, he that sees God sees everything else. *(c.1620)*

As peace is of all goodness, so war is an emblem, a hieroglyphic, of all misery. *(1622)*

God himself took a day to rest in, and a good man's grave is his Sabbath. *(1622)*

True joy is the earnest which we have of heaven, it is the treasure of the soul, and therefore should be laid in a safe place, and nothing in this world is safe to place it. *(c.1624)*

In what torn ship soever I embark,
That ship shall be my emblem of thy Ark;
What sea soever swallow me, that flood
Shall be to me an emblem of thy blood;
Though thou with clouds of anger do disguise
Thy face; yet through that mask I know those eyes,
      Which, though they turn away sometimes,
         They never will despise.

I sacrifice this Island unto thee,
And all whom I lov'd there, and who lov'd me;
When I have put our seas twixt them and me,
Put thou thy sea betwixt my sins and thee.
As the trees sap doth seek the root below
In winter, in my winter now I go,
      Where none but thee, th' Eternal root
        Of true Love I may know.

Nor thou nor thy religion dost control
The amorousness of an harmonious soul,
But thou would'st have that love thy self: As thou
Art jealous, Lord, so I am jealous now.
Thou lov'st not, till from loving more, thou free
My soul: who ever gives, takes liberty:
      O if thou car'st not whom I love
        Alas, thou lov'st not me.

Seal then this bill of my divorce to all,
On whom these fainter beams of love did fall:
Marry those loves which in youth scattered be
On fame, wit, hopes (false mistresses) to thee.
Churches are best for prayer, that have least light:
To see God only, I go out of sight:
      And to scape stormy days, I chose
        An everlasting night.
John Donne: 'A Hymne to Christ, at the Author's last going into Germany'

John Donne

From the writings of Francis Bacon:

Prosperity is the blessing of the Old Testament, adversity is the blessing of the New.

Of Adversity

God never wrought miracle to convince atheism, because his ordinary works convince it.

Atheism

A crowd is not company, and faces but a gallery of pictures, and talk but a tinkling cymbal, where there is no love.

Of Friendship

The inquiry of truth, which is the love-making, or wooing of it, the knowledge of truth, which is the presence of it, and the belief of truth, which is the enjoying of it, is the sovereign good of human nature.

Of Truth

But men must know, that in this theatre of man's life, it is reserved only for God and angels to be lookers on.

Advancement of Learning

Nature cannot be ordered about, except by obeying her.

Advancement of Learning

The end of our foundation is the knowledge of causes, and secret motions of things; and the enlarging of the bounds of human Empire, to the effecting of all things possible.

New Atlantis

The knowledge of man is as the waters, some descending from above, and some springing from beneath; the one informed by the light of nature, the other inspired by divine revelation.

Advancement of Learning

Man is not only a contributary creature, but a total creature; he does not only make one, but he is all; he is not a piece of the world, but the world itself; and next to the glory of God, the reason why there is a world. *(1625)*

As states subsist in part by keeping their weaknesses from being known, so is it in the quiet of families to have their chancery and their parliament within doors, and to compose and determine all emergent differences there. *(1625)*

Christ beats his drum, but he does not press men; Christ is served with voluntaries. *(1626)*

I neglect God and his angels for the noise of a fly, for the rattling of a coach, for the whining of a door. *(1626)*

Words Izaak Walton was to write later in *The Compleat Angler*

Good company and good discourse are the very sinews of virtue.

I love such mirth as does not make friends ashamed to look upon one another next morning.

There are offences given and offences not given but taken.

No man can lose what he never had.

Francis Bacon

16

    Philosophers have measured mountains,
Fathomed the depths of seas, of states, and kings,
Walked with a staff to heav'n, and tracèd fountains:
    But there are two vast, spacious things,
The which to measure it doth more behove;
Yet few there are that sound them, —Sin and Love.

    Who would know Sin, let him repair
Unto Mount Olivet: there shall he see
A Man so wrung with pains, that all his hair,
    His skin, his garments bloody be.
Sin is that press and vice, which forceth pain
To hurt his cruel food through ev'ry vein.

    Who knows not Love, let him assay
And taste that juice which on the cross a pike
Did set again abroach; then let him say
    If ever he did taste the like.
Love is that liquor, sweet and most divine,
Which my God feels as blood, but I as wine.

George Herbert: 'The Agony'

    O who will show me those delights on high?
Echo: *I.*
Thou Echo, thou art mortal, all men know.
Echo: *No.*
Wert thou not born among the trees and leaves?
Echo: *Leaves.*
And are there any leaves that still abide?
Echo: *Bide.*
What leaves are they? impart the matter wholly.
Echo: *Holy.*
Are holy leaves the echo then of bliss?
Echo: *Yes.*
Then tell me what is that supreme delight?
Echo: *Light.*
Light to the mind: what shall the will enjoy?
Echo: *Joy.*
But are there cares and business with the pleasure?
Echo   *Leisure.*
Light, joy, and leisure; but shall they persèver?
Echo: *Ever.*

George Herbert: 'Heaven'

POEMS OF GEORGE HERBERT SUNG AS HYMNS

Let all the world in every corner sing,
  My God and King.

The heavens are not too high,
His praise may thither fly;
The earth is not too low,
His praises there may grow.

Let all the world in every corner sing,
  My God and King.

The church with psalms must shout,
No door can keep them out;
But, above all, the heart
Must bear the longest part.

Let all the world in every corner sing,
  My God and King.
      George Herbert: 'Antiphon'.
Sung (with variations on the use of the chorus) to
LUCKINGTON, WILTON (Button), HIGH ROAD,
UNIVERSAL PRAISE and AUGUSTINE (Routley).

It is surprising how few settings of the *Antiphon* have used its original antiphonal structure. It was ignored in *Church Hymns (1871)* although Godfrey Thring included the text in its original form in his *Collection* of 1882.

The God of love my Shepherd is,
    And He that doth me feed:
While He is mine, and I am His,
    What can I want or need?

He leads me to the tender grass,
    Where I both feed and rest;
Then to the streams that gently pass:
    In both I have the best.

Or if I stray, He doth convert,
    And bring my mind in frame,
And all this not for my desert,
    But for His holy name

Yea, in death's shady black abode
    Well may I walk, not fear;
For Thou art with me, and Thy rod
    To guide, Thy staff to bear.

Nay, Thou dost make me sit and dine,
    E'en in my enemies' sight;
My head with oil, my cup with wine
    Runs over day and night.

Surely Thy sweet and wondrous love
    Shall measure all my days;
And as it never shall remove,
    So neither shall my praise.
George Herbert: 'The Twenty-third Psalm.' Sung to
UNIVERSITY and SAINT COLUMBA [Irish] (ERIN)

George Rawson was to choose some Herbert texts for the *Leeds Hymn Book* in 1853, but, like the Wesleys before him, thought he could improve on the originals. His opening verse for this text was:

The God of love my Shepherd is
    To watch me and to feed;
Since He is mine and I am His,
    What ever can I need?

18

For as the rule of all her civil actions was religion, so the rule of her religion was the Scripture; and her rule for her particular understanding of the Scripture was the church. She never diverted towards the Papist in under-valuing the Scripture, nor towards the Separatist in undervaluing the church: but in the doctrine and discipline of that church in which God sealed her to himself in baptism, she brought up her children, she assisted her family, she dedicated her soul to God in her life, and surrendered it to him in her death; and in that form of common prayer which is ordained by that church, and to which she had accustomed herself with her family twice every day, she joined with that company which was about her death-bed, in answering to every part thereof, which the congregation is directed to answer to, with a clear understanding, with a constant memory, with a distinct voice, not two hours before she died.

From John Donne's sermon at the funeral of Magdalene Danvers née Herbert

---

Christian:
Alas, poor Death! where is thy glory?
Where is thy famous force, thy ancient sting?

Death:
Alas, poor mortal, void of story!
Go spell and read how I have killed thy King.

Christian:
Poor Death! and who was hurt thereby?
The curse being laid on Him makes thee accurst.

Death:
Let losers talk, yet thou shalt die;
These arms shall crush thee.

Christian:
        Spare not, do thy worst.
I shall be one day better than before;
Thou so much worse, that thou shalt be no more.
George Herbert: 'A Dialogue-Anthem: Christian, Death'

In 1627 George Herbert mourned in Latin verse the death of his mother to whom he owed his early education and love of literature and religion. Shortly afterwards, lands in Worcestershire were granted by the Crown to George, his elder brother, and a cousin: these were sold to Henry, and George's share of the proceeds amounted to £1,000. For the first time in his life, Herbert experienced financial independence. Part of the windfall was invested with the printer Philemon Stevens and Herbert may well have used some for the fund to restore the church at Leighton Bromswold. In 1628 his stepfather remarried and Herbert found a home with his stepfather's brother, the Earl of Danby, at Dauntsey, a few miles north-east of Chippenham in Wiltshire. Some twenty miles to the south lay the village and ancient settlement of Edington, mentioned in King Alfred's will. Jane Danvers, a cousin of George's stepfather, lived with her parents at Baynton House in that parish. George and Jane met, fell in love, and were married in the twelfth-century church, often considered the best example of the Perpendicular Style in Wiltshire, on 5th March 1629.

If Thou dost give me wealth, I will restore
  All back unto Thee by the poor;
If Thou dost give me honour, men shall see
  The honour doth belong to Thee.
I will not marry; or, if she be mine,
  She and her children shall be Thine...
George Herbert: Lines from 'The Thanksgiving'

Edington Church

They rose at four; at five went to the oratory to prayers; at six said the psalms of the hour (for every hour had its appointed psalms), with some portion of the Gospel, till Mr. Ferrar had finished his Concordance, when a chapter of that work was substituted in place of the portion of the Gospel. Then they sang a short hymn, repeated some passages of Scripture, and at half-past six went to church to matins. At seven said the psalms of the hour, sang the short hymn, and went to breakfast. Then the young people repaired to their respective places of instruction. The old gentlewoman took her chair, inspecting her daughters and grandchildren as they sat at their books or other good employments in great silence, or at least avoiding all vain talking and jesting that was not convenient. No hour but had its business. Eight, nine, ten o'clock came, those hours had their several companies, that came and did as at former hours: psalms said and a head of the Concordance, the organs playing, the hymn sung at each hour, as the clock struck, that gave notice to all of the time passing. At ten, to the church to Litany every day of the week, as their bishop had given them leave. At eleven to dinner (after saying the hourly office). At which seasons were regular readings in rotation, from the Scripture, from the Book of Martyrs, and from short histories drawn up by Mr. Ferrar, and adapted to the purpose of moral instruction. Recreation was permitted till one; then the bell tolled for the boys to school, and those that had their turns came up into the great chamber again, to say their psalms and head of Concordance, sing a hymn and play on the organ whilst they sang. There old Mrs. Ferrar commonly sat till four o'clock, and, as before, each hour had its performance. Church at four for Evensong; supper at five or sometimes six. Diversions till eight. Then prayers in the oratory, where a hymn was sung, the organs playing, and afterwards all retired to their respective apartments.

Herbert's principal duty as a Canon of Lincoln Cathedral was to preach the Whit Sunday sermon there, a role he possibly undertook in person (though a deputy would have been allowed), combining the occasion with a visit to his sister Frances, his friend Nicholas Ferrar at Little Gidding, and the church of Leighton Bromswold. Nicholas Ferrar's lifestyle as a leader of this family community was a remarkable change from his earlier experience as a man of affairs. There were some forty members, rather more than half children from his own family, and that of his brother John and sister Susanne. His mother also was a member of the community. There were three schoolmasters charged respectively with teaching the children English and Latin (with an additional role of teaching English to strangers); good writing in all its branches; and singing and playing of the organ, viols and lute. Amongst other neighbourhood roles, Nicholas also used his medical knowledge to good effect. The daily routine is described in the margin, save that breakfast would have been for children and invalids only; and, after consulting with Herbert and others, regular watches were also kept through the night, where the psalms were recited antiphonally every four hours with the watchers on their knees.

Saint Andrew's Church, Bemerton

George and his new wife lived for a time at Baynton House with Jane's mother, now widowed. A little more than a year after his marriage, George Herbert was presented by the Crown with the living of Fugglestone-with-Bemerton near Salisbury and on 26th April 1630 was instituted Rector of Bemerton at Saint Andrew's Church. The Rectory, like the church, was in need of some repair; consequently it was a few months before the Herberts moved into their new home. On 19th September, Herbert was ordained priest and able to fulfil all the duties of an ordained man: curiously his curate was ordained priest a little earlier, on 23rd May. Each day would include the daily offices at ten and four; and Herbert celebrated the Holy Communion more frequently than the minimal three times a year practised in some Anglican churches.

> I cannot ope mine eyes,
> But Thou art ready there to catch
> My morning soul and sacrifice;
> That we must needs for that day make a match.
>
> My God, what is a heart?
> Silver, or gold, or precious stone,
> Or star, or rainbow, or a part
> Of all these things, or all of them in one?
>
> My God, what is a heart,
> That Thou shouldst it so eye, and woo,
> Pouring upon it all Thy art,
> As if that Thou hadst nothing else to do?
>
> Indeed, man's whole estate
> Amounts (and richly) to serve Thee;
> He did not heav'n and earth create,
> Yet studies them, not Him by whom they be.
>
> Teach me Thy love to know;
> That this new light, which now I see,
> May both the work and workman show,
> Then by a sunbeam I will climb to Thee.
>
> *George Herbert: 'Matins'*

...I visited Bemerton, and had the pleasure of officiating within the walls of that celebrated little church. The rector kindly showed me the whole Parsonage House; the parts rebuilt by Herbert were traceable... It may truly be said to stand near the Chapel, ...being distant only the width of the road, thirty-four feet, which in Herbert's time was forty feet, as the building shows. On the south is a grass-plat sloping down to the river, whence is a beautiful view of Sarum Cathedral in the distance. A very aged fig-tree grows against the end of the house, and a medlar in the garden, both, traditionally, planted by Herbert.

The whole length and breadth of the church is forty-five feet by eighteen. The south and west windows are of the date called Decorated, say 1300... A little square western turret contains an ancient bell of the fourteenth century (diameter, twenty-four inches), the daily sound of which used to charm the ploughmen from their work, that they *might offer their devotions to God with him.*

H.T. Ellacombe in a letter to 'Notes and Queries', 25th November 1850

George Herbert took his duties as a country parson very seriously. He carefully considered his role, and in doing so created a book, published posthumously, entitled *A Priest to the Temple* or *The Country Parson, his Character and Rule of Life.* Even the chapter headings show the width of his thinking . The book gives us a picture too of his own life-style at Bemerton.

Being desirous (through the mercy of God) to please Him, for Whom I am and live, and Who giveth me my desires and performances; and considering with myself that the way to please Him is to feed my flock diligently and faithfully, since our Saviour hath made that the argument of a pastor's love, I have resolved to set down the form and character of a true pastor, that I may have a mark to aim at, which also I will set as high as I can, since he shoots higher that threatens the moon, than he that aims at a tree. Not that I think, if a man do not all which is here expressed, he presently sins and displeases God; but that it is a good strife to go as far as we can in pleasing Him who hath done so much for us. The Lord prosper the intention to myself and others, who may not despise my poor labours, but add to those points, which I have observed, until the book grow to a complete pastoral.

George Herbert: From the preface to 'A Priest to the Temple' or'The Country Parson'

The Country Parson

...is exceeding exact in his life, being holy, just, prudent,temperate, bold, grave, in all his ways. And because the two highest points of life, wherein a Christian is most seen, are patience and mortification; patience in regard of afflictions—mortification in regard of lusts and affections, and the stupefying and deading of all the clamorous powers of the soul; therefore he hath throughly studied these, that he may be an absolute master and commander of himself, for all the purposes which God hath ordained him... (*The Parson's Life*)

...because country people live hardly, and therefore, as feeling their own sweat, and consequently knowing the price of money, are offended much with any who by hard usage increase their travail, the country parson is very circumspect in avoiding all covetousness, neither being greedy to get, nor niggardly to keep, nor troubled to lose any worldly wealth...(*The Parson's Life*)

...condescends even to the knowledge of tillage and pasturage, and makes great use of them in teaching, because people by what they understand are best led to what they understand not... (*The Parson's Knowledge*)

...because luxury is a very visible sin, the parson is very careful to avoid all the kinds thereof, but especially that of drinking, because it is the most popular vice...(*The Parson's Life*)

...in his house observes fasting days, and particularly...Friday his day of humiliation, which he celebrates not only with abstinence of diet, but also of company, recreation, and all outward contentments, and besides, with confession of sins and all acts of mortification... (*The Parson in his House*)

...as soon as he awakes on Sunday morning, presently falls to work, and seems to himself so as a market man is when the market day comes, or a shopkeeper when customers use to come in... (*The Parson on Sundays*)

...on Sunday...having read Divine Service twice fully, and preached in the morning, and catechized in the afternoon, he thinks he hath in some measure, according to poor and frail man, discharged the public duties of the congregation. The rest of the day he spends either in reconciling neighbours that are at variance, or in visiting the sick, or in exhortations to some of his flock by themselves, whom his sermons cannot or do not reach...(*The Parson on Sundays*)

...But specially at hard times and dearths, he even parts his living and life among them, giving some corn outright, and selling other at under rates...(*The Parson's Charity*)

...if there be any of his parish that hold strange doctrines, useth all possible diligence to reduce them to the common faith...(*The Parson's Arguing*)

...is generally sad, because he knows nothing but the Cross of Christ, his mind being defixed on it with those nails wherewith his Master was; or if he have any leisure to look off from thence, he meets continually with two most sad spectacles, sin and misery; God dishonoured every day, and man afflicted. Nevertheless, he sometimes refresheth himself, as knowing that nature will not bear everlasting droopings, and that pleasantness of disposition is a great key to do good; not only because all men shun the company of perpetual severity, but also for that when they are in company, instructions seasoned with pleasantness both enter sooner and root deeper... (*The Parson in Mirth*)

...when he is to read divine services composeth himself to all possible reverence, lifting up his heart and hands and eyes, and using all other gestures which may express a hearty and unfeigned devotion. This he doth, first, as being truly touched and amazed with the majesty of God, before whom he then presents himself; yet not as himself alone, but as presenting with himself the whole congregation, whose sins he then bears, and brings with his own to the heavenly altar to be bathed and washed in the sacred laver of Christ's blood... (*The Parson praying*)

...preacheth constantly: the pulpit is his joy and his throne...The parson exceeds not an hour in preaching, because...all ages have thought that a competency, and he that profits not in that time, will less afterwards, the same affection which made him not profit before making him then weary, and so he grows from not relishing to loathing. (*The Parson preaching*)

A pastor is the deputy of Christ, for the reducing of man to the obedience of God.
George Herbert: From 'Of a Pastor' in 'The Country Parson'

...If he be married, the choice of his wife was made rather by his ear than by his eye; his judgment, not his affection, found out a fit wife for him, whose humble and liberal disposition he preferred before beauty, riches or honour...
George Herbert: From 'The Parson's State of Life' in 'The Country Parson'

His wife is either religious, or night and day he is winning her to it. Instead of the qualities of the world, he requires only three of her: First, a training up of her children and maids in the fear of God, with prayers, and catechizing, and all religious duties. Secondly, a curing and healing of all wounds and sores with her own hands, which skill either she brought with her, or he takes care she shall learn it of some religious neighbour. Thirdly, a providing for her family in such sort as that neither they want a competent sustenation nor her husband be brought into debt.
George Herbert: From 'The Parson in his House' in 'The Country Parson'

...owing a debt of charity to the poor and of courtesy to his other parishoners, he so distinguiseth, that he keeps his money for the poor, and his table for those that are above alms. Not but that the poor are welcome also at his table, whom he sometimes purposely takes home with him, setting them close by him, and carving for them, both for his own humility and their comfort, who are much cheered with such friendliness. But since both is to be done, the better sort invited, and meaner relieved, he chooseth rather to give the poor money, which they can better employ to their own advantage, and suitably to their needs, than so much given in meat at dinner. (*The Parson's Courtesy*)

Drink not the third glass which thou canst not tame, When once it is within thee.
George Herbert: From 'The Church Porch'

...hath a special care of his church...he takes order that all things be in good repair; as walls plastered, windows glazed, floor paved, seats whole, firm, and uniform, especially that the pulpit, and desk, and communion table, and font, be as they ought for those great duties that are performed in them...the church be swept and kept clean, without dust or cobwebs, and at great festivals strewed and stuck with boughs, and perfumed with incense...there be fit and proper texts of Scripture everywhere painted...all the books...not torn or fouled, but whole, and clean and well bound... (*The Parson's Church*)

...Now, as the parson is in law, so is he in sickness also; if there be any of his flock sick, he is their physician, or at least his wife, of whom, instead of qualities of the world, he asks no other but to have the skill of healing a wound or helping the sick. But if neither himself nor his wife have the skill, and his means serve, he keeps some young practitioner in his house for the benefit of his parish...If all fail, then he keeps good correspondence with some neighbour physician, and entertains him for the cure of his parish... (*The Parson's Completeness*)

...is very exact in the governing of his house, making it a copy and model for his parish. He knows the temper and pulse of every person in his house, and accordingly either meets with their vices or advanceth their virtues... (*The Parson in his House*)

Jesu is in my heart, His sacred name
Is deeply carved there: but the other week
A great affliction broke the little frame,
E'en all to pieces; which I went to seek:
And first I found the corner where was J,
After, where ES, and next where U was graved.
When I had got these parcels, instantly
I sat me down to spell them, and perceived
That to my broken heart He was *I ease you*,
And to my whole is JESU.
George Herbert:' Jesu'

...keeps his servants between love and fear, according as he finds them, but generally he distributes it thus: to his children he shows more love than terror, to his servants more terror than love, but an old good servant boards a child...(*The Parson in his House*)

...the furniture of his house is very plain, but clean, whole, and sweet, as sweet as his garden can make; for he hath no money for such things, charity being his only perfume, which deserves cost when he can spare it... (*The Parson in his House*)

...Do well and right and let the world sink. (*The Parson and his Churchwardens*)

Herbert's friend, John Donne, sent Herbert a gift of one of his seals of the Anchor and Christ. It showed a sheaf of snakes, which was the crest of his poor family. With it came verse in English and Latin to which Herbert responded in like style.

> When all is cross, and that cross anchor grown,
> This seal's a catechism, not a seal alone.
> Under that little seal great gifts I send,
> Both works and pray'rs, pawns, and fruits of a friend.
> O may that saint that rides on our great seal,
> To you that bear His name large bounty deal.
>> *John Donne: Lines from his Poem in English to George Herbert*

Whilst it is not known when Herbert's poems were written, he certainly collected them into some kind of order during his years at Bemerton. *The Temple*, the overall name given to the collection eventually published shortly after his death, begins with this dedication.

> Lord, my first fruits present themselves to Thee;
> Yet not mine neither; for from Thee they came,
> And must return. Accept of them and me,
> And make us strive, who shall sing best Thy Name.
>> Turn their eyes hither, who shall make a gain:
>> Theirs, who shall hurt themselves or me, refrain.

Dare to be true: nothing can need a lie;
A fault which needs it most, grows two thereby.
George Herbert: From 'The Church Porch'

Love is the true price of love.
George Herbert: From 'Jacula Prudentum'

The anthology begins with a long poem *The Church Porch* followed by short poems on a wide range of religious themes.

Herbert was a musician as well as a poet; and some of the texts could well have been sung in his lifetime, perhaps by himself. But there is no evidence of music that has survived, and hymns as opposed to metrical psalms were hardly sung in Anglican worship.

There are a few seventeenth century song settings; and in the eighteenth century, the Wesleys and the Moravians drew on Herbert, much adapted, for hymnody. The use of these Herbert texts largely died out but his worth was rediscovered by a few in the 'hymnal explosion' of the second half of the nineteenth century.

> Know you, fair, on what you look?
> Divinest love lies in this book:
> Expecting fire from your eyes,
> To kindle this his sacrifice.
> When your hands untie these strings,
> Think you've an angel by the wings.
> One that gladly will be nigh,
> To wait upon each morning sigh.
> To flutter in the balmy air,
> Of your well perfumed prayer.
> These white plumes of his he'll lend you,
> Which every day to heaven will send you,
> To take acquaintance of the sphere,
> And all the smooth-fac'd kindred there.
>> And though Herbert's name do owe
>> These devotions, fairest; know
>> That while I lay them on the shrine
>> Of your white hand, they are mine.
>>> *John Donne: 'On Mr George Herbert's Book, entitled "The Temple, or Sacred Poems", sent to a Gentlewoman, by Mr. Crashaw.*

Salisbury Cathedral

Sweetest of sweets, I thank you! when displeasure
    Did through my body wound my mind,
You took me hence, and in your house of pleasure
    A dainty lodging me assigned.

Now I in you without a body move,
    Rising and falling with your wings:
We both together sweetly live and love,
    Yet say sometimes, *God help poor kings*!

Comfort, I'll die; for if you post from me,
    Sure I shall do so, and much more;
But if I travel in your company,
    You know the way to heaven's door.

George Herbert: 'Church-music'

In *Songs of Praise,* **Percy Dearmer slightly altered a Herbert text to make this verse sung to WULFRUN.**
Enrich, Lord, heart, mouth, hands in me,
With faith, with hope, with charity;
That I may run, rise, rest with thee.
The original began
Enrich my heart... and is Verse 3 of 'Trinity Sunday'

The sounds of organ, cornets and sackbuts also enriched the musical life of the Cathedral: and there is little doubt that Herbert himself joined in secular music-making and often played one part of a consort.

John Playford

A broken altar, Lord, Thy servant rears,
Made of a heart, and cèmented with tears;
    Whose parts are as Thy hand did frame;
    No workman's tool hath touched the same.
        A heart alone
        Is such a stone,
        As nothing but
        Thy power doth cut.
        Wherefore each part
        Of my hard heart
        Meets in this frame;
        To praise Thy name:
That, if I chance to hold my peace,
These stones to praise Thee may not cease.
O let Thy blessed *sacrifice* be mine,
And sanctify this *altar* to be Thine.
George Herbert: 'The Altar'
Set by John Playford in 'Psalms and Hymns in Solemn Musick' (1671)

Texts of George Herbert used as a basis of texts in the Wesleys' *Hymns and Sacred Poems (1739)*

A true Hymn
Affliction
Bitter-Sweet
Complaining
Desertion
Discipline
Doomsday
Employment
Giddiness
Grace
Gratefulness
Grieve not the Holy Spirit
Home
Longing
Man's Medley
Mattins
Misery
Praise
Prayer
Repentance
The Agony
The Banquet
The Call
The Collar
The Dawning
The Dialogue
The Elixir
The Flower
The Frailty
The Glance
The Invitation
The Method
The Reprisal
The Search
The Sigh
The Sinner
The Temper(1)
The Temper (2)
The Thanksgiving
True Praise
Vanity
Virtue

Between 1737 and 1744, the Wesleys adapted 49 texts in all: and the eighteenth-century Moravians also adapted some of Herbert's poems as hymns.

O what a thing is man! how far from power,
  From settled peace and rest!
He is some twenty sev'ral men at least
  Each sev'ral hour,

One while he counts of heaven, as of his treasure;
  But then a thought creeps in,
And calls him coward, who for fear of sin,
  Will lose a pleasure.

Now he will fight it out, and to the wars;
  Now eat his bread in peace,
And snudge in quiet: now he scorns increase;
  Now all day spares.

He builds a house, which quickly down must go,
  As if a whirlwind blew
And crushed the building: and 't is partly true,
  His mind is so.

O what a sight were man, if his attires
  Did alter with his mind,
And, like a dolphin's skin, his clothes combined
  With his desires!

Surely if each one saw another's heart,
  There would be no commerce,
No sale or bargain pass: all would disperse,
  And live apart.

Lord, mend or rather make us: one creation
  Will not suffice our turn:
Except thou make us daily, we shall spurn
  Our own salvation.

George Herbert: 'Giddiness'

When the Wesleys put together *Hymns and Sacred Poems* in 1739, they included some forty texts based on Herbert. It is fascinating to read the Wesley and original versions side by side.

Charles Wesley

HERBERT'S ORIGINAL

King of glory, King of peace,
  I will love Thee;
And that love may never cease,
  I will move Thee.

Thou hast granted my request,
  Thou hast heard me:
Thou didst note my working breast,
  Thou hast spared me.

Wherefore with my utmost art
  I will sing Thee,
And the cream of all my heart
  I will bring Thee.

Though my sins against me cried,
  Thou didst clear me;
And alone, when they replied,
  Thou didst hear me.

Seven whole days, not one in seven,
  I will praise Thee;
In my heart, though not in heaven,
  I can raise Thee.

Thou grew'st soft and moist with tears,
  Thou relentedst.
And when justice called for fears
  Thou dissentedst.

Small it is, in this poor sort
  To enrol Thee:
E'en eternity is too short
  To extol Thee.

George Herbert: Praise. Sung to GWALCHMAI,
*   LLANFAIR and BEMERTON (Wilson)*

THE WESLEY VERSION

O King of glory, King of peace
  Thee only will I love:
Thee, that my love may never cease,
  Incessant will I move!

For Thou hast granted my request,
  For Thou my cries hast heard,
Mark'd all the workings of my breast,
  And hast in mercy spar'd.

Wherefore with all my strength and art
  Thy mercy's praise I sing,
To Thee the tribute of my heart,
  My soul, my all I bring.

What, tho' my sins against me cry'd,
  Thou dids't the sinner spare:
In vain th' accuser still reply'd,
  For love had charm'd thy ear.

Thee sev'n whole days, not one in sev'n,
  Unweary'd will I praise,
And in my heart, a little heav'n,
  Thy throne triumphant raise.

Soften'd and vanquish'd by my tears
  Thou could'st no more withstand,
But when stern justice call'd for fears
  Disarm'd her lifted hand.

Small is it, in this humble sort
  Thy mercy's power to raise,
For e'en eternity's too short
  To utter all thy praise.

ANOTHER HERBERT POEM

King of glory, King of peace,
With the one make war to cease;
With the other bless Thy sheep,
Thee to love, in Thee to sleep.
Let not sin devour Thy fold,
Bragging that Thy blood is cold;
That Thy death is also dead,
While his conquests daily spread;
That Thy flesh hath lost his food,
And Thy cross is common wood.

Choke him, let him say no more,
But reserve his breath in store,
Till Thy conquest and his fall
Make his sighs to use it all;
And then bargain with the wind
To discharge what is behind.
    Blessèd be God alone,
    Thrice blessèd Three in One.

George Herbert: ' L'Envoy' from 'The Church
Militant'

HERBERT'S ORIGINAL	THE WESLEY VERSION

Teach me, my God and King,
    In all things Thee to see,
And what I do in anything,
    To do it as for Thee.

Not rudely, as a beast,
    To run into an action;
But still to Thee prepossest,
    And give it his perfection.

A man that looks on glass,
    On it may stay his eye,
Or, if he pleaseth, through it pass,
    And then the heav'n espy.

All may of Thee partake:
    Nothing can be so mean,
Which with his* tincture (for Thy sake)
    Will not grow bright and clean.

A servant with this clause
    Makes drudgery divine:
Who sweeps a room as for Thy laws
    Makes that and th' action fine.

This is the famous stone
    That turneth all to gold;
For that which God doth touch and own
    Cannot for less be told.
                    George Herbert: 'The Elexir'.
    * or *this*   *Sung to SANDYS*

Teach me, my God and King,
    In all things Thee to see;
And what I do in any thing
    To do it as for Thee!

To scorn the senses' sway,
    While still to Thee I tend:
In all I do, be Thou the Way,
    In all be Thou the End.

A man that looks on glass
    On that may fix his eye,
Or unoppos'd may thro' it pass,
    And Heav'n behind descry.

All may of Thee partake:
    Nothing so small can be,
But draws, when acted for Thy sake,
    Greatness and worth from Thee.

If done t'obey Thy laws,
    Ev'n servile labours thine;
Hallow'd is toil, if this the cause,
    The meanest work divine.

Th' elexir this, the stone
    That all converts to gold:
For that which God for His doth own,
    Cannot for less be told.

HERBERT'S ORIGINAL	THE WESLEY VERSION

Throw away Thy rod,
Throw away Thy wrath:
        O my God,
Take the gentle path.

For my heart's desire
Unto Thine is bent:
        I aspire
To a full consent.

Not a word or look
I affect to own,
        But by book,
And Thy Book alone.

O throw away Thy rod,
    O throw away Thy wrath!
My gracious Saviour and my God,
    O take the gentle path.

Then seest, my heart's desire
    Still unto Thee is bent:
Still does my longing soul aspire
    To an entire consent.

Not e'en a word or look
    Do I approve or own,
But by the model of Thy Book,
    Thy sacred Book alone.

Though I fail, I weep:
Though I halt in pace,
Yet I creep
To the throne of grace.

Then let wrath remove;
Love will do the deed:
For with love
Stony hearts will bleed.

Love is swift of foot;
Love's a man of war,
And can shoot
And can hit from far.

Who can 'scape his bow?
That which wrought on Thee
Brought Thee low,
Needs must work on me.

Throw away Thy rod;
Though man frailties hath.
Thou ar t God
Throw away Thy wrath.

George Herbert: 'Discipline'

Altho' I fail, I weep;
Altho' I halt in pace
Yet still with trembling steps I creep
Unto the throne of grace.

O then let wrath remove:
For love will do the deed!
Love will the conquest gain; with love
Ev'n stony hearts will bleed.

For love is swift of foot,
Love is a man of war;
Love can resistless arrows shoot
And hit the mark from far.

Who can escape the bow?
That which hath wrought on Thee,
Which brought the King of Glory low,
Must surely work on me.

O throw away Thy rod;
What tho' man frailties hath?
Thou art my Saviour and my God!
O throw away Thy wrath!

TWO FURTHER HERBERT TEXTS

Sweet day, so cool, so calm, so bright,
The bridal of the earth and sky,
The dew shall weep thy fall to-night;
For thou must die.

Sweet rose, whose hue, angry and brave,
Bids the rash gazer wipe his eye,
The root is ever in its grave,
And thou must die.

Sweet Spring, full of sweet days and
roses,
A box where sweets compacted lie,
My music shows you have your closes,
And all must die.

Only a sweet and virtuous soul,
Like seasoned timber, never gives;
But though the whole world turn to coal,
Then chiefly lives.

George Herbert: 'Virtue'. Sung to GAZA.
Used in 'The Compleat Angler'
by Izaak Walton

Both these texts have found their way into hymnbooks.

Come, my Way, my Truth, my Life:
Such a Way as gives us breath:
Such a Truth as ends all strife:
Such a Life as killeth death.

Come, my Light, my Feast, my Strength:
Such a Light as shows a feast:
Such a Feast as mends in length:
Such a Strength as makes his guest.

Come, my Joy, my Love, my Heart:
Such a Joy as none can move:
Such a Love as none can part:
Such a Heart as joys in love.

George Herbert:' The Call'. Sung to
TUNBRIDGE, SAVANNAH
(HERRNHÜT [Wesley]) and
COME MY WAY

HERBERT'S ORIGINAL

Come away,
　Make no delay.
Summon all the dust to rise,
Till it stir, and rub the eyes;
While this member jogs the other,
Each one whispering, *Live you, brother?*

Come away,
　Make this the day.
Dust, alas! no music feels,
But Thy trumpet; then it kneels,
As peculiar notes and strains
Cure tarantula's raging pains.

Come away,
　O make no stay!
Let the graves make their confession,
Lest at length they plead possession;
Flesh's stubborness may have
Read that lesson to the grave.

Come away,
　Thy flock doth stray,
Some to the winds their body lend,
And in them may drown a friend;
Some in noisome vapours grow
To a plague and public woe.

Come away,
　Help our decay:
Man is out of order hurled,
Parcelled out to all the world.
Lord, Thy broken concert raise,
And the music shall be praise.
　　　George Herbert: 'Doomsday'

THE WESLEY VERSION

Come to Judgment, come away!
(Hark, I hear the angel say,
Summoning the dust to rise)
Haste, resume, and lift your eyes;
Hear, ye sons of Adam, hear,
Man, before Thy God appear!

Come to Judgment, come away!
This the last, the dreadful Day.
Sov'reign author, judge of all,
Dust obeys Thy quick'ning call,
Dust no other voice will heed:
Thine the trump that wakes the dead.

Come to Judgment, come away!
Lingring Man, no longer stay:
Thee let earth at length restore,
Pris'ner in her womb no more;
Burst the barriers of the tomb,
Rise to meet Thy instant Doom!

Come to Judgment, come away!
Wide disperst howe'er ye stray,
Lost in fire, or air, or main,
Kindred atoms meet again;
Sepulchred where'er ye rest,
Mix'd with fish, or bird, or beast.

Come to Judgment, come away!
Help, O Christ, thy work's decay:
Man is out of order hurl'd
Parcel'd out to all the world;
Lord, thy broken concert raise,
And the music shall be praise.

ANOTHER HERBERT POEM

Poor silly soul, whose hope and head lie low;
Whose flat delights on earth do creep and grow;
To whom the stars shine not so fair as eyes;
Nor solid work as false embroideries;
Hark! and beware, lest what you now do measure,
And write for sweet, prove a most sour
　　　　　　　　　　　displeasure.

O hear betimes, lest thy relenting
　　　　May come too late!
To purchase heaven for repenting
　　　　Is no hard rate.
If souls be made of earthly mould,
　　　Let them love gold;
　　　If born on high,
Let them unto their kindred fly;
For they can never be at rest
Till they regain their anicient nest.
Then, silly soul, take heed; for earthly joy
Is but a bubble, and makes thee a boy.
　　　George Herbert: 'Vanity'

Herbert's *Doomsday*, besides expressing the accepted theology of his time, gives an interesting glimpse into the folk lore that the bite of the tarantula could be relieved only by an early form of music therapy. The Bemerton household included his orphaned neices, Dorothy and Margaret Vaughan, although George Herbert was to experience bereavement again when Dorothy died in 1632.

Nicholas Ferrar's cousin Arthur Woodnoth, a London goldsmith, acted as a middle-man to ensure the Little Gidding community's needs were met. He also served in helping to manage the affairs of George's stepfather, a none too easy task on behalf of so prodigal a spendthrift. At this time Woolnoth was also pondering whether he too should seek holy orders: but apparently neither Ferrar nor Herbert encouraged him. His visits both to Bemerton and Little Gidding helped keep the two friends in touch. Nicholas Ferrar translated a theological treatise by John Valdesso, a sixteenth-century chamberlain to the Pope, whose early life in court had involved insatiable perusals of chivalrous romances. The script seemed to Ferrar worth making available in English despite its Roman Catholic origin. He sought the confirmation of his friend George Herbert as to its suitability for issue. Herbert replied thus:

> My dear and deserving Brother,—Your *Valdesso* I now return with many thanks, and some notes, in which, perhaps, you will discover some care, which I forbear not in the midst of my griefs; first, for your sake, because I would do nothing negligently that you commit unto me; secondly, for the author's sake, whom I conceive to have been a true servant of God, and to such and all that is theirs I owe diligence; thirdly, for the Church's sake, to whom, by printing it, I would have you consecrate it...It is true there are some things which I like not in him, as my fragments will express, when you read them; nevertheless I wish you by all means to publish it, for these three eminent things observable therein: First, that God in the midst of Popery should open the eyes of one to understand and express so clearly and excellently the intent of the Gospel in the acceptation of Christ's righteousness (as he showeth through all his Considerations), a thing strangely buried and darkened by the adversaries and their great stumbling-block. Secondly, the great honour and reverence which he everywhere bears towards our dear Master and Lord, concluding every Consideration almost with His holy Name, and setting His merit forth so piously; for which I do so love him that, were there nothing else, I would print it, that with it the honour of my Lord might be published. Thirdly, the many pious rules of ordering our life about mortification and observation of God's kingdom within us, and the working thereof, of which he was a very diligent observer. These three things are very eminent in the author, and overweigh the defects, as I conceive, towards the publishing thereof...

Poems of George Herbert were set to music in the seventeenth century by John Blow, George Jeffreys, John Jenkins, Henry Lawes, Henry Purcell and John Wilson.

Twentieth-century composers inspired by Herbert's texts include Walford Davies, Edmund Rubbra and Ralph Vaughan Williams.

Valdesso's Consideration LXIII reads:
That the holy Scripture is like a Candle in a dark place, and that the holy spirit is like the sun. This shewed by seven conformities.
Herbert's comments include these words:
The author doth still discover too slight a regard of the Scripture, as if it were but children's meat, whereas there is not only milk there, but strong meat also...

Ferrar included a prefatory comment when he issued John Valdesso's *Divine Considerations* with this note.

> ...To have removed these few stumbling blocks, or offensive passages, by leaving them out, or by altering them, had not been the work of a Translator, but of an Author; besides the ill example of altering ancient Authors, which is one of the greatest causes of the corruption of truth and learning.

There is no monumental record to the memory of George Herbert. *He lies buried*, says Isaak Walton, *in his own church, under the altar, and covered with a gravestone without any inscription.* This, the very small old church of Bemerton, is falling into utter decay, and is quite insufficient to meet the wants of the present population. Some persons who revere the memory of George Herbert have taken the opportunity thus afforded to endeavour to raise a worthy and most appropriate monument to the memory of so good a man, by erecting a new church (thereby affording increased church accomodation to the inhabitants of Bemerton) on a site adjoining the existing small building, which, for obvious reasons it is not intended to remove.

From 'Notes and Queries' of March 26th 1859

Through his life, George had amended and rearranged his English poems; the final collection was apparently conveyed by the Reverend Edmund Duncan to Nicholas Ferrar at the beginning of 1633. A few weeks later, on 1st March, Herbert died at Bemerton Rectory. Most of his life as a priest had included a constant battle against failing health.

Arthur Woodnoth had spent some time in the closing months of Herbert's life helping him manage his affairs: in the will made a few days before his death, George appointed Woodnoth as executor and his stepfather as overseer of his affairs. When he knew he was dying, Herbert laid on Woodnoth responsibilities for looking after the interests of his wife, his nieces and the completion of the restoration of Leighton church. The role of literary executor was assumed by Nicholas Ferrar. It took some time for the trained copyists at Little Gidding to prepare the poems for the press: the prose works had not been published by the time of Ferrar's death in 1637 and it fell to Barnabas Oley, another Fellow of Clare Hall, to publish these in 1651.

Herbert's wife remarried and carefully preserved his other papers, but these were lost to us when her husband's house was destroyed during the Civil War.

For three centuries, the events of Herbert's life were preserved for posterity by Isaak Walton's biography, published in 1670. Twentieth-century scholarship has questioned some of Walton's assumptions, and provided a less extravagant story of Herbert's life: he remains one of the great English devotional poets. It was left to those in later centuries to see the possibilities of some of his texts as excellent hymns for use in Christian worship!

> Death, thou wast once an uncouth hideous thing,
>   Nothing but bones,
>   The sad effect of sadder groans:
> Thy mouth was open; but thou couldst not sing.
> ....
> But since our Saviour's death did put some blood
>   Into thy face,
>   Thou art grown fair and full of grace,
> Much in request, much sort for as a good.
>
> *George Herbert: the 1st and 4th stanzas of 'Death'*

My joy, my life, my crown!
My heart was meaning all the day,
        Somewhat it fain would say;
And still it runneth muttering up and down,
With only this, *My joy, my life, my crown!*

Yet slight not these few words:
If truly said, they may take part
        Among the best in art.
The fineness which a hymn or psalm affords
Is, when the soul unto the lines accords.

He who craves all the mind,
And all the soul, and strength, and time,
        If the words only rhyme,
Justly complains that somewhat is behind
To make His verse, or write a hymn in kind.

Whereas if th' heart be moved,
Although the verse be somewhat scant,
        God doth supply the want.
As when th' heart says (sighing to be approved)
O, *could I love!* and stops; God writeth *Loved.*

George Herbert: 'A True Hymn'

...but he that desires to excel in this kind of hagiography or holy writing, must strive by all means for perfection and true holiness, that *a door may be opened to him in heaven* Rev 4.1, and then he will be able to write, with Hierotheus and holy Herbert, a true hymn.

Henry Vaughan in the preface to 'Silex Scintillans'. Hierotheus is a mythical first-century bishop of Athens invented by Dionysus as a writer of hymns.

Thus he lived, and thus he died like a saint, unspotted of the world, full of alms-deeds, full of humility, and all the examples of a virtuous life; which I cannot conclude better than with this borrowed observation:

All must to their cold graves;
But the religious actions of the just
Smell sweet in death, and blossom
in the dust.
James Shirley

Mr. George Herbert's have done so to this, and will doubtless do so to succeeding generations. I have but this to say more of him, that if Andrew Melvin* died before him, then George Herbert died without an enemy. I will (if God shall be so pleased) that I may be so happy as to die like him.

Izaak Walton: From 'George Herbert'
* = Andrew Melville. He died in 1622. See page 10.

Ralph Vaughan Williams who chose George Herbert's texts for his *Five Mystical Songs*

Hark, how the birds do sing,
        And woods do ring!
All creatures have their joy, and man hath his.
        Yet if rightly measure,
                Man's joy and pleasure
Rather hereafter than in present is.

George Herbert: The opening stanza of 'Man's Melody'

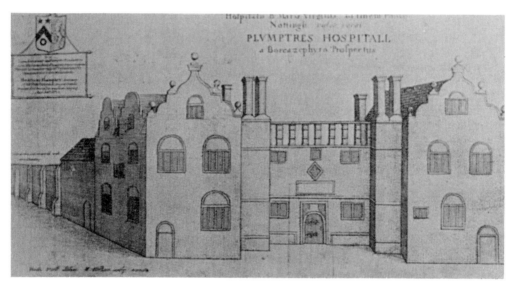

Robert Plumptre Hospital in the seventeenth century

Edward Plumptre

By letters patent dated at Nottingham the 8th July 1392, King Richard II granted a licence to John de Plumptre to found and endow a *hospital or house of God for two chaplains and thirteen agèd poor widows*. John de Plumptre was a merchant stapler: his wealth was derived principally from the export of wool. In 1650, a descendant of the founder, Dr. Huntingdon Plumptre, rebuilt the Hospital of the Virgin Mary at the Bridge-End in Nottingham. His grandson, John Plumptre, improved the property and added four new tenements; then in 1753 his son, another John, added two more, thus completing the charitable intention of the founder. Plumptre Hospital, as it came commonly to be known, was rebuilt in 1823; and the family have continued to serve this foundation through to the present day.

The lineage of Edward Hayes Plumptre can be traced, too, by direct male line to the fourteenth-century founder of the hospital. Edward's grandfather was a first cousin of that part of the family which has continued to exercise a personal interest in the ancient charity. Another earlier Plumptre, Henry, was a President of the Royal College of Surgeons. Edward's father, Edward Hallowes Plumptre, was a lawyer of the Middle Temple in London; his mother, Eliza Pitfield, hailed from Symonsbury in Dorset. There were six children from the marriage, of which Edward Hayes, born in August 1821, was the second son.

Mrs Adelaide ?
pre -1908

Prizegiving at King's College, London

Edward's elder brother Charles was called to the Bar, but gradually the courts held less and less interest for him. He had an excellent voice and between 1840 and 1850 established the first penny readings for the people. For many years he lectured on the use of the voice, publishing in 1861 *The Principles and Practice of Elocution*, which sold many editions. A younger brother, William Alfred, served as a chaplain to the Duke of Marlborough.

Edward Hayes Plumptre studied initially at home, but in 1839 he attended King's College, London. The syllabus provided religious and moral instruction in accordance with the principles of the Established Church, the Greek and Latin Classics, Mathematics, English Literature and Composition, and History. Another student at King's that year was Francis Galton, a cousin of Charles Darwin: he pioneered researches in meteorology and eugenics. Plumptre won prizes at King's College in July 1840 in Divinity, English Literature and History before going up to University College, Oxford, to gain a double first degree in Mathematics and Classics. From 1844 to 1847 he was a fellow of Brasenose College, gaining his Master of Arts degree. In June 1846, he sent a five-pound note to King's for the English Verse Prize, regretting he could not attend the presentation as he would be out of England for a while.

Plumptre was ordained deacon in 1846; and on 13th November, the council of King's College, London, appointed him as Chaplain and Lecturer in Divinity. The Principal of the college at that time was the Reverend R. W. Jelf, described by a contemporary as *par excellence the representative via media man*. The Reverend Frederick Denison Maurice was Professor of Divinity. This son of a Unitarian minister was ordained in the Established Church in 1836; but he challenged much of the accepted theology of the day. Plumptre was caught up in this conflict of ideas, the more so, perhaps, as Harriet, his chosen bride-to-be, was Maurice's youngest sister. Although Plumptre did not go all the way with Maurice, the Christian Socialist, he certainly was influenced by and interested in many of the activities of his future brother-in-law: the association made him a suspect person in the view of some of the establishment and it possibly denied him the chance of an academic life-style cloistered at Oxford or Cambridge.

In 1847, the year in which he was ordained priest, Plumptre added the role of censor to his duties at King's College. This responsibility for overseeing the resident students, and disciplining defaulters who broke college rules, gave the Chaplain a good opportunity of becoming more personally acquainted with his charges: he tried unsuccessfully to persuade

It treats politics, science, literature, as secular: but it dabbles with them, pretends to reform them by mixing a few cant phrases with them... It trembles at every social movement, at every thought which is awakened in human hearts, at every discovery which is made in the world without. But it does not tremble at its own corruptions. It can see its members indifferent to all the precepts of the Bible in their daily occupations; as shopkeepers, employers, citizens, yet if they put the Bible on their banners, and shout about the authority of the inspired book at public meetings, it asks no more; it boasts that we are *sound at heart;* it congratulates itself that spirituality is diffusing itself throughout the land.

F. D. Maurice: From the Preface to 'Patriarchs and Lawgivers in the Old Testament', 1851

the council he should retain the post, with the help of an assistant censor, when he ceased living in, following his marriage on 5th July 1848 at Hurstmonceux, Sussex, with Harriet Theodosa. But he soon found himself with extra duties teaching pre-admission theological students, and this helped to balance the family budget. The council minutes reveal that these students each paid eight guineas a term, of which Plumptre received five guineas.

In April 1848, Professor Maurice suggested that the Reverend Charles Kingsley be appointed as his assistant and introduced him to the Principal. But on 10th April, Christian Socialism was proclaimed: not only was its ardent advocate Kingsley rejected for the post but Maurice only just escaped dismissal. An uneasy truce between Principal Jelf and Professor Maurice was to hang over the college until the feud ended with Maurice evicted on grounds of teaching heretical ideas to students and generally unsettling the minds of the young. The central issue concerned Christian beliefs on the hereafter, on which subject Plumptre was to publish in 1884 a significant book *The Spirits in Prison and Other Studies on the Life after Death*. In it, he printed a letter written by Maurice in 1849 to Reverend Fenton Hort, a friend of John Ellerton, author of *Saviour, again to thy dear name we raise* and co-translator with him of some Latin hymns. This document affirmed that Maurice did not hold heretical views, at least in the terms in which he was accused.

My duty then I feel is this:–

(1) To assert that which I know, that what God has revealed, His absolute universal love in all possible ways, and without any limitation;
(2) To tell myself and all men that to know this love and to be moulded by it is *the* blessing we are to seek;
(3) To say that this is eternal life;
(4) To say that the want of it is death;
(5) To say that if they believe in the Son of God they have eternal life;
(6) To say that if they have not the Son of God they have not life;
(7) *Not* to say who has the Son of God, because I do not know;
(8) *Not* to say how long any one may remain in eternal death, because I do not know;
(9) *Not* to say that all will be necessarily raised out of eternal death, because I do not know;
(10) *Not* to judge any before the time, or to judge other men at all, because Christ has said: *Judge not, that ye be not judged;*
(11) *Not* to play with Scripture by quoting passages which have not the slightest connexion with the subject, such as *Where the tree falleth it shall lie;*
(12) *Not* to invent a scheme of purgatory, and so take upon myself the office of the Divine Judge;
(13) *Not* to deny God a right of using punishments at any time or anywhere for the reformation of His creatures;
(14) *Not* to contradict Christ's words *These shall be beaten with few, these with many stripes* for the sake of maintaining a theory of the equality of sins;
(15) *Not* to think of any punishment of God's so great as saying *Let them alone.*

It will be seen from these propositions (1) that Mr. Maurice was justified in saying that he did not hold a theory of Universalism; (2) that he excludes, to the extent of ignoring, the doctrine of a so-called Conditional Immortality; (3) that he held that God's punishments of evil, though they may include a retributive element, are also designed to be reformatory; (4) that he held that the state of death is one in which, with some exceptions, it is possible for the souls that are under punishment to turn from darkness to light, and from death to life.
A letter from (John) Frederick Denison Maurice to Fenton J. Hort written in 1849 with comment from Edward Plumptre as printed in 'The Spirits in Prison and other Studies on the Life after Death'

In 1848, too, at the request of the theological students, evening services began in the chapel. The chapel choir had for some time proved unsatisfactory both as regards the attendance of the boys and their behaviour during service. The situation was improved by the decision of the council to elect twelve boys *being the sons of clergymen or some equally respectable class* to sing daily in the chapel at the evening service and twice on Sundays in return for which they would receive free education. The following February, William H. Monk was formally appointed as Choir Director: he had been deputising for some time in this task for the Professor of Music, John Hullah, also a friend of Charles Kingsley. Hullah imported from France the Wilhelm system, using a fixed doh in teaching sight-singing which battled for many years in competition with Curwen's scheme of tonic sol-fa. Monk was to become a prolific writer of hymn tunes and the first music editor of *Hymns Ancient and Modern.*

In the middle of the nineteenth century, opportunities for women to enjoy higher education were virtually non-existent. At Oxford and Cambridge Universities, ladies were definitely not admitted. In 1828, several ladies attended lectures on Italian Life at University College, London, and four years later, two women students were registered for a course on Natural Philosophy: but it was nearly three decades before there was another registration. Some professors' wives and daughters attended a series of lectures on Geology and Genesis at King's College, London, in 1832; but any repetition was strictly forbidden. The London Mechanics' Institute admitted women to its lectures in 1830, though the committee was divided over the propriety of letting them enter by the front door. In 1842, Whitelands College was founded and in the next four years other Women's Training Colleges followed; but the educational requirements for entry were undemanding.

Against this background, the Governesses' Benevolent Institution had interested Maurice in their situation, and more specifically the need for them to be able to secure a Certificate of Competence. Many governesses had only superficial knowledge, and it was clear that if such a certificiate were to be of value, it needed to be backed by wider, higher educational opportunities for women.

It was largely on the initiative of Maurice that Queen's College, London, was founded to meet this need: its Committee of Education set up in 1847 was mostly recruited from staff at King's College, including Hullah, Sterndale Bennett and Plumptre. The College granted its first certificates in December that year and opened its doors to students on 1st May 1848.

The Committee originally had planned the age of fourteen as a minimum for entry, but when the first term began the age had been reduced to twelve, the same as that fixed by Bedford College, founded in 1849 for the higher education of women. In Queen's first year, Plumptre took the Greek class consisting of Dorothea Beale, later Headmistress of Cheltenham Ladies' College, and a friend. Dorothea recalled this class as an especially happy part of college life. William Sterndale Bennett, later a Principal of the Royal Academy of Music, provided sixty preludes and lessons *in all the keys* for his Queen's pupils.

In December 1848, the first tentative steps were taken at King's College to arrange classes for evening students: the experiment was the forerunner of an eventual Evening Class Department. Between 1849 and 1853, the students in Maurice's Theological Department were required, as a condition of taking their course, to help teach at an evening school for indigent children and adults in the densely populated area around Trafalgar Square.

The mid eighteen-hundreds marked a period of great advance in understanding the functioning of the human body; but in 1849, in a series of sermons addressed to the medical students at King's, Plumptre urged them never to forget that their patients were not mere bodies for experimentation, but whole persons.

> *The Hospital.* Ecclesiastes 7. 2. *It is better to go to the house of mourning, than to the house of feasting.*
>
> ...you consider who and what those sick people are with whom you are every day brought into contact—if you say to yourselves, till you act on the thought, almost unconsciously, without saying it—'These men and women are not here merely that we may experimentalize on them. We owe them other duties besides that of applying our professional skill to them, or learning from them. They are our brethren; they belong to the same race with us; they have the same nature, that nature which the Son of God took upon him in order to bind all men together.'
>
> *The Dissecting-Room.* Psalm 139. 14. *I will praise thee; for I am fearfully and wonderfully made; marvellous are thy works; and that my soul knoweth right well.*
>
> Very fearful and wonderful it is that life should be dependent on so complex a system; that in proportion as each power is more highly developed, the organization which is its instrument, is adapted as by a marvellous endless wisdom...

The teachers of a school may aim merely to impart information; the teachers of a college must lead their pupils to the apprehension of principles...

Frederick Denison Maurice in an inaugural lecture on the setting up of Queen's College in 1848

John Hullah

The Council having taken into consideration an Essay lately published by the Rev. Frederick D. Maurice, Professor of Divinity in King's College, and also a correspondence between the Principal and the Professor on the subject of the said Essay, and having been informed by Professor Maurice that he does not wish to make any statement in addition to his Answer to the Principal's final letter,—

Resolve—

I That in their judgment the opinions set forth, and the doubts expressed in the said Essay, and restated in the said Answer, as to certain points of belief regarding the future punishment of the wicked and the final issues of the Day of Judgment are of dangerous tendency, and calculated to unsettle the minds of the theological students of King's College.

II That the Council feel it their painful duty to declare, that the continuance of Professor Maurice's connexion with the College as one of its Professors would be seriously detrimental to its usefulness.

III That the Council, while it laments the necessity which constrains them to adopt this resolution, are bound in justice to Professor Maurice to express the sense which they entertain of the zealous and able manner in which he has discharged the duties of the two offices which he had held, and the attachment which he has at all times manifested to the College.

Resolutions of the Council of King's College, London, concerning Frederick Denison Maurice.

Work. Romans 12. 11. *Not slothful in business; fervent in spirit; serving the Lord.*

...no shrinking back from our labour because the way is less pleasant, or the difficulties greater than we expected...We must resist the temptation of short roads to arrive at results, without going through the process which leads to them. We must fight against the weariness which will sometimes come upon us, when our work brings with it that appearance of being little else than a dry and barren drudgery...*Whatsoever thy hand findeth to do, do it with thy might.*

Leisure. Philippians 4. 8. *Finally, brethren, whatsoever things are true, whatsoever things are honest, whatsoever things are just, whatsoever things are pure, whatsoever things are lovely, whatsoever things are of good report; if there be any virtue, and if there be any praise, think on these things.*

Are these pursuits worthy of the time and labour which I bestow upon them? Do they tend, in any degree, to make me wiser and better—to give me greater sympathy with what is right and good?

Extracts from four sermons on 'The Calling of a Medical Student' preached in King's College Chapel in 1849

In 1850, Plumptre found himself teaching theology to medical and military students, having given up his work with pre-admission theological students. The following year he was appointed a Select Preacher at Oxford; and also appointed an Assistant Preacher at Lincoln's Inn, an office he held until 1858. All this time Jelf and Maurice continued at loggerheads until Plumptre's brother-in-law was finally dismissed in 1853. In the reorganisation that followed at King's College, Plumptre proposed to the Principal that the subject of Pastoral Theology, concerned especially with the training of the clergy, should be upgraded, and that he should be appointed Professor. At the same time he would give up his lectures in Latin translation and his classes in Greek for beginners. This proposal was accepted and he held the Professorship until 1863. Many years later Plumptre, in the chapter *The Wider Hope in English Theology* from *The Spirits in Prison and other Studies on the Life after Death* wrote positively of Maurice in these terms:

...the three chief elements which entered into his teaching and fashioned his life...would be found, I believe:

(1) in the doctrine of the Light that lighteth every man, as it was held by Fox or Barclay in the Society of Friends;

(2) in the thoughts which Mr. Erskine's teaching had impressed on his mind as to the unconditional freeness of the Gospel, the nature of the Atonement and the purpose of all Divine Punishment; and

(3) in that which was conspicuous by its absence in their systems, the recognition of the witness borne by the policy and the sacraments of the Catholic Church to the truths they had maintained as from the standpoint at once of individuals and of humanity.

…The belief in a love which was educating men in this world, and did not cease to educate them when they had left it, might have been read between the lines in well-nigh every sermon he wrote.

Whilst others fought on wider political platforms in the cause of higher education for all, Plumptre quietly pursued the goal in the institutions in which he was placed. Maurice had to distance himself from Queen's College, as his connection with the Christian Socialist movement and his dismissal from King's frightened off parents and prospective students: but for twenty years from 1855 Plumptre was to serve there as Dean. The College had been incorporated by royal charter in 1853. In 1849 Dorothea Beale had begun teaching Mathematics and in 1854 was asked by Plumptre to help him with Latin classes. At Queen's College, the moral welfare of the girls was the responsibility of a group of lady visitors who acted as chaperons to each class. A resident lady was appointed not only to superintend discipline and household matters, but also to take some share in the education by helping pupils in the evening. Conflicts often arose between the Council, the Committee of Education and the lady visitors and lack of good communication and other differences between the parties dogged the College for many years. The heaviest burden of day-to-day matters in the school fell on the Dean. There was the delicate matter in Victorian times of including Physiology on the timetable. Plumptre suggested the lectures might be given at the Queen's College in a popular style, simplified as to suit young female students, but insisted it was a very important branch of female education which had hitherto been almost entirely neglected.

In 1856, Dorothea Beale resigned. The news shook Plumptre, who greatly respected her, and he pressed her hard to explain her reasons. These included the inefficient system of lady visitors, many of whom did not turn up to classes, the continued male domination in formulating policy, and an insistence on pulling girls out of junior classes to attend professors' lectures before they were educationally prepared for this level of teaching.

In appearance he had a very Roman face. I have seen in Roman galleries many ancient Romans like him. Especially do I remember a bust still standing in one of the courts of Pompeii. His manner was shy, but at the same time, very genial and kind; however, he certainly inspired a wholesome awe, and it was a very serious thing to be reported to the Dean.
Camilla Crudace, a student at Queen's College remembering Edward Plumptre

If there is an evil which cannot be remedied, are you right in leaving those to whom the welfare of the College is very dear to all the discomfort of feeling or imagining that there is something amiss without giving them any clue to that which, whatever it be, has been important enough to lead you to resign?
Edward Plumptre writing to Dorothea Beale in 1856.

Plumptre was also prominent in trying to secure wider evening class tuition for students working in the daytime and accepted the office of Dean of King's College Evening Class Department without extra pay, also taking a share in teaching. The intake in the autumn of 1855 was 175, enrolling as follows:

French 64	History 19
Old Testament 56	Arithmetic 16
New Testament 52	Commerce 10
Mathematics 37	Drawing 9
Latin 34	Greek 7
English 32	Chemistry 6
German 19	

Dorothea Beale

Plumptre was unhappy with any small injustice affecting an individual. One lad requested a refund of fees because the class for which he had registered was changed in time without proper notice to an occasion when circumstances prevented his attending. The refund was not easily forthcoming and Plumptre took the matter as far as a written complaint to the Council.

Little is known of Plumptre's family life at this time save for a reference to a holiday enjoyed in the English Lake District in 1856. The Plumptres remained childless.

Queen's College was staffed by visiting professors and in 1854 the level of their fees was reduced by 25% to keep the books balanced. The professors did not always turn up and their absences were a constant thorn for Plumptre. He chided them for the non-fulfilment of the promises held out in the time-table to an extent which seriously affected the character of the College and naturally led to great dissatisfaction among the pupils and parents.

In 1857, Dorothea Beale's father pressed Plumptre over the failure of Queen's to become recognized as an institution granting certificates equivalent to degrees, but Plumptre shrank from that kind of challenge.

> Your notion that the Universities might act in the matter of female education has surprised me—I cannot yet believe the older Universities prepared to step so far forward to meet the requirements of the time—still less can I conceive they would act with the London University.
>
> The formation of a Board of the first men in their respective departments of science, and no professor examining pupils from his own school, has seemed to me, for years, the measure most calculated to raise the status and remuneration of the Governess and secure the public from ignorance and pretension.

The Queen's College: as soon as possessed of a charter, was apparently in a position to carry out these views— immediately after it was recognised to this extent, I was one, who waited on its Com: to know upon what terms it would affiliate with kindred societies—suffice it to say its views appeared to that deputation too narrow to be beneficial to the public. Since that time, I have thought more and conversed with others upon the subject. I enclose you two letters from Dr. Carpenter...
I am very desirous to see some body recognized by the Governm. granting certificates equivalent to degrees. I cannot but believe that Q. Coll. has sufficient influence, if conducted upon more liberal views, to secure this standing to the Governess, with every advantage to the Institution itself, whilst delay would seem to threaten the establishment of some less effective Board.

Extracts from a letter from Miles Beale to Edward Plumptre written on 22nd June 1857

When Dorothea's new job did not work out he tried without success to persuade her to return to Queen's. Nevertheless, he watched her later career with great interest and she consulted him over plans for her history textbook.

Back at King's, in 1858, a meeting of those officially concerned with and interested in the evening classes, decided that the Christmas vacation should start after the Chaplain's lecture on 22nd December: and that it be recommended to the council that the Principal and professors invite the students of the evening classes to a soirée in January: *Tea at 7.30. Lecture on 'The Electric Light'. Speeches, conversation. At 9.00 wine and cake.*

The Chapel at King's was a low and broad building, with a bareness reflecting Anglican mainstream theology of the early eighteen-thirties. Some alterations were made in 1852 by the architect William Burges, sometime pupil of the College School and later an engineering student: in 1859 he drew up a plan for its reconstruction in the Florentine style, with the choir modelled on that of Saint Clemente of Rome. In October of that year, Plumptre wrote to the College Principal urging rebuilding. He commented that there had been bestowed on the Chapel *as small an expenditure as possible of money, thought or skill.* He declared the building to be *at variance with the principles which the College was founded to assert*, which maintained *that the union of our students in the worship of God is the condition of all true education.* There was *nothing in the Chapel to satisfy in any degree, the sense of order and beauty which is found, with varying strength, in most young men.* The Council approved the principle and asked George Gilbert Scott, the architect perhaps most responsible for the Gothic revival of the mid-nineteenth century, to make a report, He responded with a plan modelled on the lines of an ancient Christian basilica, estimating the cost at *about £3,800 or £4,800.*

I have been informed to-day that you are going to leave Casterton at Christmas. I fear from this that you have not found your work there so pleasant as you hoped. If there are any particulars connected with your change of plan which you would like to tell me, or anything as to your prospects for the future, I need not say I shall be glad to hear them.

Edward Plumptre writing to Dorothea Beale on 7th December 1857

...The plan of the book seems to be very good, and I cannot doubt that you have carried into the details the same painstaking accuracy with which we used to be familiar in your work with us.

Edward Plumptre to Dorothea Beale, for whom he wrote a reference for her application to Cheltenham Ladies' College

The existence of two ranges of iron columns in the room below the Chapel offers facilities for carrying out the idea I have suggested. It is true that we cannot safely erect massive stone columns, but I would in their place suggest double columns of metal (iron decorated with brass) in their form not unlike those in the cloister of St. John Lateran. These might carry a light clerestory with an open roof, slightly decorated with colour, as in the basilica of S. Miniato at Florence. The great difficulty is the erection of the semi-circular apse, which is essential to the basilican form; but I see means of effecting this by bracketing out with iron brackets etc. The present large windows must be divided by a columnar mullion, and should be filled with stained glass, and the Chapel of course decorated in a simple and appropriate manner, and be fitted up in a style suited to its general design.

Extract from George Gilbert Scott's letter to the Secretary of King's College, 22nd December 1859.

Plumptre also advocated the setting up of an appeal fund, offering his services as its honorary secretary, if required, and promised a personal donation of £100. There was, however, far from unanimous support from the staff for the appeal. In particular the Reverend Professor Perowne, the Censor and Divinity lecturer, was concerned that the estimates would be greatly exceeded, that the appeal for the Building Fund for King's College Hospital remained undersubscribed, and that the general character of the worship left much to be desired. Plumptre responded by circulating copies of his reply to Perowne to the entire staff. To the objection about the budget, he wrote *we must make sure it doesn't get exceeded.* If less was raised, then even less would have to be spent: but if more, then the work could be more extensive. He was *unable to recognise the force* of the reasoning in regard to the Hospital Fund. *It is, of course, obvious, that if a man's income is in any way lessened, to that extent his power to join in good work is diminished also; but I cannot see the diminuation cancels the obligation to take part in such work (the claims of which would otherwise be acknowledged) to the extent that ability remains.* On the third point he countered complaints about the services, the organ and the choir with the retort: *So long as you have the worship of the College connected with what is meagre, slovenly, unworthy, there will be want of interest and want of energy…*

The final bill came to more than £7,000 of which donations provided £6,264. Some donors presented stained glass windows depicting scenes from the Gospels and Bible characters. With the new roof and some of the oak fittings in place, the re-opening service took place on 19th June 1864 with the Bishop of London, later Archbishop of Canterbury, Dr. Archibald Tait preaching the sermon.

Edward Plumptre had the ambition to become Principal of King's College on Professor Jelf's retirement. Whilst he was short-listed, he obtained only one vote. This perhaps gives us a particular insight into his character as a very good 'Number Two'.

In 1863 he was appointed as Professor of New Testament Exegesis, the area of theology concerned with the application of particular texts within the general rules of scripture. The same year he preached the Ordination Sermon at the enthronement of the Bishop of Gloucester and was appointed a Prebendary of St. Paul's Cathedral in London.

These appointments seem to have provided sufficient remuneration for him to spend less time in actual teaching, allowing him space to begin writing hymns and poetry.

O Lord of Hosts, all heaven possessing,
Behold us from thy sapphire throne,
In doubt and darkness dimly guessing,
We might Thy glory half have known;
But thou in Christ has made us Thine,
And on us all Thy beauties shine.

Illumine all, disciples, teachers,
Thy law's deep wonders to unfold;
With rev'rent hand let Wisdom's preachers
Bring forth their treasures new and old;
Let oldest, youngest, find in Thee,
Of Truth and Love the boundless sea.

Let Faith still light the lamp of Science,
And Knowledge pass from truth to truth
And Wisdom, in its full reliance,
Renew the primal awe of youth;
So holier, wiser, may we grow,
As Time's swift currents onward flow.

Grant us, O Lord, in patience gleaning,
Thy truths in memory's shrine to store;
Reveal to us each secret meaning
Of all Thy word's divinest lore;
When round us mists of evening rise,
Shine Thou upon our wistful eyes.

Bind thou our life in fullest union
With all thy saints from sin set free;
Uphold us in that blest communion
Of all thy saints on earth with Thee;
Keep thou our souls, or here, or there,
In mightiest love that casts out fear.

*Edward Plumptre: 'Beholding as in a Glass
the Glory of the Lord' sung to NEUMARK
(BREMEN: WER NUR DEN LIEBEN
GOTT). This text combines the author's
thinking as theologian and educationalist*

Edward Plumptre

48

O Light, whose beams illumine all,
From twilight dawn to perfect day,
Shine Thou before the shadows fall,
That lead our wandering feet astray;
At morn and eve Thy radiance pour,
That youth may love and age adore.

O Way, through whom our souls draw near
To yon eternal Home of Peace,
Where perfect love shall cast out fear,
And earth's vain toil and wandering cease;
In strength or weakness may we see
Our heavenward path, O Lord, through Thee.

O Truth, before whose shrine we bow,
Thou priceless pearl for all who seek,
To Thee our earliest strength we vow,
Thy love will bless the pure and meek;
When dreams or mists beguile our sight,
Turn Thou our darkness into light.

O Life, the well that ever flows
To slake the thirst of those that faint,
Thy power to bless what seraph knows?
Thy joy supreme what words can paint?
In earth's last hour of fleeting breath
Be Thou our conqueror over Death.

O Light, O Way, O Truth, O Life,
O Jesus, born mankind to save,
Give Thou Thy peace in deadliest strife,
Shed Thou Thy calm on stormiest wave;
Be Thou our hope, our joy, our dread,
Lord of the Living and the Dead.

O mightiest Three, O holiest One,
Of all in heaven and earth the King,
All power and glory Thou has won,
To Thee all saints and angels sing;
Still serving, through the eternal rest,
They do Thy bidding, and are blest.

Edward Plumptre: 'I am the Way,
the Truth, and the Life' from '
Lazarus and other Poems', May 1864.
Sung to EATON and SAINT MARK (Elliott)

The first burst of hymns included *O light whose beams illumine all* and, for use in the newly built chapel at King's College Hospital, *Thine arm, O Lord, in days of old.* The third verse, omitted in present day hymn-books, shows how highly technical medicine was rated by Plumptre in performing modern miracles. It is generally sung to SAINT MATTHEW. Most of his work, however, in that first period of reduced teaching load was of religious poetry published under the general title *Lazarus and Other Poems.* These included one text *Gomer* about Hosea's wife; *The Song of Deborah*; *Thoughts of a Galilean Convert* and *Three Cups of Cold Water.*

Thine arm, O Lord, in days of old,
Was strong to heal and save;
It triumphed o'er disease and death,
O'er darkness and the grave;
To Thee they went, the blind, the dumb,
The palsied and the lame;
The leper with his tainted life,
The sick with fevered frame.

And lo! Thy touch brought life and health,
Gave speech, and strength, and sight;
And youth renewed and frenzy calmed
Owned Thee, the Lord of Light;
And now, O Lord, be near to bless,
Almighty as of yore,
In crowded street, by restless couch,
As by Gennesareth's shore.

Though love and might no longer heal
By touch, or word, or look,
Though they who do Thy work must read
Thy laws in Nature's book,
Yet come to heal the sick man's soul,
Come, cleanse the leprous taint;
Give joy and peace where all is strife,
And strength where all is faint.

Be Thou our great Deliverer still,
Thou Lord of life and death;
Restore and quicken, soothe and bless,
With Thine almighty breath;
To hands that work, and eyes that see,
Give wisdom's heavenly lore,
That whole and sick, and weak and strong,
May praise Thee evermore.

Edward Plumptre.

The princely David, with his outlaw-band,
Lodged in the cave Adullam…

     …The brave undaunted few,
Gathering round David, sought the mountain hold.
The sun was hot, and all day long they watched
With spear in hand and never-resting eye,
As those who wait for battle. But at eve
The eye grew dim, the lips were parched with thirst,
And from that arid rock no trickling stream
Of living water gushed. From time-worn skins
The tainted drops were poured, and fevered lips
Half-loathing drank them up. And David's soul
Was weary; the hot simoom scorched his veins;
The strong sun smote on him, and, faint and sick,
He sat beneath the shadow of the rock.
And then before his eyes a vision came,
Cool evening, meadows green, and pleasant sounds
Of murmuring fountains. Oft in days of youth,
When leading home his flocks as sunset fell,
That fount had quenched his thirst, and dark-eyed
                                    girls,
The pride and joy of Bethlehem, meeting there,
Greeted the shepherd boy, their chieftain's son…

From 'Three Cups of Cold Water', a poem about David
written in May 1864

    …Words of mystic power
Came from my lips, when o'er me poured the flood
Of surging sound, the rushing, mighty winds
Sweeping the chords of life, and stirring thoughts
That must find utterance.

From 'Gomer' written June 1864.
Gomer was the wife of the Jewish prophet Hosea

In 1863, the Dean of Westminster, the Very Reverend A. P. Stanley, had been appointed as the new Principal of Queen's. He was chosen as a figurehead to give reassurance to the parents that sound theological training could be expected there, the more so as the controversial Maurice returned that year as lecturer. A parent wrote to Plumptre *I hope there will be no objection to the request that my daughter…may have exemption from 'Church History' during the remainder of this term if it is true that Mr. Maurice is to succeed the Archbishop of Dublin as lecturer in that subject—unless indeed he is to be merely the reader of the Dean of Westminster's paper.* The Principal was, indeed, no more than a figurehead with the day-to-day administration and leadership of the College falling to Plumptre. There was pressure from the girls seeking to be allowed to perform plays, but this was met with the opposition of the Council that it is not

The Dean reported that 18 or 20 pupils of the College had intimated their intention to offer themselves for the examination held in connexion with the syndicate of the University of Cambridge for local Examinations, and was requested to inform Miss Davies, the Lady acting as Honorary Secretary of the London Committee for organising such Examination, that while the Committee had not thought it right to interpose any obstacle to the carrying out of the pupils' intentions in this matter they had left them to do so, at the discretion of their parents, without selecting any picked candidates or giving them any special training.

Minutes of the Committee of Education at Queen's College meeting on 17th November 1863

The Dean having submitted a memorial proposed to be sent to the Vice Chancellor and Senate of the University of Cambridge, requesting the extension to girls of the system of local examinations, it was resolved, that the Committee are not prepared to take any corporate action on the matter but leave it to the professors to sign or not at their discretion.

An unsuccessful effort by Edward Plumptre to secure corporate action by the Committee of Education of Queen's College in 1864. Seventeen of the professors signed the memorial as individuals

Queen's College began the Women's Education Movement undoubtedly, but it became conservative, and did not grow...

Frances M. Buss in a letter to Dorothea Beale, 13th January 1889

The Waiting Room, Queen's College, London

desirable that any dramatic performance in costume should take place within the walls of the college. Plumptre tried again on the students' behalf seeking permission for charades without costume; but these too were forbidden. At the interview when Plumptre communicated the decision to the girls, they showed considerable resentment for which they later wrote a letter of apology, but remained insistent that they should not be expected to give recitations at the School's Annual Midsummer Week Festival.

A suggested memorial to the Vice Chancellor and Senate of the University of Cambridge requesting the extension of local examination to girls was not endorsed by Queen's Committee of Education and Plumptre had to content himself with many professors signing as individuals.

When Cambridge University opened the examinations, Plumptre reported to the Committee that several pupils were intending to sit; and the resolution that no obstacles should be interposed but no special help given was hardly encouraging.

The Government set up an enquiry in 1864 to look at the state of teaching in schools and Emily Davies was quick to write to Matthew Arnold asking whether Girls' Schools were to be included in the Commission's work. On hearing this was unlikely, she drew up a memorial to the Commissioners to which Plumptre was a signatory: and which led in due course to Queen's being visited.

In 1865 Plumptre published a series of essays under the collective title *Theology and Life*. Between 1864 and 1866, he served as select preacher at Oxford and this was followed by a year as Boyle Lecturer on *Christ and Christendom*, which was very well received in the academic world. He continued to write poem after poem with a further collection published in 1866 under the title *Master and Scholar*. Emily Davies sought to raise the status of Queen's in 1866: she wanted the age of entry raised, an entrance examination instituted, so that the College was really a place of *higher* education. Plumptre's reply was negative: and Emily Davies went on to establish the College that was eventually to be Girton.

> I find among the higher class of schoolmistresses in all parts of the country a strong disposition to put themselves into friendly relations with the London Colleges. They would like their schools to be to the Colleges what the Public Schools are to the Universities, but with that view they want the Colleges to be *really* places of higher education than schools can be. Hitherto they have been more like rival schools. In fact I have heard of a case in which a girl was sent first to College, and then to school to finish. I do not see how this can be got over except by raising the age of the College students and giving them some higher kind of examination than any that is open to schools. I believe there would be no difficulty in getting these from Cambridge, if the Colleges are willing to accept what the University has to give, that is, examinations for ordinary degrees.
>
> *Emily Davies writing to Edward Plumptre*
> *in September 1866*

Curb for the stubborn steed,
Making its will give heed;
Wing that directest right
The wild bird's wandering flight;
Helm for the ships that keep
Their pathway o'er the deep;
Shepherd of sheep that own
Their Master on the throne,
Stir up Thy children meek
With guileless lips to speak,
In hymn and song, Thy praise,
Guide of their infant ways.
O King of Saints, O Lord,
Mighty, all-conquering Word;
Song of the highest God
Wielding His Wisdom's rod...

*Edward Plumptre: From 'The Earliest Christian
Hymn from the Greek of Clement of Alexandria.'*
March 1864

O Milk of Heaven, that prest
From full, o'er flowing breast
Of her, the mystic Bride,
Thy Wisdom hath supplied;
Thine infant children seek,
With baby lips, all weak,
Filled with the Spirit's dew
From that dear bosom true,
Thy praises pure to sing,
Hymns meet for Thee, our King,
⠀⠀⠀⠀⠀For Thee, the Christ;
Our holy tribute this,
For wisdom, life and bliss,
Singing in chorus sweet,
Singing in concert sweet,
⠀⠀⠀⠀⠀The Almighty Son:
We, heirs of peace unpriced,
We, who are born in Christ,
A people pure from stain,
Praise we our God again,
⠀⠀⠀⠀⠀Lord of our Peace.

Another extract from the same Hymn

The following year Plumptre wrote *March, march onwards soldiers true* for the Chaplain of the Savoy to be sung to the popular tune of Costa's MARCH OF THE ISRAELITES from the oratorio *Eli*. He was busy, too, on English versions of the works of the Greek dramatist Aeschylus, whose majesty of language was matched by the boldness of his speculation upon problems of religion.

> **I doubt whether it would be wise to raise the age limit of admission until public opinion has ripened on the matter of employment for women...**
>
> *From Edward Plumptre's reply*
> *to Emily Davies*

...Change the subtle art,
And Man's weak eyes shall search into a world
As yet unknown, where myriad forms of life,
Swarming in bough, or dust, or lake, or stream,
The subtlest tissues of the flow'ret's crown,
That golden film that forms the May-fly's wing,
The wondrous transformation of the force
That circles through all being, these shall ope
Their secret stores, and Nature, like the king
Who showed of old his armour and his gems,
His gold and silver, to the travellers come
From a far country, lead the wanderer on
Through all her treasure-chambers, one by one,
Till nought is left unshown. Nor shall there fail
Due fruit of knowledge for the use of man;
The winds shall be his servants, and the fire
Shall do his bidding, and the mighty seas,
Foam-crested, he shall pass: and subtle skill
From out the poor and common elements
Of daily use shall frame a demon-power,
As dread as are the thunderbolts of God;
And when the nations meet in fierce array,
Armed for the battle, forth from either side,
No more the clouds of arrows and of spears
Shall darken air, and speed on wings of death,
But lightning-flashes, thunder-roars, and smoke
Of myriad forms of horror.

                  Shall it be
That this advance in knowledge will but bring
New strength for evil? I have dreamt my dream;
And still, it seems, there comes, as end of all,
The fiercer discord and the mightier hate.
Shall this be all the progress?...

Words put into the mouth of Roger Bacon, sitting at a desk dressed as a Franciscan friar, barefooted at St. Ebbe's, Oxford, at sunrise in the winter of 1267. From Edward Plumptre: 'Master and Scholar'

...let slip an opportunity for stating briefly the grounds on which I have been led to the conclusion that that wonderful poem came into the literature of Israel through the intercourse with the people of Southern Arabia, of which the visit of the Queen of Sheba was the great representative instance.

From the appendix to 'Theology and Life': 'The Authorship of the Book of Job'

                 ...I, who, poor,
Bereaved of father, mother, home, have found
Safe shelter here...

             ...All the threefold way
Of Grammar, Logic, Rhetoric, I leave
As childish things behind me, and I press
On to the great Quadrivium, where I know
Thy counsels will not fail me. How I fare
In music thou hast heard. Each day from thee
I learn the mystic powers and subtle laws
Of Numbers; and my hand is skilled to trace
The circles and triangles, whence we learn
To measure earth and heaven...

Part of the scholar's reply at St. Ebbe's in 1267

...Nay, father, 'tis not that I love thee less,
But, as thou taughtest, love the truth yet more,
That thus I speak. I come to pay my debt:
Thou gav'st me knowledge of the things of earth,
The wonders of this mighty universe;
I bring thee knowledge of the things of God,
The peace that passeth knowledge. Hear my tale,
The witness as of one who once was blind
And now sees clearly. Bertholdt's words of love
First drew me to him, yes, his love for thee:
And so I stayed and listened...

Words from the scholar on his return to St. Ebbe's
as his master is dying in 1294

Draw near, my son;
The hour is past, and that unwonted strength—
The flashing of the beacon ere it die—
Has left me faint and feeble. Eyes are dim,
Voice fails me, and the dews of death are chill.
Yet lift me; draw my couch from out the shade
Close to yon casement. I would fain behold
In the far East, once more, the orient blaze,
That vision of the glory of the Lord,
The token of the Love that streams alike
On evil and on good. Yes, fair and bright,
This crowning glory of the circling year,
This bright midsummer morn of Barnabas!
Well hast thou timed thy journey, faithful friend,
True son of comfort!
Lo! the shadows flee;
The glory of the Presence comes apace
With healing in its wings the golden light
Floods all the azure of that sapphire sea!
Jam lucis orto sidere! At last
The day-star has arisen!

Bacon's dying words to his scholar on St. Barnabas Day, 1294

But lightening-flashes, thunder-roars, and smoke
Of myriad forms of horror. **London during the Blitz - 1940**

Rejoice ye pure in heart,
Rejoice, give thanks, and sing;
Your orient banners wave on high,
The cross of Christ your King.

Bright youth and snow-crowned age,
Strong men and maidens meek,
Raise high your free, exulting song,
God's wondrous praises speak.

Yes, onward, onward still,
With hymn, and chant, and song,
Through gate, and porch, and columned aisle,
The hallowed pathways throng.

With ordered feet pass on;
Bid thoughts of evil cease,
Ye may not bring the strife of tongues
Within the Home of Peace.

With all the angels choirs,
With all the saints on earth,
Pour out the strains of joy and bliss,
True rapture, noblest mirth.

Your clear Hosannas raise,
And Hallelujahs loud,
Whilst answering echoes upward float,
Like wreaths of incense cloud.

With voice as full and strong
As ocean's surging praise,
Send forth the hymns our fathers loved,
The psalms of ancient days.

Yes, on through life's long path,
Still chanting as ye go,
From youth to age, by night and day,
In gladness and in woe.

Still lift your standard high,
Still march in firm array,
As warriors through the darkness toil
Till dawns the golden day.

At last the march shall end
The wearied ones shall rest;
The pilgrims find their Father's home,
Jerusalem the Blest.

Then on, ye pure in heart,
Rejoice, give thanks, and sing:
Your orient banner wave on high,
The cross of Christ your King.

Praise Him who reigns on high,
The Lord whom we adore,
The Father, Son and Holy Ghost,
One God for evermore.
Edward Plumptre: 'Processional'.
May 1865 sung to DAY OF PRAISE
(Steggall)

And there was no more sea:
So spake the Prophet of the golden lips,
Whose vision, clear and free,
Saw the far depths of that Apocalypse.

From each cavernous deep,
Where storms come not, and tempest wave is dumb,
The forms of them that sleep
Shall rise undying when the Judge shall come.

And then, its history o'er,
The great, wide sea shall flee and pass away,
And many a golden shore,
Long hidden, greet the bright, eternal day.

*No Sea!...*And shall the earth
Lose his love bride, with all her countless smiles?
Shall that diviner birth
Destroy the beauty of her myriad isles?

No! Far as man may dream
The wondrous glory yet to be revealed,
Still on the eye shall gleam
The emerald waters as a crystal field;

Still on the golden isles
The brightness of the Lord of light shall shine,
And still the countless smiles
Illume the face of that clear hyaline.

Only the drear expanse
Of waters barren, stormy, fathomless,
Shall meet no more our glance,
Shall leave the new-born earth our souls to bless.

No more the treacherous wave
Shall whelm poor wanderers in the homeless deep,
The dark and lonely grave
Where thousand shipwreked souls have slept their
sleep.

We know not how the light
Shall flow when neither sun nor moon shall shine;
And yet no shade of night
Shall mar the glory of the blaze divine.

We know not how the streams
Of those great rivers shall flow wide and free;
And yet the Prophet's dreams
Proclaim aloud, *There shall be no more sea.*

We know not...but the veil
Which hides it from our sight shall one day lift,
And, where in vision pale
As yet the darkness and the storm-clouds drift,

God shall make all things new,
And shoreless sea shall join with sealess shore;
And cleansèd eyes shall view
Might, wisdom, mercy, met for evermore.

Edward Plumptre: Extracts from 'And there was no more Sea'. From
'Master and Scholar etc. etc.' April 1865

In 1868, Plumptre finally gave up the Chaplaincy of King's College which he had held for over twenty years and took up the role, probably through the good offices of the Archbishop of Canterbury, of Rector of Pluckley in Kent. He also had charge of the neighbouring parish of Pevington; but as the population of the two together was only 777, his reponsibilties were not particularly onerous.

Pluckley Church

In 1870, a committee at Queen's examined a proposal to dispense with the services of a Librarian. Plumptre found himself in a minority of one and prepared his own report. He believed the presence of a Lady in the Library authorised to maintain order and entrusted with the care of the books, giving them out to pupils and seeing them returned and replaced had proved favourable to study and kept the library from loss. To such a lover of books as Plumptre, the saving of £60 stipend in this area was outweighed by the educational loss and he was compelled to look on the majority report as a false opinion.

Plumptre continued his scholarly output as a member of the Old Testament Company of Revisors of the Bible and as a side benefit he published a book of numerous Biblical Studies, including a review of the Psalms of the sons of Korah, authorship of the Book of Job, the old age of Isaiah, and the Babylonian Captivity. He also included amongst New Testament subjects Simon of Cyrene, a Philippian Sisterhood and the old age of Saint Peter.

> The work went on well, and within thirteen months of their arrival they were able to hold a solemn assembly for laying the foundation. Once again the priests appeared in their apparel, and blew their silver trumpets, and the Levites, the sons of Asaph, made music with their cymbals. The traditions of the Temple had not been forgotten, and the service was renewed *after the pattern of the ordinance of David,* and the old antiphonal chants were revived, and the people joined in the loud Hallelujahs with a great shout. With that shout, however, there was mingled a strangely discordant sound of wailing and lamentation. Some there were in that crowd old and grey-haired, *priests, and Levites, and chiefs of the fathers*, who had passed the limit of the threescore years and ten, and with them the memory of the past was stronger than their exultation in the present. They had seen the *first house*, the *holy and beautiful house.* They had gone with the *multitude that kept holy-day* to the house of God; and now they stood there, the last survivors of a race that had passed away, and they could not restrain their grief. *They wept with a loud voice; and many shouted aloud for joy; so that the people could not discern the noise of the shout of joy from the noise of the weeping of the people: for the people shouted with a loud voice, and the noise was heard afar off.* The emotion was natural and claims our sympathy, but it contained the germ of a perilous evil. That brooding over the vanished glory of the past led them, as it has led so many others, to be negligent and inactive in the present, and became an excuse for a selfish and cowardly apathy.
>
> *Edward Plumptre: From 'Biblical Studies':*
> *'The Babylonian Captivity', 1870.*

For *Church Hymns* (1871), Plumptre wrote his hymn on the Transfiguration, *Behold, they gain the lonely height,* sung to WAIN-WRIGHT. Stanley remained an absentee Principal, a figurehead with the day-to-day leadership of Queen's College falling to Plumptre. When the Council finally sought Stanley's resignation in 1872, he wrote: *I certainly understood when I accepted the post that such occasional lectures as I was able to give was all that was expected of me.*

Back in 1861, George Wythes had bought an estate at Bickley, then in Kent, and had sold it off in two-acre and five-acre plots for the building of large houses with extensive grounds. It was to the Church of Saint George built in 1863 in this affluent area that Plumptre moved as Vicar ten years later.

In 1873, the Council at Queen's appointed the Revd. J. Llewelyn Davies as the new Principal. The brother of Emily Davies, he sought to give Queen's a status his sister had dreamed for it, and which was beyond Plumptre's imagination. Plumptre was an excellent teacher, a good disciplinarian, an effective reconciler, but, despite generally liberal views, was neither innovator nor real educational visionary. Plumptre meanwhile served as Greenfield Lecturer and Examiner at Oxford University. Llewelyn Davies made some progress with the Queen's Committees, but just as they were beginning to make some vital decisions, he resigned. The Council turned again to the amiable Plumptre, who was appointed Principal in 1874.

Behold, they gain the lonely height,
The Master and the favoured three,
And through the thickest gloom of night
The glory of the Lord they see.

He prays, and lo! the wondrous cloud
Enwraps Him in its robe of fire;
And they on earth, in terror bowed,
Look upward, fainting with desire.

What forms are these that, floating near,
Hold converse with their Lord on high?
The prophet old, the Tishbite seer,
Why speak they now of Calvary?

Yea, seer and prophet witness gave
That all their work on earth was done:
For He, the Christ, was strong to save,
And all that they had hoped was won.

What wonder that the eager heart
Should seek to stay the flight of time;
And, from that vision loath to part,
Still linger on the loftier clime?

Ah, vain the dream! The morning clear
Brings back earth's weary life again;
The heavenly voice no more they hear,
But murmuring cries of doubt and pain.

Yet still within each faithful breast
There dwells the thought of what shall be;
That vision of the eternal rest,
That cloud of Love's deep mystery.

So grant us, Lord, through mists of night,
To see Thee in Thy glory clad;
Make us Thy children, heirs of light,
And with Thy gladness make us glad.
Edward Plumptre: From 'Church Hymns'

This perhaps finally determined that Queen's College should not develop into a Ladies' College and become part of the University of London; but should be effectively a girls' school as it remains to this day. Three years on, Plumptre ended his long association with Queen's, and passed the reins back to Llewelyn Davies who accepted a second stint as Principal. Plumptre had lost one last battle with the Committee. The elderly Resident Lady was replaced by Eleanor Grove, an aggressive feminist, an appointment not to his liking.

In 1875, Plumptre had been awarded a Doctorate of Divinity by Glasgow University. In 1877 he began to edit the magazine *Bible Educator,* a task undertaken until 1879. In 1878 however, he spent the Lent term abroad for the sake of his health. In 1879 he was also appointed Examining Chaplain to the Archbishop of Canterbury. At long last, in 1881, the Church of England offered Edward Plumptre preferment as Dean of Wells. He gave up his association of nearly forty years with King's College and a Plumptre Memorial Fund was instituted to offer a prize of £125 or thereabouts for the study of the English language by students of the Theological Department.

At Wells he became involved not only in his specific work as Dean but, with Canon Bernard, virtually refounded the Choir School; he lectured frequently in the Theological College and became involved in the life of the city, its hospital, workhouses and almshouses. Another interest was the Somerset Discharged Prisoners' Aid Society which had a hospice at Wells. He continued to write poetry and a new anthology *Things old and new* was published in 1884.

> Not thine the exile's weary lot to tread
> The stairs of others, as with bleeding feet,
> Nor yet in lonely wanderings still to eat
> The doled-out bitter gifts of others' bread:
> Thine rather is it to have nobly led
> When others halted or would fain retreat,
> To steer the State, though fierce the storm-winds beat,
> On to the wished-for haven, sails full spread.
> Unlike in outward fortunes, yet we trace
> In thee and in our Dante many a line
> Of inward likeness, sharing each the grace
> Aye given to those that seek Truth's inmost shrine,
> The will that stands four-square to Fortune's blows,
> Thoughts that age ripens, hope that wider grows.
> *Edward Plumptre: 'A Parallel'*

In the *Standard* of 9th January 1883 a letter to Giánbattista Giuliani from the Liberal statesman, William Gladstone, was printed, and Plumptre picked up this reference to Dante to write a poem *A Parallel.* Gladstone wrote: *In the school of Dante I have learned a great part of that mental provision, however insignificant it be, which has served me to make the journey of life up to the term of nearly seventy-three years.* Other subjects for poems in the anthology include John Bunyan and his masterpiece telling of a pilgrim's progress; a silver wedding day; the funeral service of Catherine Tait, wife of the Archbishop of Canterbury; the revocation of the Edict of Nantes; Rome under the Emperor Decius; the contemporary debate about ritual in the Church of England; the Franco-Prussian War of 1870; and the life of the Duke of Albany. Hymns included one for Harvest Thanksgiving, a text on the Transfiguration, a processional, and verses for choral and dedication festivals. There are two poems about America, one sparked off by George Herbert's lines:

> Religion doth on tiptoe stand,
> Ready to pass to the American strand.

Five and twenty summers lie behind you in the past,
Since the solemn words were spoken that made you one for life;
Five and twenty summers, coming slowly, fleeting fast,
Binding still, with links of silver, the husband and the wife.

Joys and griefs in that dim distance now are blended into one,
Each building up the fabric of the love and peace of home;
Rest and labour, health and sickness, have reared it, stone by stone,
And the house shall stand unshaken, though winds beat and waters foam.

Ah! we know not, and we ask not; the times are in His hand
Who orders all things well for all loving hearts and true;
And the years shall bring the peace which we cannot understand,
Life's welcome euthenasia, be they many years or few.

Edward Plumptre: Two extracts from 'A Silver Wedding Day'

O wondrous Birth, O heavenly Word,
Of God begotten, Lord of Lord;
O awful Babe, O glorious Child,
Man's nature bearing undefiled,
In whom, thus veiled from mortal eye,
We own Incarnate Deity.

In wondrous ways to eye and heart
He doth His risen self impart;
In that new life, so full, so rare,
All things that live may claim their share;
Flowers round His glorious footsteps spring,
Birds chant their carols to the King.

¤   ¤   ¤   ¤   ¤   ¤   ¤

¤   ¤   ¤   ¤   ¤   ¤   ¤

The star once more their friend and guide,
They wend their homeward way,
And leave fierce Herod to his rage,
To threaten and to slay;
With wailing cry the stern command
Is heard through Bethlehem's coast,
And mothers yield their infant sons
To join the martyr's host

Nations twain hath Christ united,
Jew and Greek alike invited,
All are welcome there;
And the new wine now is filling
Souls that with new thoughts are thrilling,
Claiming each its share.

Edward Plumptre: Verses selected from his
translations of 'The Sarum Missal' choosing
a piece from the sections for Christmas,
Epiphany, Easter, and Whitsuntide

Four names of honour mark a week of light,—
Names of high place on history's noblest scroll,—
And through the ages as they onward roll
Shall shine like stars in azure vault of night;
First, he who told the tale of tyrant might
That urged the quest of sad Evangeline;
The sage who fearless wrought in Truth's deep mine,
Seeking the Law that orders all things right;
The poet-friend whose clarion voice was heard,
A call to freedom for the toiling slave;
And he whose story many a heart has stirred
To keep the track of statesmen wise and brave;
We may not meet again, yet still the past
For me shall live as long as life shall last.

Edward Plumptre: 'New England Memories'

The second celebrates four Americans Plumptre had the joy of meeting. *New England Memories* remembers Longfellow, Emerson, Whittier and Bancroft. It is from Whittier's poem *The Brewing of Soma* that the hymn *Dear Lord and Father of mankind* is culled: the Quaker's condemnation of elaborate ritual and music in worship—the foolish ways of the text—is an interesting example of a hymn taken out of its original context.

Plumptre in his anthology turns also to a Buddhist idyll of Vasadavatta and translates from the work of Adam of St. Victor, the twelfth-century Parisian author of liturgical poetry and from that of his contemporaries.

Although written in 1865, another poem included in the 1884 publication is *The Emperor and the Pope* about Trajan and Gregory which ends with the lines:

See, they lead him from his dungeon,
Bent with age and cramped with fetters;
And around his limbs his raiment
Hangs in scanty folds and tattered.
White his hair with years and sorrow,
Worn his face with pain and watching;
But his eyes still keep their brightness,
And his spirit knows no terror,
Though around him whispered murmurs
Tell of coming death and torture.

Dark-bowed sophists, priests and soldiers,
Servants of the mighty Caesar;
Men who bow before their idols,
Jove or Neptune or Quirinus;
Slaves who own no God but Mammon,
Doubters, of all creeds long weary,—
These are joined in league against him;
For they know their craft endangered,
Know that in him dwells a spirit,
Mighty, loving, strong to conquer,
Which will war against their falsehood,
Till their shrines are all deserted,
And through temple's shattered columns
Roam, for throng of eager pilgrims,
Dog and wolf, and pard and panther;
Blow, for clouds of wafted incense,
Mists and vapours from the marshes.

Edward Plumptre: Opening lines of 'The Martyr'
recounting the persecution of Christians under the
Emperor Decius.

For all who give to child or saint
A cup of water as they faint,—
For these be sure that all is well,
I hold the keys to Death and Hell.

His note printed after the poem in the first edition of *Things Old and New* reveals the author's continuing interest in life beyond mortal death.

"The popularity of the story thus told, as meeting the cravings for the wider hope which were repressed but not extinguished by the mediaeval theology which had its starting-point in the teaching of Augustine is seen:

(1) By its prominence in the life of St. Gregory as given in the *Golden Legend...* ,where the answer to the Pope's prayer is given in a form that deserves special notice.

> Thenne answerd a voys fro God, saying:
> I have now herd thy prayer, and have spared
> Tragan fro the payne perpetuelly. By thys thus,
> as somme saye, the payne perpetuell due to Tragan
> as a mescreaint ('unbeliever') was somedele taken
> awaye, but for all that he was not qoyte from
> the pryson of helle: for the sowle may well be
> in helle, and fele there no payne, by the mercy
> of God.

(2) By the equal prominence given to it in the *Vision of Piers Ploughman...* , the great storehouse of the freer thoughts that were struggling in the minds of Englishmen in the fourteenth century, with the noticeable addition that the Pagan Emperor was saved:

> Nought through preiere of a Pope
> But for his pure truth.

(3) A yet nobler representative of mediaeval thought is found in the great Florentine poet who, for the most part accepts the condemnation of the heathen, because unbaptized, with an unpitying coldness. I quote the story as told by him in the *Purgatorio...*:

> There was wrought out the glory great and high
> Of that great prince of Rome whose excellence
> Gregorius moved to his great victory
> (To Trajan, Emperor, I this praise dispense).
> And a poor widow stood beside his rein,
> Bowed down with many a tear and grief intense;
> And round about him 'twas all thronged with train
> Of mounted knights, and eagles all of gold
> In the wind fluttering, glittered clear and plain.
> Among them all that wretched woman told
> Her tale, so seemed it, 'I for vengeance call
> For my son's death that turns my heart's blood cold.'
> And he replied, 'Wait thou till it befall
> That I return; and she 'Nay, good my Lord',
> Answered as one with grief impatient all,
> 'If thou return not'...'Who comes next,' his word
> So ran, 'will do it for thee.' She, 'The good
> Of others will not help thee, when 'tis heard
> That thou thine own neglectest.' 'Let thy mood',
> Said he, 'be glad: at once the right, I do;
> So justice wills ; me pity hath subdued.'

John Greenleaf Whittier

The tale is carried to its close when Dante finds the soul of Trajan in Paradise, and seeks to reconcile the salvation of the Emperor with the traditional dogma of the schoolmen by an ingenious variation from the popular version of the story. Trajan, as he tells the tale, had been actually restored to life, and the soul had come back to the body, and so there was an opportunity given for faith in Christ, and for the baptism without which salvation was impossible.

> The glorious soul of whom I tell the praise,
> Returning to his flesh for briefest hour,
> Believed in Him who could direct his ways,
> And so, believing, glowed with fiery power
> Of love unfeigned, that, when he died again,
> He was thought worthy of this blissful bower."

Hymnwriter John Ellerton, a contemporary of Plumptre, also showed concern about the fate of those dying without a life of conventional religious observance. Plumptre traced the ambivalent views of Christian theologians down the ages in his *The Spirits in Prison, and other Studies on the Life after Death*, also published in 1884.

The year 1885 was probably the high spot of the Dean's time at Wells. Cathedral and City celebrated the bicentenary of the consecration of the illustrious Bishop Thomas Ken and the anniversary of the Trial of the Seven Bishops. The new window on the north aisle of the choir was first seen by the public on 29th June. The sermon was preached by the Right Reverend Dr. Alexander, Bishop of Derry, and the husband of the hymnwriter Cecil Frances Alexander, author of *There is a green hill far way*. By 1888, Plumptre's sensitive two-volume biography of *Thomas Ken* was published.

In proposing the toast of the 'Health of the Dean of Wells', his lordship spoke with admiration of their grand cathedral, their bright service ...the distinguished ability which Dr. Plumptre had shown in his early youth, and reminding them how the Dean of Wells had thoroughly fulfilled the promise of those early days in the theologian, the critic, the scholar and the poet, he said that anyone who heard his most practical and instructive catechising in the Cathedral on the preceding day must have seen how fitted he was for the work to which God had called him. The Dean had been very active in getting up the present glorious festival and in bringing it to a happy end, and he cordially proposed his health.

From an account in the 'Wells Journal' of the lunch which formed part of the Ken celebrations. The toast was proposed by the Bishop of Derry.

Thomas Ken

Before many days had passed Ken was called to bear his part in one of the closing scenes of the tragedy. Monmouth, who, with Lord Grey, a German officer, and others, most of whom took other directions in the course of the flight, had fled from Sedgmoor before the battle was over, belying by this cowardice the promise of courage given in his French campaign, had been taken, after two days' wandering, by the King's troops near Cranbourne Chase, at a spot which still bears the name Monmouth's Close, lying in a ditch, covered with brambles, half dead with hunger and fatigue, was allowed but a short shrift, and managed to exhibit in the compass of a few days all his characteristic vices of vacillation, falsehood, faithlessness. He pleaded for his life with an abject pusillanimity, threw all the blame on his associates, asserted that he had signed the unpardonable proclamation without reading it, half hinted that he might, if his life was spared, go back to the religion in which his early years had been trained (it

Wells Cathedral

was characteristic of both parties to that interview —
July 13 — that the nephew should have thought this the
surest path to his uncle's clemency), grovelled on the
ground in prostrate and tearful humiliation, and finally,
when all hope was gone, rose, with some touch of the
courage of despair, to prepare for the inevitable end.
The 15th of July was fixed for his execution. The
intervening hours were spent in piteous appeals to the
King, the Queen, and ministers, for life on any terms.
The only reply was significant enough. Roman Catholic
priests were sent to prepare him for his death. When he
rejected their ministrations, Ken was sent for by James
to give such spiritual counsels as the case required, and
with him were associated his friends Francis Turner,
Bishop of Ely, and George Hooper, now Rector of
Lambeth, and at Monmouth's own request, Tenison,
afterwards Archbishop of Canterbury. Ken and Turner
were with him during the night, and at his wish, all four
accompanied him to the place of execution. They found
it hard to rouse his conscience to activity, or to elicit the
full confession which was, in their eyes, the note of a
true repentance. He seemed at first insensitive to the

When they had to deal with the excesses of the rich, they might suppose them to be the result of a deliberate love of pleasure and self-indulgence; in the strictest sense, it was the lust of the flesh, the desire of the eye, and the pride of life...

...the drunkenness of the poor: they rather endeavoured to escape from evils by narcotising and drugging themselves with spirits, that they for a few moments might stupify themselves, so that they did not remember the evils against which they had to struggle.

From a sermon by Edward Plumptre on Temperance as reported in the 'Wells Journal' of 8th October 1885.

misery and death that he had brought upon his followers, and declared that he had *nothing on his conscience, and had wronged no man.* He would not admit that he had been wrong in leaving his wife for Lady Henrietta. He had been forced, when too young to give an intelligent consent, into a marriage which was no marriage. This had led to a reckless license of life, from which he had been rescued by the new attachment for one who was worthy of his love, and to whom he had been faithful.

Part of Edward Plumptre's biography of 'Thomas Ken' in which the night before the execution of the Duke of Monmouth is described

Plumptre was an active supporter of the Temperance Movement. Besides his preaching on this theme, he produced an unusual pamphlet suggesting that if William Shakespeare had lived in the nineteenth century, he would most likely have been a total abstainer.

I shall seem, perhaps, to be pushing the licence of enquiry almost beyond its legitimate limits, when I announce my intention to *supoena*, as it were, the great dramatist to give his evidence on the Temperance question...

...there are words of Shakespeare's which are often on the lips of those who deride, or obstruct, either the moral or legislative action contemplated by the Church of England Temperance Society. Almost as familiar as the platitude that *you can't make men sober by Act of Parliament* is the quotation flung at the abstainer: – *Dost thou think, because thou are virtuous, that there shall be no more cakes and ale? (Twelfth Night, II. 3).* That seems to the quoter, as it seemed to Sir Toby Belch, to be a sufficient answer to all remonstrances on the degradation which excess in drink brings with it. Yes; but has the quoter read his Shakespeare? Does he recollect how the rollicking pot-valiant knight is described? Listen to Olivia's questions and the Clown's answers when the knight reels in 'half-drunk' as the stage directions have it.

Olivia: What's a drunken man like, fool?
Clown: Like a drowned man, a fool and a madman; one draught above heat makes him a fool; the second mads him; and a third drowns him.
Olivia: Go thou and seek the coroner, and let him sit o' my coz; for he's in the third degree of drink; he's drowned. Go, look after him.
Clown: He is but mad yet, madonna.

In the leaflet Plumptre quotes seven other plays to make his case that, had he then been alive, Shakespeare would have been found in the chair at the Stratford branch of the Church of England Temperance Society!

A particular innovation during Plumptre's period of office at Wells Cathedral was the introduction of gas lighting. He had a wide vision of the role of cathedrals in their diocese and, at a time when some politicians were flying the kite of disestablishing the Church, he read a paper to the Church Congress at Plymouth.

The illumination of the Nave is a great success; in every part—even in the shadow of the great columns—there is ample light to read the smallest print, while the general effect is striking and beautiful. The capitals of the clustered columns, the grand mouldings of the bays and of the arcading of the triforium, and the quaint and grotesque heads which protrude from the wall above the nave arches, stand out in bolder relief, and the lofty vaulting seems to gain in altitude. The light is obtained from brackets— the gift of the Dean—on the columns on either side of the Nave...

From the 'Wells Journal',
24th September 1885

Do I then despair of the future of our Cathedrals, or content myself with the Cassandra utterance of one who sees 'rocks ahead'. Far otherwise than that. So far as I can feebly act myself, so far as I can advise others, my counsel would be 'Do not depend on legislation'. Do not wait for it. Be content for the present with the day of small things. Prophesy once more to the four winds, and bid them breathe life into whatever in ourselves and our systems has become ossified and dead. Invite preachers from within and from without who have the gift of utterance. Let special services for children win the rising generation of our future masters to feel that the Cathedral is their home, that there, at any rate, they can find a 'free and open' Church. Revive the other services so that they may be musically and otherwise, not by Act of Parliament or Episcopal decree, but by their own completeness, the standard of ritual to the diocese. Let each member of the Cathedral find in the history of the past and the opportunities for the present, that which shall prompt him to higher aims and more resolute activities. Let the Dean be as the father of his choir boys, and the Chancellor see that his schools are efficient and well organised, and the Precentor do his best to make the choral element of worship, in the highest liturgical acts as well as in daily worship, in the hymns, which win the hearts of the people, as well as the anthems, which satisfy the expert, as near perfection as may be attainable. Where there is a theological college, let the Cathedral dignitaries do what they can to help its students. Let Prebendaries and Honorary Canons remember that the distinction of which they are justly proud, involves also the duties of brotherhood and co-operation. Let all alike remember that the people of the Cathedral city and of the Diocese, are, in the truest sense, their neighbours, and have the first claim on their thoughts, time and money. If we do these things, then, with or without Acts of Parliament, we shall make our Cathedrals a praise and glory in the land, instead of a bye-word and proverb of reproach. For each and all, there is the counsel which Aelfric of York gave of old, as a master to his scholars, *Esto quod es* – 'Be that thou art'.

There is no such quaint, strange, and wholly delightful Deanery, as the great rambling ancient house, built round two inner courts, and crying out for a hierarchic income to maintain it worthily: which stands near the wonderful west end of the great church: and in which you may very easily lose yourself, and wander about up and down unexpected flights of steps and along great corridors. Its peaceful garden, an unoverlooked expanse of grass and trees, lightened in June with the blaze of flowers: can Winter ever come there? Here is the enviable home of the Very Rev. E. H. Plumptre, D. D.: a man worthy to stand among the foremost of the Anglian Hierarchy for learning, eloquence, and large and liberal views. Nor does it fail to commend him to many earnest souls, that his wife is the sister of the saint and prophet, Maurice...

It is difficult to arrive at Wells by railway: but a man of resolution, who is content to change his train at several road-side stations, and who is prepared to give up a large part of the day to travel, may make sure of ultimately reaching the little city amid its environment of deep Southern green.

...As the hour of worship draws near, the *Dean's Verger* presents himself at the Deanery, duly robed, and bearing the accustomed poker: and the Dean, in his surplice, follows him across the velvety green to a lesser western door. It is all very pleasant in high Summer, and it looks well: but how in Winter sleet and storm? In a little while the Voluntary peals out: the surpliced train enters the exquisite Choir with all reverence and the beautiful worship is worthily rendered.

...only the strong good sense and reasonableness, which are his marked characteristics, could have prevented one holding his doctrinal views from becoming in some measure a suspect theologian: as Arnold, Whately, and Stanley became with not more reason. But the Dean's own teaching, and that of others, have leavened the intelligence of the country: and it is perfectly certain that those who incline to a larger hope than could once have been, are thoroughly entitled to their place in the Church of England. Archbishop Tait, wise and strong man, publicly thanked God that the honest Anglican cleric might legally cherish and express the hope that it some way, and some time, which only presumption would define, Good is to vanquish Evil at the last. And even the stupidest Philistine, though holding Plumptre to be a somewhat dangerous man, and though ready to repeat in a somewhat spiteful whisper *Maurice's brother-in-law, you know*; will now in most cases acknowledge that *The Dean means well.* Plumptre is, as everybody knows, a poet as well as a theologian:...Many, indeed, have looked for his further elevation: and the legend is probably true that the connection with Maurice prevented his getting one of the great Professorships of Divinity...

From 'Celebrities at Home: Edward Plumptre' in 'The World', August 12, 1885

Wells in Victorian Times

The Dean continued work on the English version of *Divina Commedia*, the story of an imaginary journey through Hell, Purgatory and Paradise under the guidance of Reason and Faith, and probably the greatest poem of the Middle Ages, written by the Florentine Dante Alighieri. Indeed, Plumptre was recognised as the greatest Dante scholar of his day.

He also wrote *For all thy countless bounties* to mark the Jubilee Year of Queen Victoria and found time to be a regular contributor to *The Contemporary Review*, to give the Cambridge University sermons *Movements in Religious Thought*, including one on Agnosticism which was well reviewed in *The Spectator*, and to write a book on confession and absolution.

In 1889 he wrote the hymn *Thy Hand, O God, has guided*, widely used since as an ecumenical hymn, but essentially addressed to the various wings of the Anglican Church. Tunes include ST. THEODULPH(VALET WILL ICH DIR GEBEN), CRUGER (Herrnhüt) and THORNBURY.

That year he suffered bereavement by his wife's death. His last publication in 1890 was of the plays by the Athenian tragic poet Sophocles, of whom Euripides said: *He paints men as they are; I paint them as they ought to be.*

He died on 1st February 1891 and is buried in Wells Cathedral. There is a memorial brass in the north aisle of the choir beneath Ken's window and a tombstone of Aberdeen granite with a cross laid upon it. Amongst his bequests was £1,000 towards restoration of an ancient building as a College Library; £2,000 for the education of choristers, and a sum to rebuild Wells Cottage Hospital, where his arms are carved in stone. This memorial is in keeping with the Hospital set up by his forefathers' actions in earlier centuries.

Mortals needs must bear
The chances which the Gods on high
         shall give;
But those who fall upon self-chosen ills,
As thou has fallen, they have little claim
To pardon or compassion. Thou art fierce,
And wilt not list to one who counsels thee,
And, if one give advice in pure good will,
Thou hatest him, and deemest him a foe.
Yet I will speak, invoking holy Zeus who
         reigns,
The guardian of all oaths. Be sure of this,
And write it in the tablets of thy mind,
Thy pain has come to thee by will of Gods.
In that thou cam'st too near to Chryse's
         guard,
The serpent who in secret keeps his watch
Over the unroofed precincts of her shrine...
From Sophocles: 'Philoctetes' translated by Edward Plumptre. The extract is part of a speech by Neoptolemos, son of Achilles, addressed to Philoctetes.

Thy Hand, O God, has guided
Thy flock, from age to age;
The wondrous tale is written,
Full clear, on every page;
Our fathers own'd Thy goodness,
And we their deeds record;
And both of this bear witness,
One Church, one Faith, one Lord.

Thy heralds brought glad tidings
To greatest, as to least;
They bade men rise, and hasten
To share the great King's feast;
And this was all their teaching
In every deed and word,
To all alike proclaiming
One Church, one Faith, one Lord.

When shadows thick were falling,
And all seem'd sunk in night,
Thou, Lord, didst send Thy servants,
Thy chosen sons of light.
On them and on Thy people
Thy plenteous Grace was pour'd,
And this was still their message,
One Church, one Faith, one Lord.

Through many a day of darkness,
Through many a scene of strife,
The faithful few fought bravely,
To guard the Nation's life.
Their Gospel of redemption,
Sin pardon'd, man restored,
Was all in this enfolded,
One Church, one Faith, one Lord.

And we, shall we be faithless?
Shall hearts fail, hands hang down?
Shall we evade the conflict?
And cast away our crown?
Not so: in God's deep counsels
Some better thing is stored;
We will maintain, unflinching,
One Church, one Faith, one Lord.

Thy Mercy will not fail us,
Nor leave Thy work undone:
With Thy right Hand to help us,
The Victory shall be won;
And then, by men and angels,
Thy Name shall be adored,
And this shall be their anthem,
One Church, one Faith, one Lord.
                    Edward Plumptre

Thick clouds from censers waved by fair-haired boys,
The two tall candles lit on either hand,
Prayers in a speech that none can understand,
Bright robes, rich tones, that thrill the sense with joys,
Teaching that neither heart nor brain employs:–
Is it for these we leave our fathers' ways,
Turn to poor pageants of the bygone days,
As though the man should play with childhood's toys?
Shall we not rise and ask for curb of law
To check what else will grow without restraint?
Shall not her voice the stubborn wills o'erawe
That lead the sheep astray and spread the taint?
Surely in vain our martyrs strove and bled,
If forms of errors old their dark spells round us spread.
      Edward Plumptre: 'Ritualism: Counsel for the Prosecution'

Nay, judge not rashly. To their Master they
Or stand or fall, as He discerns aright:
It were ill done to crush with arm of might
Whom He may welcome in His own great day.
Weak souls there are, for whom the Truth's pure ray,
Cloudless and clear, o'ertakes the feebler sight,
Whose spirit craves the softer, broken light
Of rainbow hues that in the sunset play.
Perchance these rites may bring to those who dwell
In the dull life of city's crowded street,
A vision of the glories that excel,
A foretaste of Heaven's harmonies complete.
Be not too quick the strife of forms to end,
Lest thou, against thy will, Christ's little ones offend.
          Edward Plumptre: 'Ritualism: Counsel for the Defence'

Ken Memorial Window and Plumptre plaque, Wells Cathedral

Robert Bridges

Robert Bridges

Robert was born on 23rd October 1844 as the fourth son and eighth child of John Thomas Bridges at the family home of Roselands at Walmer in Kent. His father was a gentleman farmer whose family had prospered in the county for several generations. Robert's direct male ancestor was the Reverend John Bridges (or Brydges) who was Rector of Harbledown, just west of Canterbury, from 1579 to 1589. His mother Harriet Elizabeth was a daughter of Reverend Sir Robert Afflick, who, after serving as vicar of Silkstone near Barnsley in Yorkshire, succeeded in 1833 as fourth baronet and lived thereafter at Dalham Hall, a few miles east of Newmarket in Suffolk.

As in most well-to-do homes, the young Robert was cared for by a nurse. Catherine is recalled in a poem written in 1921 entitled *Kate's Mother.*

> Long ago—when as yet the house where I was born
> was the only home I knew and I no bigger then
> than a mastiff-dog may be, and little of clothing wore
> but shirt and trews and shoes and holland pinafore:
> then was my father's garden a fairy realm of tree-
> worship, mimic warfare and ritual savagery
> and past its gates a land of peril and venture lay
> my field of romance the steep beach of the wild sea
> whither might I go wander on high-days for long hours
> tended at every step by a saint, a nurse and mate
> of such loving devotion patience and full trust
> that of all Catharines she hath been my only Kate.
>
> *Robert Bridges: From 'Kate's Mother'*

...my mother used to amuse us younger children with tales of her own childhood. A merry, gameson spirit was not the least of her charms, and that she had been so universal a favourite in her girlhood may have been greatly due to the original pranks with which she would enliven any society whose dulness or gravity provoked her. Among the various scenes of her fund of stories Finedon was one. Her grandfather had once been rector of the parish, and the family associations were continued by occasional visits to Hall or Rectory, in days that seemed to the younger generation to have been unusally supplied with a dignified and long-lived aristocracy of generals, baronets, and divines, whose features were familiar to me among the many miniatures, silhouettes, and other little portraits, mementos of personal affection, that hung in my mother's rooms, and in their eighteenth-century fashions, kindled our imaginations of a strange and remote world...

Robert Bridges recalling his mother in a memoir introducing the poems of his friend Digby Mackworth Dolben.

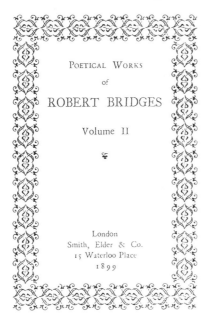

POETICAL WORKS

of

ROBERT BRIDGES

Volume II

London
Smith, Elder & Co.
15 Waterloo Place
1899

Frontispiece of 1899 volume of Robert Bridges' *Poetical Works*

Bridges gives us a further word picture of the garden of his childhood home and the outlook over the North Sea in an earlier poem *Elegy: The Summer-House on the Mound.* Nearby was Walmer Castle, a coastal fort erected on the orders of King Henry VIII around 1540. In the early 1700s it became the home of the Warden of the Cinque Ports and was so occupied by the Duke of Wellington, often seen about by the young Bridges.

...mother espying one of these old-fashioned gentlemen taking a nap by the open window of a garden-room, drew his pigtail through to the outside, and shut the sash down upon it. Her freak, inspired by simple delight in the prospect of the mighty anger and fuss that would ensue when the hero awoke, was fully successful, and the consequent disturbance went on rippling with amusement in her memory for at least seventy-five years. I should lack piety and humour if I neglected this opportunity of according to the absurdity a renewed lease of life.

Robert Bridges writing of his mother in a memoir introducing the poems of his friend, Digby Mackworth Dolben.

There grew two fellow limes, two rising trees,
Shadowing the lawn, the summer haunt of bees,
Whose stems, engraved with many a russet scar
From the spear-hurlings of our mimic war,
Pillar'd the portico to that wide walk,
A mossy terrace of the native chalk
Fashion'd, that led thro' the dark shades around
Straight to the wooden temple on the mound.
There live the memories of my early days,
There still with childish heart my spirit plays;
Yea, terror-stricken by the fiend despair
When she hath fled me, I have found her there;
And there 'tis ever noon, and glad suns bring
Alternate days of summer and of spring,
With childish thought, and childish faces bright,
And all unknown save but the hour's delight.

High on the mound the ivied arbour stood,
A dome of straw upheld on rustic wood:
Hidden in fern the steps of the ascent,
Whereby unto the southern front we went,
And from the dark plantation climbing free,
Over a valley look'd out on the sea.
That sea is ever bright and blue, the sky
Serene and blue, and ever white ships lie
High on the horizon steadfast in full sail,
Or nearer in the roads pass within hail,
Of naked brigs and barques that windbound ride
At their taut cables heading to the tide.

Robert Bridges: From 'Elegy: The Summer-House on the Mound'

The observant lad, later in the poem *Kate's Mother*, gives a detailed account of one of his earliest day's out when he and an elder sister were taken by the nurse to visit her elderly mother for tea.

A blazing afternoon in splendor of mid-July
Kate and my elder sister and I trudged down the street
past village pond and church, and up the winding lane
came out beside the windmill on the high cornland
where my new world began. A wheel-worn sunken track
parted the tilth, deep rugged ruts patch'd here and there
with broken flints raked in from strewage of the ground,

baked clay fissured by drought, as splinter'd rock unkind
to a child's tread, and on either hand the full-grown corn
rose up a wall above me, where no breeze might come
nor any more sight thence of the undulating sweep
of the yellow acres nor of the blue main below.

¤ ¤ ¤ ¤ ¤

For difficulty and roughness and scorch of the way
then a great Bible-thought came on me: I was going
like the Israelites of old in the desert of Sin,
where forty years long they journey'd in punishment:
'twas such a treeless plain as this whereon they went,
this torrid afternoon under the fiery sun
might be the forty years; but I forgat them soon
picking my way to run on the low skirting banks
that shelved the fields, anon foraging mid the ranks
fending the spikey awns off from my cheeks and eyes
wherever I might espy the larger flowers, and pull'd
blue Cockle and scarlet Poppy and yellow Marigold,
whose idle blazonry persists to decorate
the mantle of green and gold which man toileth to weave
for his old grandmother Earth...

¤ ¤ ¤ ¤ ¤

(O how interminable to me seem'd that way!)

¤ ¤ ¤ ¤ ¤

...'twas a storeroom of wonders, but my eyes returned
still to the old dame, she was the greatest wonder of all,
the wrinkles innumerable of her sallow skin,
her thin voice and the trembling of her patient face
as there she swayed incessantly on her rocking-chair
like the ship in the clock: she had sprung into my ken
wholly to enthrall me, a fresh nucleus of life-surprise
such as I knew must hold mystery and could reveal:
for I had observed strange movement of her cotton skirt
and as she sat with one knee across the other, I saw
how her right foot in the air was all a-tremble and jerked
in little restless kicks: so when we sat to feast
about the table spredd with tea and cottage cakes
whenever her eye was off me I watched her furtively
to make myself assured of all the manner and truth
of this new thing, and ere we were sent out to play
(that so Kate might awhile chat with her mother alone)
I knew the SHAKING PALSY...

Robert Bridges: Extracts from 'Kate's Mother'

Flocks and herds shall bleed no more,
Stanched the flood of reeking gore,
Lo ! He comes from Heaven above;
   Victim to His Father's love.

¤   ¤   ¤   ¤   ¤

While to Heaven thy pious love
Duly vows the sacred dove,
And upon thy bosom lies
   More than dove-like sacrifice.

Verses 2 and 4 from 'Sion, ope Thy hallowed
dome' in 'The Child's Christian Year'

Sundays were strictly observed in the Bridges' household with the children required to learn by heart poems and hymns commended by John Keble in *The Child's Christian Year*, much of which was a very inferior kind of verse. Bridges' father died in 1853 and his considerable estates were sold, leaving a financial provision for Robert which was to allow him freedom from an absolute necessity to earn a living. One of Robert's last childhood memories from that seaside home at Walmer overlooking busy shipping lanes was in March 1854 when the first naval vessels powered by steam were assembling to sail to the Baltic.

One noon in March upon that anchoring ground
Came Napier's fleet unto the Baltic bound:
Cloudless the sky and calm and blue the sea,
As round Saint Margaret's cliff mysteriously,
Those murderous queens walking in Sabbath sleep
Glided in line upon the windless deep:
For in those days was first seen low and black
Beside the full-rigg'd mast the strange smoke-stack,
And neath their stern revolv'd the twisted fan.
Many I knew as soon as I might scan,
The heavy *Royal George*, the *Acre* bright,
The *Hogue* and *Ajax*, and could name aright
Others that I remember now no more;
But chief, her blue flag flying at the fore,
With fighting guns a hundred thirty and one,
The Admiral ship *The Duke of Wellington*,
Whereon sail'd George, who in her gig had flown
The silken ensign by our sisters sewn.
The iron Duke himself,—whose soldier fame
To England's proudest ship had given her name,
And whose white hairs in this my earliest scene
Had scarce more honour'd than accustom'd been,—
Was two years since to his last haven past:
I had seen his castle-flag to fall half-mast
One morn as I sat looking on the sea,
When thus all England's grief came first to me,
Who hold my childhood favour'd that I knew
So well the face that won at Waterloo.
Robert Bridges: From 'Elegy: The Summer-House on the Mound'

That year his mother married again, this time the Reverend John Edward Nassau Molesworth, who, when he was at Saint Martin's, Canterbury, had pioneered the *Penny Sunday Reader*. Robert's stepfather in 1854 was Vicar of Rochdale in Lancashire and this became his new family home. Then, like the Duke of Wellington before him, Robert was sent to Eton for school days of happy memory. Although a serious lad, he enjoyed athletic activities, including boating on the nearby Thames, and ended his schooldays as Captain of his House.

It was in studying the poetry of the Roman poet Ovid that Bridges became excited by the beauty of poetic form, confirmed for him in the English language especially through the works of John Milton and John Keats. Perhaps the poets he read together with the friendship of Vincent Coles and Digby Dolben were the especially significant factors in Bridges' schooldays.

> Down he plunges, king of waters, foaming over Boveney Weir,
> Dear to swimmer, dear to rower, dear in Spring, in Summer dear;
> Other streams for other oarsmen—all our homage this one claims,
> Gliding through the grassy meadows, broad and bright, the silver Thames.
> *Up and down the river—all the summer long,*
> *Skim the river reaches—sing the river song.*
>
> First of March, with snow and tempest, bids the eight-oars strip and row,
> First of March to first of August sees the eight-oars come and go;
> Eight-oars, four-oars, gigs and cedars—many boats with many names—
> Flying, racing, lounging, floating—up and down the silver Thames.
> *Up and down the river—all the summer long,*
> *Skim the river reaches—sing the river song.*
> *Verses chosen from 'A River Song' in a nineteenth century issue of the*
> *'Eton College Chronicle'*

Him the Almighty Power

Hurled headlong flaming from th' ethereal sky
With hideous ruin and combustion down
To bottomless perdition, there to dwell
In adamantine chains and penal fire
Who durst defy th' Omnipotent to arms.

¤   ¤   ¤   ¤   ¤

A dungeon horrible, on all sides round
As one great furnace flam'd; yet from those flames
No light, but rather darkness visible
Serv'd only to discover sights of woe,
Regions of sorrow, doleful shades, where peace
And rest can never dwell, hope never comes
That comes to all.

¤   ¤   ¤   ¤   ¤

Mammon led them on,

Mammon, the least erected Spirit that fell
From heav'n, for ev'n in heav'n his looks and thoughts
Were always downward bent, admiring more
The riches of heaven's pavement, trodden gold,
Than aught divine or holy else enjoy'd
In vision beatific.

John Milton: Passages from Book 1 of 'Paradise Lost'

Or on the tabled sward all day
Match your strength in England's play,
Scholars of Henry, giving grace
To toil and force in game or race;

¤   ¤   ¤   ¤   ¤

Or whether with naked bodies flashing
Ye plunge in the lashing weir; or dashing
The oars of cedar skiffs, ye strain
Round the rushes and home again;—

Or what pursuit soe'er it be
That makes your mingled presence free,
When by the schoolgate 'neath the limes
Ye muster waiting the lazy chimes;

¤   ¤   ¤   ¤   ¤

For you shall Shakespeare's scene unroll,
Mozart shall steal your ravished soul,
Homer his bardic hymn rehearse,
Virgil recite his maiden verse.

Now learn, love, have, do, be the best;
Each in one thing excel the rest:
Strive: and hold fast this truth of heaven—
To him that hath shall more be given.

Robert Bridges: Selected verses from 'Founder's Day'
written for the 450th anniversary of Eton College
in 1890

...I was then reading Shakespeare for the first time, and my imperfect understanding hindered neither my enjoyment nor admiration. I also studied Milton, and carried Keats in my pocket. But Dolben, though I cannot remember that he had any enthusiasm for Shakespeare, was more widely read in poetry than I, as he was also more abreast with the taste of the day. Browning, Mrs Browning, Tennyson and Ruskin were the authors of whom he would talk; and among the poets he ranked Faber, a Romanized clergyman, of whose works I have nothing to say, except that a maudlin hymn of his, when Digby showed it me, provoked my disgust...

Robert Bridges: From a memoir
introducing the poems of
Digby Mackworth Dolben

Season of mists and mellow fruitfulness,
  Close bosom-friend of the maturing sun;
Conspiring with him how to load and bless
  With fruit the vines that round the thatch-eaves run;
To bend with apples the moss'd cottage-trees,
  And fill all fruit with ripeness to the core;
    To swell the gourd, and plump the hazel shells
  With a sweet kernel; to set budding more,
And still more, later flowers for the bees,
Until they think warm days will never cease,
    For Summer has o'erbrimm'd their clammy cells.

John Keats: The opening lines of 'Ode to Autumn'

John Keats

Vincent Stuckey Stratton Coles was born in the old rectory of Shepton Beauchamp in Somerset five months after Robert's birth at Walmer. His father James Stratton Coles was parson and squire and his mother, a daughter of west-country banker Vincent Stuckey, was attracted to the Tractarian movement. In 1858 he arrived at Eton, deeply influenced by High Church ideas, shortly after confirmation at Martock Church. Despite his intense religious convictions and lack of aptitude for games, he established several friendships, including one with Bridges. He suffered from some fairly rough bullying, and once all the boys of Mr Hales' house were docked of a holiday for sousing Coles and his belongings. By 1862 he possessed copies of John Mason Neale's *Sequenticæ ex Missalibus Germanicis, Anglicis, Gallicis, aliisque Medii Collectæ* and soon afterwards Mone's *Hymni Latini Medii Ævi*. In later life, after serving as Rector of Shepton Beauchamp on the death of his father, a model parish of the Catholic revival, he was Librarian and then Principal of Pusey House, preached often in London's St. Paul's Cathedral, visited South Africa to assess what a mission to that country might achieve, served as Warden of the Community of the Epiphany at Truro and as Diocesan Chaplain to Bishop Gore in Oxford. He too became a hymnwriter and his texts include *We pray thee, heavenly Father* for use at Holy Communion and *Ye who own the faith of Jesus* for the Feast Day of Saint Mary the Virgin.

Vincent Stuckey Coles...was preëminent for his precocious theological bent and devotion to *the cause* ...was indeed the recognised authority, and our leader in so far as universal esteem and confidence could give any one such a position amongst us...

From a memoir by Robert Bridges acting as a preface to the poems of Digby Mackworth Dolben. It concerns the small group of Pusey-ites at Eton

May the Mother's intercessions
On our homes a blessing win,
That the children all be prospered,
Strong and fair and pure within,
Following our Lord's own footsteps,
Firm in faith and free from sin.

For the sick and for the aged,
For our dear ones far away,
For the hearts that mourn in secret,
All who need our prayers to-day,
For the faithful gone before us,
May the holy Virgin pray.

Vincent Coles: Verses 4 and 5 of 'Ye who own the faith of Jesus' sung to
DEN DES VATERS SINN GEBOREN

Coles' *Act of Devotion* has echoes of words also found in the Methodist Covenant Service:

O my God, I am not my own, but Thine; take me for Thine own, and make me in all things to do Thy blessed will. O my God, I give myself to Thee, for joy or for sorrow, for sickness or for health, for life or for death, for time or for eternity. Make me and keep me Thine own, through Jesus Christ our Lord.

...As I happened to be captain of the house, I was able without inconvenience to discharge those duties of elder relative which are so specially obnoxious to Eton boys. I enrolled Dolben among my fags, and looked after him...

He was tall, pale, and of delicate appearance, and though his face was thoughtful and his features intellectual, he would not at that time have been thought good-looking. Indeed he was persistently teased by the little boys for his appearance, his neglectful dress, his abstracted manner, and his incapacity for games at ball...

For, different as we were in physical temperament, different as boys could be, we were both of us terribly serious, determined, and of artistic bent, and had come through the same sort of home-teaching to the same mental perplexity. We satisfied our natural bias towards art by poetry, but the magnitude of the religious problems which we had been led up to face was occupying our attention; it involved both our spiritual and practical interests in life. A sectarian training had provided us with premisses, which, so long as they remained unquestioned, were of over-whelming significance: they dominated everything: the logical situation was appalling: the ordinary conventions of life were to us merely absurd: we regarded the claim of the church in the same way as Cardinal Newman had elaborated it in his writings; and we were no doubt indirectly influenced by his views, though I had never myself read any controversial books, and had little taste for them. We were in fact both of us Pusey-ites, and if we reacted somewhat differently to the same influences, yet neither of us at that time doubted that our *toga virilis* would be the cassock of a priest or the habit of a monk.

From Robert Bridges' memoir introducing the poetry of Digby Mackworth Dolben

Digby Mackworth Dolben, a cousin of Robert Bridges, born in February 1848, arrived in Eton in 1862 from Finedon Hall in Northamptonshire. His father inherited a strong Protestant tradition and young Dolben was educated from infancy in the strictest religious creeds and motives. On arrival at a private school in Cheam, he was an evangelist amongst his schoolfellows, who included Wentworth Beaumont Hankey who preceded him at Eton by one term. Bridges described him as of a different species, a saint among the little ruffians. Like Bridges, he was a poet, and despite the age difference, they became close friends.

Digby was drowned in 1869 in a swimming accident, but many years later Bridges was to honour his old schoolfriend in editing a volume of his poetry.

Eton College

Was it a dream—the outline of that Face,
Which seemed to lighten from the Holy Place,
Meeting all want, fulfilling all desire?
A dream—the music of that Voice most sweet,
Which seemed to rise above the chanting choir?
A dream—the treadings of those wounded Feet,
Pacing about the Altar still and slow?
Illusion—all I thought to love and know?
   Strong Sorrow-wrestler of Mount Calvary,
Speak through the blackness of Thine Agony,
Say, have I ever known Thee? answer me!
Speak, Merciful and Mighty, lifted up
To draw those to Thee who have power to will
The roseate Baptism, and the bitter Cup,
The Royal Graces of the Cross-crowned Hill.
   Terrible Golgatha—among the bones
Which whiten thee, as thick as splintered stones
Where headlong rocks have crushed themselves away,
I stumble on—Is it too dark to pray?
Digby Mackworth Dolben: 'Good Friday'

Lilies, lilies not for me,
Flowers of the pure and saintly—
I have seen in holy places
Where the incense rises faintly,
And the priest the chalice raises,
Lilies in the altar vases,
    Not for me.

   Leave untouched each garden tree,
Kings and queens of flower-land.
When the summer evening closes,
Lovers may-be hand in hand
There will seek for crimson roses,
There will bind their wreaths and posies
    Merrily.

   From the corn-fields where we met
Pluck me poppies white and red;
Bind them round my weary brain,
Strew them on my narrow bed,
Numbing all the ache and pain.—
I shall sleep nor wake again,
    Best forget.
Digby Mackwoth Dolben: 'Poppies'

From falsehood and error,
From darkness and terror,
From all that is evil,
From the power of the devil,
From the fire and the doom,
From the judgement to come—
Sweet JESU, deliver
Thy servants for ever.
Digby Mackworth Dolben: 'A Prayer'

I was also abhorrent towards Ruskin, for I thought him affected, and was too ignorant of painting to understand his sermonizing; nor could I imagine how another could presume to tell me what I should like or dislike...

I loved some of Tennyson's early lyrics, and had them by heart, yet when I heard *The Idylls of the King* praised as if they were the final attainment of all poetry, then I drew into my shell, contented to think that I might be too stupid to understand, but that I could never expect as good a pleasure from following another's taste as I got from my own...

As for Browning, I had no leanings towards him; but when Digby read me extracts from *Saul*, I responded fairly well...

Our instinctive attitudes towards poetry were very dissimilar, he regarded it from the emotional, and I from the artistic side...

What had led me to poetry was the inexhaustible satisfaction of form, the magic of speech, lying as it seemed to me in the masterly control of the material: it was an art which I hoped to learn...

I was related through my mother with both Dolbens and Mackworths, indeed my mother's great-grandmother in the direct male line was a Dolben, so that I myself am in some fractional part a Dolben...
Extracts from Robert Bridges' memoir introducing the poems of Digby Mackworth Dolben

I was myself leaving at Election, but I stayed on after term was over in order to entertain my younger brother, who came to spend a few days with me, in making excursions on the river, and hearing the music at S. George's, where Dr. Elvey had allowed me to compile the anthem list for the week, so that my brother, who was an enthusiastic musician, might hear some of the earlier church music.

Robert Bridges: From a memoir introucing a volume of Digby Mackworth Dolben's poetry

Bridges was a great lover of music, so it is not surprising that he found his way in the latter part of his schooldays to St. George's Chapel, a sumptuous Gothic building in the grounds of Windsor Castle. St. George's was founded by King Edward III as the chapel of the Order of the Garter. Its carved stools in the choir are overhung with the banners of the present occupants of the Order. Bridges often attended the first part of Evensong especially for the opportunity to hear early English choral music. He sat in the north aisle or in the organ loft, slipping out after the anthem to be back at the college not too late for five o'clock school.

> Old Thunder***s is dead, we weep for that,
> He sings for aye his lowest note, B Flat.
> Unpursed his mouth, empty his mighty chest,
> His run is o'er, and none may bar his rest.
> We hope he is not d—d, for if he be
> He's on the wrong side of the middle sea.
> Nay we are sure if weighed he will not fail
> Against the Devil to run down the scale;
> While even three-throated Cerberus must retreat
> From one that bellows from his sixteen feet:
> Or should he meet with Peter at the door,
> He'll seize the proper key as heretofore,
> And by an easy turn he'll quickly come
> From common time straight to *ad libitum*.
> This is the equal temperament of Heaven,
> Sharps, crotchets, accidentals, all forgiven,
> He'll find his place directly, and perspire
> Among the bases of the Elysian quire.
>   Fear, dwellers on the earth, this acquisition
> To the divine etherial ammunition;
> O thunder is let loose, a very wonder
> Of earthborn, pitiless, Titanic thunder:
> We who remain below and hear his roar,
> Must kneel and tremble where we laughed before.

Robert Bridges: 'Epitaph on a Gentleman of the Chapel Royal'
written in 1869

The Pre-Raphaelite Brotherhood was founded in 1848 by three young artists, Dante Gabriel Rossetti (also a poet), John Everett Millais and William Holman Hunt, who sought to react against anecdotal and unimaginative work by the Royal Academy of the day by abandoning the rules of art established by Sanzio Raphael (1483-1520), and by expressing with vitality and freshness genuine Biblical ideas and painting from nature. Their ideas spilled over into other art forms.

From Eton the young Bridges went to Corpus Christi College, Oxford, where he was moved by Pre-Raphaelite more than Tractarian ideas. At Oxford, Bridges began a friendship with the poet Gerard Manley Hopkins, who came up to Balliol the same year. Their friendship was sustained by frequent correspondence until Hopkins died of typhoid in 1889. Bridges issued a complete edition of his poems in 1918. Much of Hopkins' poetry makes use of the device of 'sprung rhythm', as found in alliterative poetry written in Old and Middle English. In 1866, Hopkins became a Roman Catholic and in 1868 began training as a Jesuit, serving as a priest in Ireland and England before undertaking a teaching assignment. Bridges was saddened at his friend's decision to become a Roman, with which cause he had no sympathy; but they remained close in the ensuing years.

> Come then, your ways and airs and looks, locks, maiden gear,
>   gallantry and gaiety and grace,
> Winning ways, airs innocent, maiden manners, sweet looks,
>   loose locks, long locks, lovelocks, gaygear, going gallant,
>   girlgrace—
> Resign them, sign them, seal them, send them, motion them
>   with breath,
> And with sighs soaring, soaring síghs deliver
> Them; beauty-in-the-ghost, deliver it, early now, long before
>   death
> Give beauty back, beauty, beauty, beauty back to God, beauty's
>   self and beauty's giver.
> See: not a hair is, not an eyelash, not the least lash lost; every hair
> Is, hair of the head, numbered.
> Nay, what we had lighthanded left in surly the mere mould
> Will have waked and have waxed and have walked with the wind
>   what while we slept,
> This side, that side hurling a heavyheaded hundredfold
> What while we, while we slumbered.
> O then, weary then why should we tread? O why are we so
>   haggard at the heart, so care-coiled, care-killed, so fagged,
>   so fashed, so cogged, so cumbered,
> When the thing we freely fórfeit is kept with fonder a care,
> Fonder a care kept than we could have kept it, kept
> Far with fonder a care (and we, we should have lost it) finer, fonder
> A care kept.—Where kept? Do but tell us where kept, where.—
> Yonder.—What high as that! We follow, now we follow.—
>   Yonder, yes yonder, yonder,
> Yonder.

Gerard Manley Hopkins: From 'The Golden Echo'
('Maidens' Song' from 'St. Winefred's Well')

In 1866 Robert's younger brother Edward died. They were very close and the bereavement devastated Robert, perhaps explaining why the degree he obtained in Literae Humaniores was only of second class despite his excellent brain. The event plunged him into deep sorrow and he recounted that it considerably altered the hopes and prospects of his life. It took the gilt from acting as stroke in his college boat which was second on the river and of a visit to Paris for a regatta there.

The young Bridges both loved and could afford to travel. After leaving college Robert spent nine months in Germany becoming fluent in the language. His companion William Sanday, son of a well known cattle and sheep breeder, was a theologian who lectured at Oxford until 1869; his life's work was to be dedicated to a scientific study of the New Testament. Other trips while Bridges was in his twenties were to Egypt,

As to the relation of Poetry to Religion. True Religion, the conviction and habit of a personal communion between the soul and God, is of too unique and jealous a temper to allow of any artistic predominance and yet we find the best expression of it in Poetry: indeed the poetic expression of the spiritual life is of such force that its beauty may hold the mind in slavery to false ideals.

I believe it to be greatly due to this that the English people are still mentally enslaved to a conception of God altogether unworthy and incompatible with our better notions: and, if it is the old Hebrew poetry which is greatly responsible for this delusion, then it seems reasonable to look to our own poets for our release.

On this general question of religion I shall take only that one point. We have spiritually outgrown the theology of the Reformation, and our churches, in endeavouring to make their obsolete ideas work, find their most effective agent in the beauty of our English translation of the Old Testament which, while secular art was in decay, captured the artistic susceptibility of the people.

Robert Bridges: From 'The Necessity of Poetry'

Syria and the Netherlands. He went to Italy with Harry Wooldridge, the painter, musician and critic with whom he shared lodgings in London at 50 Maddox Street off Regent Street. Wooldridge had at first been articled at Lloyds but had swapped his office desk for an easel at the Royal Academy School. His Academy paintings were always well hung; his work included decorating stained glass and furniture; an accomplished singer, he was chosen to re-edit Chappell's *Popular Music of the Olden Time* in 1893. In 1895 he was appointed Slade Professor of Fine Art at Oxford.

In 1869 Bridges entered Saint Bartholomew's Hospital as a medical student. If that seems an unexpected way forward, it can perhaps best be explained by his love of the pursuit of all knowledge; though who can measure another man's motives? With his trips abroad, he seems to have pursued his studies in a leisurely fashion but qualified as Bachelor of Medicine in 1874.

Medicine had not separated Bridges from poetry and in 1873 he published his first collection. He chose Basil Montagu Pickering to print it, probably because their recent type-facsimile edition of *Paradise Lost* commended itself to him. Later, Bridges rejected many of these poems, including the delightful piece about Adam and Eve which begins *Her eye saw, her eye stumbled.* His own definitive choice of what should be retained was decided in Book 2 of the six-volume edition of his poetry published about the turn of the century.

50 Maddox Street, London

Her eye saw, her eye stumbled:
　Her fingers spread and touched it:
It was so ripe it tumbled
　Off in her hand, that clutched it.

She raised it up to smell it:
　Her jealous tongue ran o'er it:
Ere the thought rose to quell it,
　Her keen teeth closed and tore it.

There as she stood in wonder,
　And smacked the flavour fruity,
She scanned it o'er and under,
　And marvelled at its beauty.

'It's fair', she said, 'and fairest
　Just where the sun's rays strike it;
The taste's the strangest, rarest;
　It's bitter, but I like it.'

¤　　　¤　　　¤　　　¤

To man she brought it, bitten,
　She brought it, she the woman,
The fruit, of which 'tis written
　The eating should undo man.

'Taste, taste!' she cried, 'thou starvest;
　Eat as I ate, nor fear it,
For of all the garden's harvest
　There's nothing like or near it.

'Fair to the eyes, and fairest
　Just where the sun's rays strike it:
But oh! the taste's the rarest,
　It's bitter, but thou'lt like it.

¤　　　¤　　　¤　　　¤

He took the fruit she gave him,
　Took it for pain or pleasure:
There was no help could save him,
　Her measure was his measure.

Through her teeth's print, the door of it,
　He sent his own in after;
He ate rind, flesh, and core of it,
　And burst out into laughter.

'Tis fair', he cried, 'and fairest
　Just where the sun's rays strike it:
The taste's the strangest, rarest.
　It's bitter, and I like it.'

Robert Bridges: From 'Poems 1873'

O Golden Sun, whose ray
My path illumineth:
Light of the circling day,
Whose night is birth and death:

That dost not stint the prime
Of wise and strong, nor stay
The changeful ordering time,
That brings their sure decay:

Though thou, the central sphere,
Dost seem to turn around
Thy creature world, and near
As father fond are found;

Thereon, as from above
To shine, and make rejoice
With beauty, life and love,
The garden of thy choice,

To dress the jocund Spring
With bounteous promise gay
Of hotter months, that bring
The full perfected day;

To touch with richest gold
The ripe fruit, ere it fall;
And smile through cloud and cold
On Winter's funeral.

Now with resplendent flood
Gladden my waking eyes,
And stir my slothful blood
To joyous enterprise.

Arise, arise, as when
At first God said LIGHT BE!
That He might make us men
With eyes His light to see.

Scatter the clouds that hide
The face of heaven, and show
Where sweet Peace doth abide,
Where Truth and Beauty grow.

Awaken, cheer, adorn,
Invite, inspire, assure
The joys that rise thy morn,
The toil thy noons mature:

And soothe the eve of day,
That darkens back to death;
O Golden Sun, whose ray
Our path illumineth!
Robert Bridges:
'Morning Hymn'
first printed in the pamphlet
issued in 1879

...I will merely state that it is not unusual for a casualty physician to see 150 patients in less than two hours; and I shall not be using extravagant language if I call this quick work, and say that very great accuracy cannot be arrived at in such hasty proceedings. Indeed, it is not easy to see what he can be supposed to do except work miracles, considering that if he had only to take down the patients' names and addresses he would be over-occupied; and yet his duties are very distinctly understood. A metaphor is usually employed to define them. If a casualty physician were to complain of the number of cases he has to see, he would probably be told that he is not supposed to attend to them or prescribe for them very much; that the surgery is the filter of the hospital, or that he himself is the filter. It is in vain to point out that filtering is of necessity a process slow in proportion to its efficacy, while the quick filtering of patients is almost unintelligible. Making bricks without straw cannot be compared to it; that is done every day, but filtering quickly is a contradiction in terms. And yet filter he must, and filter quickly too; and be prepared to hear his quick filtrate shamefully ill-spoken of in the wards and in the out-patient rooms. But this theory of a system, which breaks down as soon as it is seriously examined ...vanishes like smoke when a physician finds himself face to face with some 200 paupers, who are many of them seriously ill, some mortally, many but slightly, but nearly all with considerable bodily inconvenience or pain, which, unless disease be a joke, and this the whole constitution of our Hospital forbids us to suppose, entitles them to his patient attention and investigation, and demands his skill and advice. He will decide at once that what he has to do is the best that can be done under the circumstances, and he will make the best of a bad business, and take it patiently, even when his filtrate comes bubbling back into the surgery from the steward's office because there is no vacant bed, or from from the out-patient room because it was not filtered before eleven a.m.

Robert Bridges: From 'An Account of the Casualty Department' in the 1878 'St. Bartholomew's Hospital Reports'

I found to-day out walking
    The flower my love loves best.
What, when I stooped to pluck it,
    Could dare my hand arrest?

Was it a snake lay curling
    About the root's thick crown?
Or did some hidden bramble
    Tear my hand reaching down?

There was no snake uncurling,
    And no thorn wounded me;
'Twas my heart checked me, sighing
    She is beyond the sea.

Robert Bridges: this poem printed in the 1899 edition was born in the 1873 volume.

In 1876 he published a collection of twenty-four sonnets under the title *The Growth of Love*, which was superseded by a new version in 1889 of seventy-nine sonnets. He printed sixty-nine of them in his definitive edition in 1898 noting: *It was not my wish to offer these sonnets to the public, but since they have been published in America without my permission...and have been mentioned in professional criticism, I have thought it wise to come to their rescue...cutting out ten, and amending the worst places in others where I could.*

O flesh and blood, comrade to tragic pain
And clownish merriment; whose sense could wake
Sermons in stones, and count death but an ache,
All things as vanity, yet nothing vain:
The world, set in thy heart, thy passionate strain
Reveal'd anew; but thou for man didst make
Nature twice natural, only to shake
Her kingdom with the creatures of thy brain.

    Lo, Shakespeare, since thy time nature is loth
To yield to art her fair supremacy;
In conquering one thou hast so enrichèd both.
What shall I say? for God—whose wise decree
Confirmeth all He did by all He doth—
Doubled His whole creation making thee.

Robert Bridges: 'Sonnet 21' from 'The Growth of Love' (1898 Edition)

In 1877, Bridges was appointed Casualty Physician at Saint Bartholomew's Hospital. When his stepfather died that year, he made a home for his mother and himself at 52 Bedford Square. That year, too, the Hospital for Sick Children's new building was completed nearby, and in 1878, Bridges started work at Great Ormond Street. He stayed only briefly, moving on to serve at the Great Northern Hospital then located in Caledonian Road which runs from King's Cross to Holloway.

He remained there until, overcome with pneumonia, he retired from medical practice, wintering in Italy in 1881.

Meanwhile, in 1879, Bridges made friends with the poet-parson and church historian Reverend Richard Dixon, a bond that was to last until Dixon's death in 1909. Dixon also loved painting and appreciated the early efforts of the Pre-Raphaelites. The son of a noted Wesleyan preacher, he served, after curacies in London, as Vicar of Hayton and later as Vicar of Warkworth.

'I rode my horse to the hostel gate,
    And the landlord fed it with corn and hay:
His eyes were blear, he limped in his gait,
    His lip hung down, his hair was gray.

'I entered in the wayside inn,
    And the landlady met me without a smile;
Her dreary dress was old and thin,
    Her face was full of piteous guile.

'There they had been for threescore years,
    There was none to tell them they were great,
Not one to tell of our hopes and fears;
    And not far off was the churchyard gate.'
Richard Dixon: 'I rode my horse to the hostel gate'

Bridges himself continued to write and publish poems in pamphlet, including a volume printed in 1884 by another new friend the Reverend C. H. Daniel, who had access to agreeable typefaces. The typography and decoration used for his work was of great concern and interest to Bridges and he became learned in typography as well as in his numerous other fields of expertise.

When Bridges returned from Italy, he sought a new home for his mother and himself, leaving London for Yattendon Manor in a Berkshire village a few miles from the river at Streatley.

52 Bedford Square, London

O Peace, O Dove, O shape of the Holy Ghost,
    I would not vex thee with too subtle thought,
Put thee in fear by hopes, send thee to coast
    Regions unknown for what I dearest sought.
To rough delights I would not open course,
    Nor thy composure fray with vague desire,
Nor aspiration hold that did thee force
    Nor move a step that I could not retire.

Nay, nay, I pray thee, close thy startled eye,
    Compose again thy self-stirred plumes, nor aim
At other station, in timidity
    Of fancied plots, which here I all disclaim.
Well, fly then! for perchance from heavenward flight
    Gentler on me thou mayst again alight.
Richard Watson Dixon: 'To Peace'

continued from page 84 margin
...With the lowest estimate of female garrulity, one must recognise the grandeur of the feat accomplished in giving separate audience to the troubles of 150 women in three-hours and a quarter...though I learned to enforce laconicism by making them stand with their tongues out much longer than was necessary for medical diagnosis I yet find that an average female case lasted one-fiftieth of a minute longer than a male case...

...in the prevalence of sore throats, those who complained of them were set on one side till a long enough row of them had been collected to justify my rising from my seat to visit them all at once with the spatula...

I will leave it to the reader, if he has any further taste for figures, to calculate the rule-of-three sum, if in thirty-five years, 0 patients increase to 190,000, how many will 190,000 have become at the end of the world? It is probable that before that time, a necessity will arise of reforming our Casualty Department...

...deducting income-tax, which promises to be a permanent charge, the sum paid to the casualty physician per patient is about 7/10d per patient (just under 1/3rd of a new penny)...This fee presents an amusing discrepancy with the 30,000 and odd guineas which the Royal College of Physicians might consider us annually entitled to. There are extremes certainly which do not meet, and it seems a pity that there is no resting-place in the wide interval which separates them. For instance, if the patients were to fee us sixpence a visit, which is not much considering that many of them owe their complaints to drinking eight pennyworth of beer a day, we should each of us draw from them an income of over £750 per year.

Further extracts from 'An Account of the Casualty Department' in 'Saint Bartholomew's Hospital; Reports' for 1878'

When men were all asleep the snow came flying,
In large white flakes falling on the city brown,
Stealthily and perpetually settling and loosely lying,
  Hushing the latest traffic of the drowsy town;
Deadening, muffling, stifling its murmurs failing;
Lazily and incessantly floating down and down:
  Silently sifting and veiling road, roof and railing;
Hiding difference, making unevenness even,
Into angles and crevices softly drifting and sailing.
  All night it fell, and when full inches seven
It lay in the depth of its uncompacted lightness,
The clouds blew off from a high and frosty heaven;
  And all woke earlier for the unaccustomed brightness
Of the winter dawning, the strange unheavenly glare:
The eye marvelled—marvelled at the dazzling whiteness;
  The ear hearkened to the stillness of the solemn air;
No sound of wheel rumbling nor of foot falling,
And the busy morning cries came thin and spare.
  Then boys I heard, as they went to school, calling,
They gathered up the crystal manna to freeze
Their tongues with tasting, their hands with snowballing;
  Or rioted in a drift, plunging up to the knees;
Or peering up from under the white-mossed wonder,
'O look at the trees!' they cried, 'O look at the trees!'
  With lessened load a few carts creak and blunder,
Following along the white deserted way,
A country company long dispersed asunder:
  When now already the sun, in pale display
Standing by Paul's high dome, spread forth below
His sparkling beams, and awoke the stir of the day.
  For now doors open, and war is waged with the snow;
And trains of sombre men, past tale of number,
Tread long brown paths, as toward their toil they go:
  But even for them awhile no cares encumber
Their minds diverted; the daily word is unspoken,
The daily thoughts of labour and sorrow slumber
At the sight of the beauty that greets them, for the charm
      they have broken.
Robert Bridges: 'London Snow'

There is a hill beside the silver Thames,
Shady with birch and beech and odorous pine:
And brilliant underfoot with thousand gems
Steeply the thickets to his floods decline.
       Straight trees in every place
       Their thick tops interlace,
And pendant branches trail their foliage fine
       Upon his watery face.

¤   ¤   ¤   ¤   ¤

A rushy island guards the sacred bower,
And hides it from the meadow, where in peace
The lazy cows wrench many a scented flower,
Robbing the golden market of the bees:
       And laden barges float
       By banks of myosote;
And scented flag and golden flower-de-lys
       Delay the loitering boat.

¤   ¤   ¤   ¤   ¤

Where is this bower beside the silver Thames?
O pool and flowery thickets, hear my vow!
O trees of freshest foliage and straight stems,
No sharer of my secret I allow:
       Lest ere I come the while
       Strange feet your shades defile;
Or lest the burly oarsman turn his prow
       Within your guardian isle.

Robert Bridges: Selected stanzas from
'There is a hill beside the silver Thames'

O Youth whose hope is high,
Who dost to Truth aspire,
Whether thou live or die,
O look not back nor tire.

Thou that art bold to fly
Through tempest, flood and fire,
Nor dost not shrink to try
Thy heart in torments dire:

If Thou canst Death defy,
If thy Faith is entire,
Press onward, for thine eye
Shall see thy heart's desire.

Beauty and love are nigh,
And with their deathless quire
Soon shall thine eager cry
Be numbered and expire.

Robert Bridges: From a poem by Théophile Gautier, itself based on the
English of Thomas Moore in 'The Epicurean'

During the 1880s and 1890s Bridges continued to show a considerable interest in the detailed techniques of poetry:

Most readers will observe that I have avoided using the term Iambic of blank verse. I believe that it was applied to English verse from a misconception, and I am sure that it leads to nothing but confusion. Before any one calls the feet in English blank verse iambs let him consider in what respect they are entitled to the name. A Greek or Latin iambus is a foot of two syllables, the first of which is always short, and the second always, at least by position, long, while the accent is as often on the first as on the second. The so-called English iambus, whatever its commonest condition may be, may have either of its syllables short, or long, or both may be short, or both long, while the stress is always on the last. There is nothing in common between the classical and the English feet except what is common to all disyllabic feet; the English iambs might for this be as well called trochees or spondees; and if the consideration be added that in the Greek and Latin iambus the first syllable is reckoned to be exactly half the value of the second—just as a crotchet is half a minim—it is plain that it must be better to renounce altogether the attempt to readjust a term, which means something so remotely and definitely different from that to which we would apply it.

Robert Bridges: From 'On the
Use of Greek Terminology in
English Poetry', part of
'Milton's Prosody'

The full list of plays by Bridges in this period in their order of writing comprises:

Nero (The First Part), **first printed 1885. Dedicated to Thomas Barlow, M.D.**

Palicio, **written 1883, first printed 1890. Dedicated to William Bridges, Robert's cousin.**

The Return of Ulysses, **written 1884, first printed 1890. Dedicated to the musician, C. Hubert Parry.**

The Christian Captives, **written 1886, first printed 1890. Dedicated to the Bishop of Peterborough.**

The Humours of the Court, **first printed 1893. Dedicated to Reverend William Sanday.**

Achilles in Scyros, **first printed 1890. Dedicated to Samuel Gee, M.D.**

The Feast of Bacchus, **first printed 1889. Dedicated to Reverend C. H. Daniel.**

Nero (The Second Part), **first printed 1894. Dedicated to Andrew Lang.**

Bridges made the dedications in memory of old friendships when he had completed the group of plays.

In 1883, the poet wrote *Prometheus the Firegiver,* a masque in the Greek manner from the story in ancient mythology.

When in 1884 Bridges married Mary Monica Waterhouse, he acquired a renowned architect as father-in-law. Alfred Waterhouse, son of a Quaker household, built Manchester Town Hall, the Natural History Museum in South Kensington, the City and Guilds Institute in nearby Exhibition Road, as well as hospitals, banks, court houses, hospitals, halls and colleges. He restored the ancient buildings at Staple Inn in London, served as Treasurer of the Artists' General Benevolent Institution and founded the Society for Checking the Abuses of Public Advertising.

Eros and Psyche, Bridges' narrative poem in twelve measures was printed in 1885, with a revised edition issued in 1894. It is taken from the ancient legend principally as recorded by the second century Roman author and philosopher Lucius Apuleius. Bridges located the story in Crete, into which setting he allowed himself a description of the atmospheric phenomena which followed the disastrous eruption of the volcano Krakatoa in Sunda Strait, Indonesia, in 1883. The twelve measures follow the months of the year. In spring, from March to May, the story is told of Psyche's earthly parentage, how she is worshipped by men and persecuted by Aphrodite and then loved and carried off by Eros. The summer quarter tells how Psyche's sisters, snaring her to destruction, are themselves destroyed. After Psyche's autumn wanderings, her winter trials end with her reception in heaven.

> Fair was the sight; for now, though full an hour
> The sun had sunk, she saw the evening light
> In shifting colour to the zenith tower,
> And grow more gorgeous ever and more bright.
> Bathed in the warm and comfortable glow,
> The fair delighted queen forgot her woe,
> And watch'd the unwonted pageant of the night.
>
> Broad and low down, where late the sun had been
> A wealth of orange-gold was thickly shed,
> Fading above into a field of green,
> Like apples ere they ripen into red,
> Then to the height a variable hue
> Of rose and pink and crimson freak'd with blue,
> And olive-border'd clouds o'er lilac led.
>
> High in the opposèd west the wondering moon
> All silvery green in flying green was fleec't;
> And round the blazing South the splendour soon
> Caught all the heaven, and ran to North and East;
> And Aphrodite knew the thing was wrought
> By cunning of Poseidon, and she thought
> She would go see with whom he kept his feast.
>
> *Robert Bridges: Stanzas from 'Eros and Psyche'*

Bridges wrote his first verse play in 1885. *Nero* deals with the earlier part of the Emperor's reign up to the point of the assassination of his mother Agrippina Augusta. When it was reprinted in 1901, Bridges wrote: *This play was not intended for the stage, as the rest of my plays are. It was written as an exercise in dramatic qualities other than scenic...*

Wanton with long delay the gay spring leaping cometh;
The blackthorn starreth now his bough on the eve of May:
All day in the sweet box-tree the bee for pleasure hummeth:
The cuckoo sends afloat his note on the air all day.

Now dewy nights again and rain in gentle shower
At root of tree and flower have quenched the winter's drouth:
On high the hot sun smiles, and banks of cloud uptower
In bulging heads that crowd for miles the dazzling south.

Robert Bridges: 'April, 1885'

For his tragedy *The Christian Captives* written in 1886, Bridges turned to events c.1420 which were also dealt with in the play *El Principe Constante* by the seventeeth-century Spanish dramatist and poet Pedro Calderon de la Barca with whose work Bridges was familiar. The captives are held by the King of Fez and form the chorus for Bridges' verse-play. Besides the King, other participants are his general, the Princes of Portugal, Ferdinand and Enrique (grandchildren of John of Gaunt), Prince Tarudante of Morocco, and Princess Almeh, the King's daughter.

The hatred each side had of the other's religion (for the absolute truth of Islam or of Christianity must be defended by their adherents) leads to acts of cruelty which the perpetrators would not otherwise countenance. But for the religious divide, the acts of kindness which sometimes break through would seem to be the natural norm for most of the participants. The play centres on Princess Almeh, first enthralled by the polyphonic singing of the Christians and later by the returned love of the captured Prince Ferdinand and her secret acceptance of Christianity; by the love for Almeh of the King's general who has known her from childhood, and of her father's will that she should marry Prince Tarudante of Morocco to cement a military alliance. Bridges directs that the captives' chorus should sing the Latin hymn *Jesu dulcis memoria* set by Gregorio Allegri (1582-1652) and one of the Anerio brothers. In the 1902 edition of the play, he notes *its use would be an anachronism, but it is one that would never be observed, and it may therefore fairly be allowed.*

The Devil wore a crucifix:
"The Christians they are right,"
The Devil said, "So let us burn
A heretic to-night,
A heretic to-night."
Sydney Carter: From a song lyric written in 1961

'Twas last night, Sala, as I lay long awake
Dreamily hearkening to the ocean murmur,
Softer than silence, on mine ears there stole
A solemn sound of wailful harmony:
So beautiful it was that first I thought
This castle was enchanted, as I have read
In eastern tales; or else that 'twas the song
Of people of this land, who make the sea
Their secret god, and at midnight arise
To kneel upon the shore, and his divinity
Trouble with shrilling prayer: or then it seemed
A liquid-voicèd choir of spirits that swam
Upon the ocean surface, harp in hand,
Swelling their hymns with his deep undersong.
That was the Christian captives.

Robert Bridges: Princess Almeh to General Sala ben Sala in 'The Christian Captives'

Nay, I ask
How, being a Christian, thou professest arms.
Why hast thou come against us, with no plea
Save thy religion, and that happy gospel
Thou hast trampled on in coming, Peace on earth?

Robert Bridges: Princess Almeh to Prince Ferdinand in 'The Christian Captives'

It is not likely that Milton wrote the whole of *Paradise Lost* without discovering the defects and regretting the limitations of his prosody. After having carried it consistently through that long poem, we should not expect, however, that he would depart much from it in any poems which he might afterwards write; but we might look to find him not so strict with himself, and either admitting new licences or developing his old rules to form new rhythms.

As a matter of fact, *Paradise Regained* and *Samson Agonistes* are just in this condition. They are written generally by the same laws of prosody as *Paradise Lost*, but both contain new licences and *Samson Agonistes* new rhythms, which show in what direction Milton thought well to modify and expand his own laws...

Robert Bridges: From "On the Prosody of 'Paradise Regained' and 'Samson Agonistes'"

In 1885 Henry Charles Beeching was appointed to the living of Yattendon, where he ministered for fifteen years. The parish duties were not heavy, and he was able to give most of his time to the literary work he loved. Like Bridges, he regarded the work of John Milton highly, and he published an edition of his work in 1900. He also wrote poetry himself and his *Love in a Garden* was published in 1895. In 1900, he went on to become Professor of Pastoral Theology at King's College, London, to which role Edward Plumptre had been appointed in 1853. He completed his ministry as Dean of Norwich.

There seems little doubt that Beeching and Bridges were in regular communication about the work of John Milton. It was the technique of the writing which was of especial interest to Bridges and he published various papers on this subject, and on prosody generally over the years.

Ó how cómely it ís, and hów revíving,
Tó the spírits of júst men lóng oppressed,
When Gód put into the hands of their deliverer
Púts invíncible might.

An illustration from John Milton's 'Samson Agonistes' chosen by Robert Bridges to show Milton's use of new rhythms

Green leaves panting for joy with the great wind rushing through:
A burst of the sun from cloud and a sparkle on valley and hill,
Gold on the corn, and red on the poppy, and on the rill
Silver, and over all white clouds afloat in the blue.

Swallows that dart, a lark unseen, innumerous song
Chirruped and twittered, a lowing of cows in the meadow grass,
Murmuring gnats, and bees that suck their honey and pass:
God is alive, and at work in the world:— we did it wrong.

Human eyes, and human hands, and a human face
Darkly beheld before in a vision, not understood:—
Do I at last begin to feel as I stand and gaze
Why God waited for this, then called the world very good?
H. C. Beeching: 'A Summer Day'

John Milton

Bread of the world in mercy broken,
Wine of the soul for sinners shed,
Christ, by whose death's mysterious
token
Thy church is stay'd and comforted;
Hear thine own words in blessing
spoken,
Thy table see in memory spread:
Bread of the world in mercy broken,
O may our souls by Thee be fed.
*Robert Bridges from the original by
Reginald Heber. Written for the
village choir of Yattendon Church
because Heber's original words did
not suit Bridges and did not seem
to make good sense. Set by H. Ellis
Wooldridge to Louis Bourgeois'
tune for GENEVAN PSALM 118*

In January 1888, the Bridges' daughter, Elizabeth, was christened at Yattendon. That year, Bridges sorted his collection of English motets, madrigals and part songs in the Novello edition so as to bind them into a single volume with background notes about the composers.

Early 1888 also saw the Bridges in Italy again, travelling by way of Arles, the Riviera and Cornice to visit Genoa, Pisa and Florence. They were accompanied by Bridges' neice, Mary Plow, who was afterwards to marry Yattendon's incumbent.

In 1889, Bridges had his *The Feast of Bacchus* privately printed by the Reverend C. H. Daniel. The author's source was the Roman dramatist Publius Terence whose story was itself taken from Menander's *Heautontimorumenos*. For a Christian audience, Bridges considered only about a sixth of Terence's original Latin suitable, and Bridges translated this for use in the domestic comedy about two neighbours, Menedemus, an Athenian gentleman, and his wife, and Chremes, a retired Ionian sponge-merchant, and their offspring.

When the play was reprinted for wider circulation in 1894, Bridges wrote a detailed note about the metre, summed up by *a natural emphasizing of the sense gives all the rhythm that is intended.* He concluded that he *had been told that it will be said by the critics to be prose; but that if it were printed as prose, they might pronounce it to be verse; and this is the effect aimed at; since a comic metre which will admit colloquial speech without torturing it must have a loose varying rhythm.*

By 1893, there were enough new poems for another collection to be printed by Mr. Daniel. Bridges noted later that it was published contemporaneously with an American edition, according to the requirements of the international copyright law. Many like *The Winnowers, The Garden in September, Larks, The Palm Willow, Asian Birds, January, A Robin, Nighingales, North Wind in October, First Spring Morning,* and others not titled are about country life. But poems of human relationships have their place too.

My eyes for beauty pine,
My soul for Goddës grace:
No other care nor hope is mine;
To heaven I turn my face.

One splendour thence is shed
From all the stars above:
'Tis namèd when God's name is
said,
'Tis Love, 'tis heavenly Love.

And every gentle heart,
That burns with true desire,
Is lit from eyes that mirror part
Of that celestial fire.
*Robert Bridges from a madrigal
by Michael Angelo (No. 8 in
'Guasti') used in the comedy
'The Humours of the Court'*

The Humours of the Court,
published in 1893 is based on two
Spanish comedies which Bridges
had read: *El secreto á voces* by
Pedro Calderon de la Barca and *El
perro del hortelano* by Lope Felix de
Vega Carpio. The first suggested
his plot and the second a
particular scene. The Court is that
of Ricardo, Duke of Milan.

I never shall love the snow again
     Since Maurice died:
With corniced drift it blocked the lane,
And sheeted in a desolate plain
     The country side.

The trees with silvery rime bedight
     Their brances bare.
By day no sun appeared; by night
The hidden moon shed thievish light
     In the misty air.

We fed the birds that flew around
    In flocks to be fed:
No shelter in holly or brake they found.
The speckled thrush on the frozen ground
    Lay frozen and dead.

We skated on stream and pond; we cut
    The crinching snow
To Doric temple or Arctic hut;
We laughed and sang at nightfall, shut
    By the fireside glow.

Yet grudged we our keen delights before
    Maurice should come.
We said, In-door or out-of-door
We shall love life for a month or more,
    When he is home.

They brought him home; 'twas two days late
    For Christmas day:
Wrapped in white, in solemn state,
A flower in his hand, all still and straight
    Our Maurice lay.

And two days ere the year outgave
    We laid him low.
The best of us truly were not brave,
When we laid Maurice down in his grave
    Under the snow

Robert Bridges:'I never shall love the snow again'

Since to be loved endures,
    To love is wise:
Earth hath no good but yours,
    Brave, joyful eyes:

Earth hath no sin but thine,
    Dull eye of scorn:
O'er thee the sun doth pine
    And angels mourn.
Robert Bridges

There was no lad handsomer than Willie was
The day that he came to father's house:
There was none had an eye as soft an' blue
As Willie's was, when he came to woo.

To a labouring life though bound thee be,
An' I on my father's ground live free,
I'll take thee, I said, for thy manly grace,
Thy gentle voice an' thy loving face.

'Tis forty years now since we were wed:
We are ailing an' grey needs not to be said:
But Willie's eye is as blue an' soft
As the day when he wooed me in father's croft.

Yet changed am I in body an' mind,
For Willie to me has ne'er been kind:
Merrily drinking an' singing with the men
He 'ud come home late six nights o' the se'n.

...The dreamy butterflies
With dazzling colours powdered
   and soft glooms,
White, black and crimson stripes,
   and peacock eyes,
Or on chance flowers sit,
With idle effort plundering one
   by one
The nectaries of deepest-throated
   blooms.
  Robert Bridges: From 'The
  Garden in September'

An' since the children be grown an' gone
He 'as shunned the house an' left me lone:
An' less an' less he brings me in
Of the little he now has strength to win.

The roof lets through the wind an' the wet,
An' master won't mend it with us in's debt:
An' all looks every day more worn,
An' the best of my gowns be shabby an' torn.

No wonder if words hav' a-grown to blows;
That matters not while nobody knows:
For love him I shall to the end of life,
An' be, as I swore, his own true wife.

An' when I am gone, he'll turn, an' see
His folly an' wrong, an' be sorry for me:
An' come to be there in the land o' bliss
To give me the love I looked for in this.
      Robert Bridges:'A Villager'

And at all times to hear are
   drowsy tones
Of dizzy flies, and humming
   drones,
With sudden flap of pigeon wings
   in the sky,
Or the wild cry
Of thirsty rooks, that scour ascare
The distant blue, to watering as
   they fare
With creaking pinions, or—on
   business bent,
If aught their ancient polity
   displease,—
Come gathering to their colony,
   and there
Settling in ragged parliament,
Some stormy council hold in the
   high trees.
  Robert Bridges: From 'The
  Garden in September'

Beautiful must be the mountains whence ye come,
 And bright in the fruitful valleys the streams, wherefrom
  Ye learn your song:
Where are those starry woods? O might I wander there,
 Among the flowers, which in that heavenly air
  Bloom the year long!

Nay, barren are those mountains and spent the streams:
 Our song is the voice of desire, that haunts our dreams,
  A throe of the heart,
Whose pining visions dim, forbidden hopes profound,
 No dying cadence nor long sigh can sound,
  For all our art.

Alone, aloud in the raptured ear of men
 We pour our dark nocturnal secret; and then,
  As night is withdrawn
From these sweet-springing meads and bursting boughs of May,
 Dream, while the innumerable choir of day
  Welcome the dawn.
     Robert Bridges: 'Nightingales'

Bridges noted an error in one poem, indicating in later editions that the poem he had begun *Pink-throated linnet* had been amended to *Flame-throated robin,* whose song the stanzas described! For the bicentenary celebrations of the composer Henry Purcell, cut off from life when still in his thirties, the poet wrote an *Ode to Music,* which was set by C. Hubert Parry and performed at the Leeds Festival in 1895.

Myriad-voiced Queen, Enchantress of the air,
Bride of the life of man! With tuneful reed,
With string and horn and high-adoring quire
Thy welcome we prepare.
In silver-speaking mirrors of desire,
In joyous ravishment of mystery draw thou near,
With heavenly echo of thoughts, that dreaming lie
Chain'd in unborn oblivion drear,
Thy many-hearted grace restore
Until our isle our own to be,
And make again our Graces three.

Robert Bridges: From 'Ode to Music' written for the Bicentenary
Commemoration of Henry Purcell

Bridges also wrote *A Hymn of Nature*, an ode written for music, set also by C. Hubert Parry and performed at the Gloucester Festival in 1898.

In the eighteen-nineties, a great deal of talent was brought together in the choir of Yattendon Church, of which Bridges was precentor for many years. Here *The Yattendon Hymnal* was born.

> The origin of this book was my attempt, when precentor of a village choir, to provide better settings of the hymns than those in use.
>
> When I gave up my office, I printed the first twenty-five hymns for the convenience of the choir, and also for the sake of the tunes by Jeremy Clark, which I had been at some pains to restore, and for the preservation of the tunes composed on our behalf by Professor Wooldridge.
>
> My choice of music had so far been limited to tunes, for which suitable words were to be found in *Hymns Ancient & Modern*; but by the time that these first tunes were printed, I determined to continue the book free of this restriction, and, from whatever source, to provide words for tunes which I had hitherto been unable to use. I then became aware of a real cause for the absence of most of these tunes from the common hymnals: *there were no words of any kind to which they could be sung*. Having already translated some of the old Latin hymns for their proper melodies, I was thence led on to the more difficult task of supplying the greater need of these other tunes; the result being that over forty of these hundred hymns have english words newly written by myself. Almost all of these new hymns are in some sense translations, for even where an original hymn could not be followed in its entirety, as an old Latin hymn generally may be, there was usually a foundation to begin upon, and I never failed to find the music conditioning, dictating, or inspiring the remainer. I did not willingly engage in this, nor until I had searched in word-books of all kinds; a fruitless labour, unless for the

...But I am concerned in combating the general proposition that modern music, by virtue of a declamatory method, is able satisfactorily to interpret almost any kind of good poetry...the repetitions in music and poetry are incompatible ...Musical declamation must mean that the musical phrase is not chosen, as the earlier musicians might have chosen or invented it, chiefly for the sake of its own musical beauty, in correspondence with the *mood* of the words, and merely fitting the syllables; but that it is invented also to follow the verbal phrase in correspondence with some notion of rhetorical utterance, or natural inflection of speech enforcing the sense, and in so far with lesser regard to its own purely musical value...when a declamatory musical movement is once started, the musician has very few means of bringing it to a conclusion...the very rhythms of poetry and choral music are different in kind...the most beautiful effects in poetry are obtained by suggestion ...Because in the musical drama that must be sung which should be spoken, why try to make that seem to be spoken which should be sung?

Robert Bridges: From the
Preface to 'Ode to Music' as
printed in 'The Shilling
Garland'

Sources and composers of items in
The Yattendon Hymnal in order of
date. Where more than one item
appears, the number used is given
in brackets:

Plainsong Melodies:
  Sarum use (9)
  Ambrosian (2)
  Later plainsong (2)
Heinrich Isaac, 1490
Strasbourg Psalter before 1540
German of the same date
Louis Bourgeois , 1550 (13)
Christopher Tye, 1550
Crespin's Psalters c. 1560 (3)
Thomas Tallis, 1560 (7)
French Genevan Psalter,
                   after 1560
Setting by Claude Goudimel, 1565
English, 16th century (4)
Settings by George Kirkbye,
                   1592 (2)
Setting by John Farmer, 1592
Setting by Richard Allison, 1599
Italian, 16th Century
Hans Leonhard Hassler, 1600
Thomas Campion, 1613
Orlando Gibbons, 1623 (8)
Henry Lawes, 1638
Johann Crueger, 1640 (4)
English & Scotch, 1600-1650 (7)
German, 17th century (2)
Jeremy Clark 1700 (9)
William Croft 1710 (4)
English, 18th century (4)
J. S. Bach, settings mostly of
                   earlier melodies (8)
H. E. Wooldridge (6 plus 1 setting)

A choir that cannot sing
unaccompanied cannot sing at
all...
  *Robert Bridges: From Preface
  to Notes in 'The Yattendon
                   Hymnal'*

hope begotten thereof that my practice in versifying and
my love for music may together have created something
of at least relative value.
  Robert Bridges: From Preface to Notes in 'The Yattendon Hymnal'

The contents of *The Yattendon Hymnal* were determined
principally for musical rather than theological or literary
reasons. The preface bears the name of H. Ellis Wooldridge as
well as Bridges and begins:

Among the old melodies which it is the chief object of
this book to restore to use, some will be found which
will be quite new to the public, while others will be
familiar though in a somewhat different form; and since
the sources whence all the tunes are taken are well
known, and have been already largely drawn upon by
the compilers of Psalters and Hymnals, any melody
which is new in this book may be considered as having
been hitherto overlooked or rejected, while in the
alternative case it is to be understood that the original
cast of the melody has at some former time been altered,
(frequently to suit the English common metre to which
it was not at first conformable,) and is now restored.

The plain-song tunes...and the few other old tunes
which do not fall into either of the two above-
mentioned classes, were included for the sake of their
settings.

With respect to the vocal settings in four parts it may be
said that, in the numerous cases in which such settings
were not added by the composer of the melody, the
editors have done their best to supply the want in a
suitable manner, and with some attempt towards the
particular qualities of workmanship upon which much
of the beauty of the old vocal counterpoint depends; and
this latter aim has also governed the composition of the
six tunes not derived from old sources which have been
included in the work.

This book is offered in no antiquarian spirit. The
greater number of these old tunes are, without question,
of an excellence which sets them above either the
enhancement or ruin of Time, and at present when so
much attention is given to music it is to be desired that
such masterpieces should not be hidden away from the
public, or only put forth in a corrupt and degraded form.
The excellence of a nation in music can have no other
basis than the education and practice of the people; and
the quality of the music which is most universally sung
must largely determine the public taste for good or ill.
  *Robert Bridges and H. Ellis Wooldridge: From the Preface to 'The
                   Yattendon Hymnal'*

The only nineteenth century melodies in the book were by Wooldridge and were especially written for the Yattendon choir in which the composer also sang. The hymns thought to need new tunes were:

Lord, thy word abideth (Henry Baker)
Lead, kindly light (John Newman)
I heard the voice of Jesus say (Horatius Bonar)
King of Glory, King of Peace (George Herbert)
Far from my heav'nly home (Henry Lyte)
Hark! how all the welkin rings (Charles Wesley)

It will be noted Bridges had no place for *herald angels* on grounds of Biblical accuracy; and on musical grounds, altered:

Pleased as Man with man to appear
Jesus, our Immanuel here.

to:

Pleased as Man with man to dwell
Jesus, our Emmanuel.

Most four-part arrangements in the book were made either by Wooldridge or Mary Bridges, with two by Charles Wood.

Bridges desribed his approach to writing his texts thus:

The unusual method which I was constrained to follow, that is of writing words to suit existing music, has its advantages. In some cases…the musician, out of despair or even contempt for the doggrel offered to him, has composed a fine tune quite independent of the words to which it was dedicated, and such tunes have been silent ever since they were composed: while even when a melody has been actually inspired by a particular hymn, the attention of the composer to the first stanza has not infrequently set up a hirmos, or at least a musical scheme of feeling, which, not having been in the mind of the writer of the words, is not carried out in his other stanzas: indeed, as every one must have observed, the words of hymns have too often been written with insufficient attention to the conditions which a repetition of any music to every stanza must impose. To get rid of such discrepancies between words and music is advantageous to both, and although this treatment cannot of course be applied to english hymns,—which it is not allowable to alter, except in cases of glaring unfitness or absurdity, such as would if uncorrected cause the neglect of a good hymn,—yet, where the hymn has to be translated from a foreign language, some reconstruction is generally inevitable, and it can follow no better aim than that of the mutual enforcement of words and music. And the words owe a courtesy to the music; for if a balance be struck between the words and

Congregational singing of hymns is much to be desired; but, though difficult to obtain, it is not permissible to provoke it by undignified music. Its only sound musical basis is good melody: good melodies should therefore be offered to the people, such as it has been the object of this book to bring together; and they should have as much freedom and variety of rhythm as possible.

A hymn-book which is intended entirely for congregational use must be faulty in one of two ways; either it will offer for congregational singing hymns whose sacred and intimate character is profaned by such a treatment, or it will have to omit some of the most beautiful hymns in the language: but congregations differ much, not only with regard to the music in which they are capable of joining, but also as to the sort of words which best express their religious emotion.
Robert Bridges: Extracts from Preface to Notes in 'The Yattendon Hymnal'

This fine hymn has been kept out of use by the second line of the second stanza, *with inextinguishable blaze.* This cannot be sung: in altering it I have departed from the original as little as possible.
Robert Bridges: From Notes to 'The Yattendon Hymnal' about Charles Wesley's 'O Thou who camest from above'. Bridges' revised text read: 'With ever-bright undying blaze'

98

There can be little doubt that it is the *hymn tune* from which Dr. Miller says that he *partly took* his famous ROCKINGHAM. His acquaintance with Bishopthorpe is confirmatory. Much is thereby explained. It is easy to see how Dr. M. came to write a popular tune, if he vulgarized the work of a man of genius: also why Rockingham has won the favour of musicians; because the force of Clark's melodious invention supports the coarse fabric of Dr. M.'s garment. He certainly concocted a tune which any congregation can sing, and one which, alas! the average english congregation is never tired of singing. His maudlin composition is still chosen by our church musicians to be sung to the most sacred words.

Robert Bridges discusses the use of ROCKINGHAM with 'When I survey the wondrous cross' in the notes to 'The Yattendon Hymnal' about Jeremiah Clark's tune BROMLEY. (ROCKINGHAM is also known by the names CATON and COMMUNION [Miller])

I state here once for all that in musical matters I offer my opinion with becoming humility.
Robert Bridges in a footnote in 'The Yattendon Hymnal'

music of hymns, it will be found to be heavily in favour of the musicians, whose fine work has been unscrupulously altered and reduced to dulness by english compilers, with the object of conforming it in rhythm to words that are unworthy of any music whatever. The chief offenders here are the protestant reformers, whose metrical psalms, which the melodies were tortured to fit, exhibit greater futility than one would look for even in men who could thus wantonly spoil fine music.
Robert Bridges: From the Preface to Notes in 'The Yattendon Hymnal'

The texts and extracts of Bridges' hymns are almost all given in the version in *The Small Hymnbook*, the words edition of *The Yattendon Hymnal*, indicated by the author as his correct edition, sometimes with unusual spellings.

Now cheer our hearts this eventide,
Lord Jesus Christ, and with us bide:
Thou that canst never set in night,
Our heav'nly Sun, our glorious Light.

May we and all who bear thy name
By gentle love thy cross proclaim,
Thy gift of peace on earth secure,
And for thy Truth the world endure.
Robert Bridges: After 'Ach bleib bei uns, Herr Jesu Christ' by Dr Nicholaus Selnecker, German sixteenth-century preacher and professor of theology for Bach's setting of an anonymous 1659 melody in the 'Vierstimmige Choralgesänge'

O gladsome light, O grace
Of God the Father's face,
Th' eternal splendour wearing;
Celestial, holy, blest,
Our Saviour Jesus Christ,
Joyful in thine appearing:

Now, ere day fadeth quite,
We see the evening light,
Our wonted hymn outpouring;
Father of might unknown,
Thee, his incarnate Son,
And holy Spirit adoring.

To Thee of right belongs
All praise of holy songs,
O Son of God, Lifegiver:
Thee, therefore, O most high,
The world doth glorify,
And shall exalt for ever.
Robert Bridges: From the Greek sometimes attributed to Sophronius, a seventh-century Patriarch of Jerusalem. The tune is a melody by Louis Bourgeois as set by Claude Goudimel. The tune NUNC DIMITTIS, to which the hymn is sometimes sung today, is based on Goudimel's harmonies with some changes

The King, O God, his heart to Thee upraiseth;
With him the nation bows before thy face:
With high thanksgiving Thee thy glad Church praiseth;
Our strength thy spirit, our trust and hope thy grace.

Unto great honour, glory undeservèd,
Hast Thou exalted us, and drawn Thee nigh:
Nor, from thy judgments when our feet had swervèd,
Didst Thou forsake, nor leave us, Lord most high.

In Thee our fathers trusted and were savèd,
In Thee destroyèd thrones of tyrants proud;
From ancient bondage freed the poor enslavèd:
To sow thy truth pour'd out their saintly blood.

Us now, we pray, O God, in anger scorn not,
Nor to vainglorying leave, nor brutish sense.
In time of trouble thy face from us turn not,
Who art our rock, our stately sure defence.

Unto our minds give freedom and uprightness;
Let strength and courage lead o'er land and wave.
To our souls' armour grant celestial brightness,
Joy to our hearts, and faith beyond the grave.

Our plenteous nation still in power extending,
Increase our joy, uphold us by thy Word;
Beauty and wisdom all our ways attending,
Goodwill to man and peace thro' Christ our Lord.

Robert Bridges : Adapted for the year of the Queen's Jubilee from Psalm 21
in Robert Tailour's 'Fifti Select Psalms' for Louis Bourgeois' melody to
Marot's Twelfth Psalm in a setting by H. Ellis Wooldridge. DONNE
SECOURS (GENEVAN PSALM 12) is a unison setting and the hymn is
also sung to WELWYN

Rejoice, O land,
Rejoice, O land,
In God thy might,
In God thy might.
His will obey, Him serve aright,
Him serve aright.
For thee the saints uplift their voice,
Uplift their voice.
Fear not, O land, in God rejoice,
In God rejoice.

Glad shalt thou be, with blessing crown'd.
With joy and peace thou shalt abound.
Yea, love with thee shall make his home,
Until thou see God's kingdom come.

He shall forgive thy sins untold.
Remember thou his love of old.
Walk in his way, his word adore,
And keep his truth for evermore.

Robert Bridges. Sung in the 1890s in Wells Cathedral,and written for the
original version of Thomas Tallis' Canon, which leads to the repeated
words as set out in Verse 1. It is sometimes sung today in the unextended
form to WAREHAM

*The Yattendon Hymnbook is
printed in the music types of Peter
Walpergen and the Roman and
Italic of Bishop Fell.*

The form and size of the book were
determined by the type, chosen
because it was the only one that I
could find of any beauty; and I
wished that my book should in this
respect give an example, and be
worthy both of the music and its
sacred use.
*Robert Bridges: From Preface
to Notes in 'The Yattendon
Hymnal'*

The cheapness is not the direct
cause of the ugliness of our
common hymn-books, nor is their
ugliness the cause of their
cheapness. If many copies of a
book are sold, they can be sold
cheaply; if only a few, then the
initial expense, which is much the
same whether the book be
beautiful or ugly, must be shared
between those few buyers and the
author. But thus it comes about
indirectly for cheapness to be the
cause of meanness and ugliness,
because in a larger market, there
is greater indifference to artistic
excellence of all kinds, and from
habit a preference for what is
inferior. In a large edition this
book could be sold as cheaply as
another.
*Robert Bridges in a footnote in
'The Yattendon Hymnal'*

There is one novelty which I am responsible for introducing, namely the four-part vocal settings of certain early plainsong melodies. The later plain-song tunes...are, I suppose, as fit for this treatment as any other tunes of the same date; but in the case of the earlier melodies, which were composed before the invention of any complete system of harmony, it is generally agreed that they should be sung in unison, in fact the more elaborate of them cannot be sung otherwise. To give four-part settings of any of these early tunes calls therefore for an explanation, which I will give as briefly as possible.

When these tunes are sung, they are usually accompanied, and this implies a harmonic treatment. Now the best harmonic treatment which they can have is the Palestrinal, because that was the earliest complete system, and therefore the nearest to their time, and also because we may rely on the truth of its interpretation of the modes for the reason that Palestrina had never heard any music that was not modal. A modern musician, if he attempts to go back beyond Palestrina, must draw on his imagination, and while his aim must be to produce something artistically and technically less perfect than Palestrina's system, his work, when it is done, will carry neither authority nor conviction.

If then we take Palestrina's harmonic interpretation of the modes, it seems to me that there can be no objection to giving vocal parts to the simpler hymns. If it is preferred to sing them in unison, the modal settings will be a guide to the accompanist. But it is my opinion that such settings as I offer will really please, and they may possibly do something to bring these tunes, which have a unique, unmatchable beauty, into favour with choirs that dislike the effort and waste of unison singing.

continued in opposite margin

O sacred head sore wounded,
    Defiled and put to scorn:
O kingly head surrounded
    With mocking crown of thorn!
What sorrow mars thy grandeur?
    Can death thy bloom deflower?
O countenance, whose splendour
    The hosts of heav'n adore.

Thy beauty long-desirèd,
    Hath vanisht from our sight.
Thy power is all expirèd,
    And quencht the light of light.
Ah me! for whom Thou diest,
    Hide not so far thy grace:
Show me, O love most highest,
    The brightness of thy face.

I pray thee, Jesus, own me,
    Me, Shepherd good, for thine;
Who to thy fold hast won me,
    And fed with truth divine.
Me guilty, me refuse not,
    Incline thy face to me,
This comfort that I lose not,
    On earth to comfort Thee.

In thy most bitter passion
    My heart to share doth cry,
With Thee for my salvation
    Upon the cross to die.
Ah! keep my heart thus movèd
    To stand thy cross beneath,
To mourn Thee, well belovèd,
    Yet thank Thee for thy death.

My days are few, O fail not,
    With thine immortal power,
To hold me, that I quail not
    In death's most fearful hour.
That I may fight befriended,
    And see in my last strife
To me thine arms extended
    Upon the cross of life.

Robert Bridges: Based on 'Salve caput cruentatum' from 'Salva mundi' ascribed to Saint Bernard. Tune: PASSION CHORALE, a harmonisation by J. S. Bach of a tune by Hans Leonhard Hassler (1564-1612) originally written for secular use. The tune is also known as O HAUBT VOLL BLUT UND WUNDEN and as HERLICH THUT MICH VERLANGEN

O Prince of Peace, who man wast born
That Thou mightst die to succour us,
My foolish tears do not Thou scorn,
But be my comfort, Christ Jesus.

Forgive my fears, my wretched moan,
For me it was Thou wroughtest thus;
Thou madest God and man at one:
So be my comfort, Christ Jesus.

For all Thou would'st make friend of foe,
Yet will my sin torment me thus:
My heavy guilt hath laid me low:
But be my comfort, Christ Jesus.

Give courage now to meet my strife;
Let me not lie in languor thus:
Raise me again to better life,
And be my comfort, Christ Jesus.

And when to die it is my day,
Thou, on the cross that diedst for us,
Leave me not then in that hard fray,
But be my comfort, Christ Jesus.

Robert Bridges: Adapted from 15th century MS in the Lambeth Library
'Jhesus, that sprung of Jesse root', described by Bridges as one of the best
pre-reformation vernacular hymns to survive. The tune SONG 5 by
Orlando Gibbons was found by Bridges in George Wither's 'Hymns and
Songs of the Church', 1623

Ah, holy Jesu, how hast thou offended,
That man to judge thee hath in hate pretended?
By foes derided, by thine own rejected,
    O most afflicted.

Who was the guilty? Who brought this upon thee?
Alas, my treason, Jesu, hath undone thee.
'Twas I, Lord Jesu, I it was denied thee:
    I crucified thee.

Lo, the good Shepherd for the sheep is offer'd;
The slave hath sinnèd, and the Son hath suffer'd;
For man's atonement, while he nothing heedeth,
    God intercedeth.

For me, kind Jesus, was thy incarnation,
Thy mortal sorrow, and thy life's oblation:
Thy death of anguish and thy bitter passion,
    For my salvation.

Therefore, kind Jesu, since I cannot pay Thee,
I do adore Thee, and will ever pray Thee
Think on thy pity and thy love unswerving,
    Not my deserving.

Robert Bridges. Retranslated from a meditation by Saint Anselm. The
original was used for the German text 'Herzliebster Jesu' in 15 stanzas by
Johann Heerman (1585-1647). The melody by J. Crüger (1598-1662) is set
by H. Ellis Wooldridge. Another adaptation is named in some hymnbooks
HERZLIEBSTER JESU

continued from opposite margin
These settings offer no difficulty
of execution; *all that is necessary is*
that the under voices should know
the melody: and though this is not
generally thought requisite in a
modern hymn, it is asking nothing
extra of a choir that would sing the
plain-song tunes; for even if they
are sung in unison, they must first
be known by heart (otherwise
their rhythmical freedom, which
defies notation, and is indis-
pensable to their beauty, cannot be
approached), and when once a
choir has got thus far, the under
parts, being phrased with the
melody, will easily follow it.
Robert Bridges: From Preface
to Notes in 'The Yattendon
Hymnal'

Palestrina presents his
***Masses* to Pope Julius III**

102

Thee will I love, my God and king,
 Thee will I sing,
 My strength and tower:
For evermore Thee will I trust,
  O God most just
  Of truth and power.
   Who all things hast
   In order placed,
Yea, for thy pleasure hast created;
   And on thy throne
   Unseen, unknown,
   Reignest alone
In glory seated.

Set in my heart thy love I find;
  My wandering mind
 To Thee Thou leadest:
My trembling hope, my strong desire
  With heavenly fire
 Thou kindly feedest.
  Lo, all things fair
  Thy path prepare,
Thy beauty to my spirit calleth,
  Thine to remain
  In joy and pain,
  And count it gain
Whate'er befalleth.

O more and more thy love extend,
  My life befriend
 With heavenly pleasure;
That I may win thy paradise,
  Thy pearl of price,
 Thy countless treasure.
  Since but in Thee
  I can go free
From earthly care and vain oppression,
  This prayer I make
  For Jesu's sake
  That Thou me take
In thy possession.

Robert Bridges, with a first line suggssted by Psalm 145 for an old French melody, reconstructed by Louis Bourgeois in 1543, used as GENEVAN PSALM 138. Set by Mary Bridges. Also sung today to CROSSINGS

Yattendon Church

All my hope on God is founded;
 He doth still my trust renew,
Me thro' change and chance He guideth,
 Only good and only true.
  God unknown,
  He alone
Calls my heart to be his own.

Pride of man and earthly glory,
   Sword and crown betray his trust:
What with care and toil he buildeth,
   Tower and temple fall to dust.
      But God's pow'r,
      Hour by hour,
   Is my temple and my tow'r.

God's great goodness aye endureth,
   Deep his wisdom passing thought:
Splendour, light and life attend him,
   Beauty springeth out of nought.
      Evermore
      From his store
   New-born worlds rise and adore.

Daily doth th' Almighty Giver
   Bounteous gifts on us bestow.
His desire our soul delighteth,
   Pleasure leads us where we go.
      Love doth stand
      At his hand;
   Joy doth wait on his command.

Still from man to God eternal
   Sacrifice of praise be done,
High above all praises praising
   For the gift of Christ his Son.
      Christ doth call
      One and all:
   Ye who follow shall not fall.

Robert Bridges, based on Joachim Neander, the first poet of the Reformed
Church in Germany. The music was of a proper German melody,
sometimes also ascribed to Neander, but noted by him as a well-known
melody. It was set by H. Ellis Wooldridge. It is also sung to MEINE
HOFFNUNG, based on a later form of the same melody with different
setting; and to MICHAEL (Howells) and GROESWERN

Christ's loving children, for his hope abiding,
Active in gladness, or in hymns adoring;
Be we as servants that await a Master
      Sorely delaying.

Happy those servants, whether He returneth
At dead of midnight, or at early morning:
Happy those servants, if He only find them
      Faithfully watching.

Father of mercies, give us holy comfort
Here in our pains, and Paradise hereafter:
Where in eternal vision uncreated
      Joy never endeth.
         Amen.

Robert Bridges: Words based in mood only of a Latin text ascribed to Saint
Gregory the Great for a melody from 'Leofric's Collectarius'

The duteous day now closeth,
Each flower and tree reposeth,
　　Shade creeps o'er wild and wood:
Let us, as night is falling,
Our God our maker calling,
　　Give thanks to Him, the giver good.

Now all the heav'nly splendour
Breaks forth in starlight tender
　　From myriad worlds unknown:
And man, the marvel seeing,
Forgets his selfish being
　　For joy of beauty not his own.

His care he drowneth yonder
Lost in th' abyss of wonder;
　　To heav'n his soul doth steal:
This life he disesteemeth,
The day it is that dreameth,
　　That doth from truth his vision seal.

Awhile his mortal blindness
May miss God's loving-kindness,
　　And grope in faithless strife:
But when life's day is over
Shall death's fair night discover
　　The fields of everlasting life.
Robert Bridges. From the German 'Nun ruhen alle Wälder' of Paul
Gerhardt (1607-1676), his hymn for use on the occasion of going to bed.
The tune was J. S. Bach's setting of a German melody adapted for the
words 'In allen meinen Thaten'. Bridges' text is sung today to
INNSBRUCK (O WELT ICH MUSS DICH LASSEN [Bach])

All praise be to God, whom all things obey,
From angels and men for ever and aye:
　　Who sendeth on earth the powers of his throne,
His providence good and love to make known.

His angels are they of countenance fair,
The arm of his strength, his hand of kind care:
　　His message of peace to us they reveal,
His wisdom most high they seal or unseal.

'Twas they of their art taught David to sing;
And faith evermore hath knelt at his spring.
　　Thro' them the world doth with music abound
Of viols and reeds and horns of rich sound.

By Martyrs of old they stood in the flame,
And bade them not flinch, but call on God's name.
　　Thro' torment, thro' shame, thro' darkness of death
They led without fear the sires of our faith.
Robert Bridges: Verses from 'Children's Hymn of Angels' for the tune of
Psalm 67 in Crespin's Psalter, 1560

Christ hath a garden walled around,
A Paradise of fruitful ground,
Chosen by love and fenced by grace
From out the world's wide wilderness.

Like trees of spice his servants stand,
There planted by his mighty hand;
By Eden's gracious streams, that flow
To feed their beauty where they grow.

Awake, O wind of heav'n, and bear
Their sweetest perfume thro' the air:
Stir up, O south, the boughs that bloom,
Till the belovèd Master come:

That He may come, and linger yet
Among the trees that He hath set;
That He may evermore be seen
To walk amid the springing green.

Adapted by Robert Bridges from a text by Isaac Watts, 'We are a garden walled around' for a tune by W. Leighton in 'Tears or Lamentations of a Sorrowful Soul', 1614, re-set by H. Ellis Wooldridge

That exiles here awhile in flesh
Some earnest may our souls refresh
Of that pure life for which we long,
Some foretaste of the heav'nly song.

Robert Bridges: Verse 6 of 'This day the first of days was made', a translation of 'Primo dierum omnium' ascribed to Saint Gregory the Great. Sung to a proper Sarum plainsong melody set by Mary Bridges. The original was in universal Sunday use at Nocturns or Matins. Sung also to ANDERNACH

Rejoicing may this day go hence,
Like virgin dawn our innocence,
Like fiery noon our faith appear,
Nor know the gloom of twilight drear.

Robert Bridges: Verse 7 of 'O splendour of God's glory bright'. a translation of 'Splendor Paternæ gloriæ' by the fourth-century writer Saint Ambrose. Sung to a Proper Sarum plainsong melody set by Mary Bridges. Also sung to WAREHAM

Our senses with thy light inflame:
Our hearts to heav'nly love reclaim:
Our bodies' poor infirmity
With strength perpetual fortify.

Robert Bridges: Verse 4 of 'Come, O Creator Spirit, come', a translation and revision of 'Veni Creator Spiritus' a text current by the tenth century. For VENI CREATOR in a setting by Mary Bridges. The proper Sarum tune is probably earlier than the text: the tune was first written for 'Hic est verus Dei', the Ambrosian Easter hymn

Bridges wrote of Louis Bourgeois, whose tunes especially inspired him: *A name come, with the slow justice of time, out of long obscurity to high esteem...He was imprisoned by his employers for his musical innovations in 1551, and having suffered Calvin for sixteen years, seems to have lost his appointment and left Geneva on account of Calvin's opposition to his desire to introduce part-singing.* **Claude Goudimel, whose pupils in Rome included Nanini and Palestrina, settled in Paris in 1555. Having made part-settings of Bourgeois' melodies, he was suspected of heresy, and was massacred in the horrible bloodshed of Saint Bartholomew's Day, 1572.**

Christ to their homes giveth his peace,
  And makes their loves his own.
But ah, what tares the Evil one
  Hath in his garden sown.

Sad were our lot, evil this earth,
  Did not its sorrows prove
The path whereby the sheep may find
  The fold of Jesu's love.

Robert Bridges: Verses 3 and 4 of 'Happy are they, they that love God', a
free translation of 'O quam juvat frates, Deus' by Charles Coffin, who lived
from 1676 to 1749 and was appointed Rector of Paris University in 1718.
Set by Mary Bridges to a melody by William Croft (1678-1727). Sung also
to BINCHESTER, using the same melody with different harmonies

Love of the Father, love of God the Son,
From whom all came, in whom was all begun;
Who formest heav'nly beauty out of strife,
Creation's whole desire and breath of life.

Thou the all-holy, Thou supreme in might,
Thou dost give peace, thy presence maketh Right;
Thou with thy favour all things dost enfold,
With thine all-kindness free from harm wilt hold.

Robert Bridges: Verses 1 and 2 from the twelfth-century Latin text 'Amor
patris et filii veri splendor', to be sung to Orlando Gibbons' SONG 22 in
George Wither's 'Hymns and Songs of the Church', 1623. When Gibbons
wrote the tune, he took little notice of the originally written words which
show no trace of the strong cæsura in the first line of the music (O Lord of
Hosts and God of Israel!) while the syncopated bass plays havoc with the
second line (Thou who between the Cherubims dost dwell)

Lifespring divine, and bond of all,
Abiding in Thyself unmoved,
By change of thy created light
Our mortal times determining,

Accord to us an evening fair,
Whereby our life fall not in shade;
That so our souls in holy death
Forestall thy gift of endless day. Amen.

Robert Bridges: From 'Rerum Deus tenax vigor', a hymn from the seventh
century or earlier. For an Ambrosian melody to three hymns of the lesser
hours, Terce, Sext and Nones

Our mortal being purify
To be thy praise, thy temple fair;
That holy fire of heav'nly love
Flame forth and kindle all the world.

Robert Bridges: Verse 2 of a translation of 'Nunc sancte nobis spiritus', an
anonymous early hymn which begins in Bridges' version
'O Holy Spirit, Lord of Life' for an ancient anonymous tune

As well as the completion of *The Yattendon Hymnal,* 1899 saw the issue of the second of the six-volume edition of Bridges' poetry. Book 1, published the previous year, had reproduced *Prometheus the Firegiver, Eros and Psyche* and *The Growth of Love.* Book 2 brought together the shorter poems, including several written some years earlier but not previously published. The texts included *Eclogue II: Giovanni Dupré,* a poem first printed in *The Cornhill Magazine,* in the form of a conversation between Lawrence and Richard about the artist of Santa Croce as they watch his funeral procession pass. Much of his work had been fashionable but mediocre. Two portions spoken by Richard provide the flavour:

> I can tell
> All as we walk. A poor woodcarver's son,
> Prenticed to cut his father's rude designs
> (We have it from himself), maker of shrines,
> In his mean workshop in Siena dreamed;
> And saw as gods the artists of the earth,
> And long'd to stand on their immortal shore,
> And be as they, who in his vision gleam'd,
> Dowering the world with grace for evermore.
> So, taxing rest and leisure to one aim,
> The boy of single will and inbred skill
> Rose step by step to academic fame.
>
> ¤   ¤   ¤   ¤   ¤   ¤
>
> Yet he made one thing
> Worthy of the lily city in her spring;
> For while in vain the forms of beauty he aped,
> A perfect spirit in himself he shaped;
> And all his lifetime doing less than well
> Where he profess'd nor doubted to excel,
> Now, where he had no scholarship, but drew
> His art from love, 'twas better than he knew:
> And when he sat to write, lo! by him stood
> The heavenly Muse, who smiles on all things good;
> And for his truth's sake, for his stainless mind,
> His homely love and faith, she now grew kind,
> And changed the crown, that from the folk he got,
> For her green laurel, and he knew it not.

In very different style is the Jubilee Song, *Regina Cara,* for music, written for 1897, which ends:

> In wisdom and love firm is thy fame:
> Enemies bow to revere thy name:
> The world shall never tire to tell
> Praise of the queen that reignèd well.

O FELIX ANIMA, DOMINA PRAECLARA
AMORE SEMPER CORONABERE
REGINA CARA.

I have sown upon the fields
Eyebright and Pimpernel,
And Pansy and Poppy-seed
Ripen'd and scatter'd well,

And silver Lady-smock
The meads with light to fill,
Cowslip and Buttercup,
Daisy and Daffodil;

King-cup and Fleur-de-lys
Upon the marsh to meet
With Comfrey, Watermint,
Loose-strife and Meadowsweet;

And all along the stream
My care hath not forgot
Crowfoot's white galaxy
And love's Forget-me-not:

And where high grasses wave
Shall great Moon-daises blink,
With Rattle and Sorrel sharp
And Robin's ragged pink.

Thick on the woodland floor
Gay company shall be,
Primrose and Hyacinth
And frail Anemone,

Perennial Strawberry-bloom,
Woodsorrel's pencilled veil,
Dishevel'd Willow-weed
And Orchis purple and pale,

Bugle, and blushes blue,
And Woodruff's snowy gem,
Proud Fox-glove's finger-bells
And Spurge with milky stem.

High on the downs so bare,
Where thou dost love to climb,
Pink Thrift and Milkwort are,
Lotus and scented Thyme;

And in the shady lanes
Bold Arum's hood of green,
Herb Robert, Violet,
Starwort and Celandine;

And by the dusty road
Bedstraw and Mullein tall,
With red Valerian
And Toadflax on the wall,

*Robert Bridges' poem
'The Idle Flowers'
is continued in the
margin of the next page*

continued from previous page
Yarrow and Chicory,
That hath for hue no like,
Silene and Marrow mild
And Agrimony's spike,

Blue-eyed Veronicas
And grey-faced Scabious
And downy Silverweed
And striped Convolvulus:

Harebell shall haunt the banks,
And thro' the hedgerow peer
Withwind and Snapdragon
And Nightshade's flower of fear.

And where men never sow,
Have I my Thistles set,
Ragwort and stiff Wormwood
And straggling Mignonette,

Bugloss and Burdock rank
And prickly Teasel high,
With Umbels yellow and white,
That come to kexes dry.

Pale Chlora shalt thou find,
Sun-loving Centaury,
Cranesbill and Sinjunwort,
Cinquefoil and Betony:

Shock-headed Dandelion,
That drank the fire of the sun:
Hawkweed and Marigold,
Cornflower and Campion.

Let Oak and Ash grow strong,
Let Beech her branches spread;
Let Grass and Barley throng
And waving Wheat for bread;

Be share and sickle bright
To labour at all hours;
For thee and thy delight
I have made the idle flowers.

But now 'tis Winter, child,
And bitter northwinds blow,
The ways are wet and wild,
The land is laid in snow.

Robert Bridges:
'The Idle Flowers'

A young man, another Old Etonian, William Johnston Stone, who in his short life taught briefly at Radley College and Marlborough College, was to play a significant role in Bridges' future work. His published paper *On the Use of Classical Metres in English* explains his dream which brought him to Yattendon in the late 1890s. His poem of thanks for hospitality to Mary Bridges gives a vivid picture of the occasion:

> Dear Mrs Bridges,
>   I cannot
> Say farewell to Yattendon
>   All the charm of it undefined,
>   Undefinable,—and to
>
> Those less indefinite pleasures,
>   Reading in sunny places
> Weighty theologists' remarks,
>   With divided attention;
>
> Submitting to a kind critic,
>   Patient, unprejudiced, sound,
>   Sheets of dull matter, ill written
> Nor at all better expressed;
>
> Or receiving a just rebuke
>   For misuse of an adverb,
> Conversational wholly un-
>   justfiable adverb;
>
> Games unintelligently played,
>   Played against better informed,
>   Vastly more ready intellects,
> Playing and coming off worst;
>
> Or with antagonist fitter
>   Prancing in the racket-court,
> Or watching the village recruits
>   Turning round several times.
>
> I cannot quit it all without
>   Indistinctly telling you
> In Pherecratians coupled
>   With yet uglier in name
>
> Glyconics—together the lines
>   (See the scansion above this)
> Are asclepiad in rhythm—
>   How delightful it all was.

William Stone writing from The Briary Cottage, Eton, to Mrs Bridges after a visit to Yattendon

It was in fulfilling a promise that he would one day test Stone's theory that Bridges began writing English poems in classical prosody in 1903 (though he penned a letter to his doctor friend Thomas Barlow in this form in 1902). Bridges' interest in language had also led him to devise his own system of phonetic spelling, over which he was to fight for acceptance without success. It was through this cause that he began a long friendship with the lexicographer, Henry Bradley. He had begun work on the *Oxford English Dictionary* in 1883, became joint-editor in 1889 and succeeded James Murray as senior editor in 1915.

Another commission early in the new century was for a masque to be performed by the ladies of Somerville College, Oxford, at the inauguration of their new building in 1904. He turned to Greek mythology for his theme, telling the story of Persephone. Here is the ode to proceed the entry of Demeter at the beginning of the third Act concerned with Persephone's restoration for which Demeter has worked so hard:

O that the earth, or only this fair isle wer' ours
    Amid the ocean's blue billows,
With flow'ry woodland, stately mountain and valley,
    Cascading and lilied river;
Nor ever a mortal envious, laborious,
    By anguish or dull care opprest,
Should come polluting with remorseful countenance
    Our haunt of easy gaiety.
For us the grassy slopes, the country's airiness,
    The lofty whispering forest,
Where rapturously Philomel invoketh the night
    And million eagar throats the morn;
With doves at evening softly cooing, and mellow
    Cadences of the dewy thrush.
We love the gentle deer, the nimble antelope;
    Mice love we and springing squirrels;
To watch the gaudy flies visit the blooms, to hear
    On ev'ry mead the grasshopper.
All thro' the spring-tide, thro' the indolent summer,
    (If only this fair isle wer' ours)
Here might we dwell, forgetful of the weedy caves
    Beneath the ocean's blue billows.
Robert Bridges: 'Ode' to proceed the entry of Demeter at the beginning of Act III of 'Demeter'

The first experiment in English poetry in classical prosody took the form of a letter to Lionel Muirhead, a friend since schooldays at Eton. The opening stanza explains the purpose of the letter:

Now in wintry delights, and long fireside meditation,
'Twixt studies and routine paying due court to the Muses,
My solace in solitude, when broken roads barricade me
Mudbound, unvisited for months with my merry children,
Grateful t'ward Providence, and heeding a slander against me
Less than a rheum, think of me to-day, dear Lionel, and take
This letter as some account of Will Stone's versification.

I always seem to see man as the center of concentric spheres, the nearest to him being the *circle* of common sense and matter-of-fact, beyond this the circle of science and intellect, & beyond that, stretching out to infinity, the realm of imagination...
From a letter from Robert Bridges to Henry Bradley written on 2nd October 1901

As to the phoenetics, I think you understand my attitude pretty well. My state of mind with regard to spelling reform is a sad bundle of contradictions. The problem *looks* to me insoluble; and yet I am convinced that it cannot be really insoluble, but will sometime get solved in some way of which I have no conception. I am afraid this lame-winged scepticism with a sort of optimsm behind it is too characteristic of my way of thinking in general, but I seem unable to get out of it...I do not think your notation will find many friends among scientific phoneticians, but it may be useful, on account of its beauty and ingenuity, in attracting the attention of some who have been accustomed to look on phoenic spelling as a barbarous foolery...
From a letter written to Robert Bridges by Henry Bradley while on holiday in Bournemouth on 17th March 1903

The object of this paper will be an attempt to realize a dream, which has I suppose at one time or another been present to most of us, that classical metres might find a place in our language not merely distantly similar to that which they held in Latin and Greek, but really and actually the same, governed by rules equally strict and perfect, and producing on the ear the same pure delight. Every one who has tried has failed...
William Johnson Stone: From 'On the use of Classical Metres in English' read at King's College, Cambridge

110

These experiments in quantative verse were made in fulfilment of a promise to William Johnson Stone that I would some day test his theory. His premature death converted my consent into a serious obligation. This personal explanation is due to myself for two reasons: because I might otherwise appear firstly as an advocate of the system, secondly as responsible for Stone's determination of the lengths of English syllables. Before writing quantitive verse it is necessary to learn to *think* in quantities. This is no light task, and a beginner requires fixed rules. Except for a few minor details, which I had disputed with Mr. Stone, I was bound to take his rules as he had elaborated them; and it was not until I had made some progress and could think fairly well in his prosody that I seriously criticized it. The two chief errors that I find in it are that he relied too much on the quality of a vowel in determining its syllabic length, and that he regarded the *h* as *always* consonantal in quality...

...Though the difficulty of adapting our English syllables to the Greek rules is very great, and even deterrent—for I cannot pretend to have attained to an absolutely consistent scheme —yet the experiments that I have made reveal a vast unexplored field of delicate and expressive rhythms hitherto unknown in our poetry: and this amply rewarded me for my friendly undertaking.
Robert Bridges: From the preface to 'Poems in Classical Prosody'

We, whose first memories reach half a century backward,
May praise our fortune to have outliv'd so many dangers,—
Faultiness of Nature's unruly machinery or man's—;
For, once born, whatever 'tis worth, LIFE is to be held to,
Its mere persistence esteem'd as rèal attainment,
Its crown of silver reverenc'd as one promise of youth
Fruiting, of existence one needful purpose accomplish'd:
And 'twere worth the living, howe'er unkindly bereft of
Those joys and comforts, throu' which we chiefly regard it:
Nay,—set aside the pleasant unhinder'd order of our life,
Our happy enchantments of Fortune, easy surroundings,
Courteous acquaintance, dwelling in fair homes, the delight of
Long plann'd excursions, the romance of journeying in lands
Historic, of sèeing their glory, the famous adornments
Giv'n to memorial Earth by man, decorator of all-time,
(—As wè saw with virginal eyes travelling to behold them,—)
Her gorgeous palaces, V her tow'rs and stately cathedrals;
Where the turrets and domes of pictured Tuscany slumber,
Or the havoc'd splendours of Rome imperial, or where
Glare the fretted minarets and mosks of trespassing Islam,
And old Nilus, amid the mummied suzerainty of Egypt,
Glideth, a godly presence, consciously regardless of all things,
Save his unending toil and èternal recollections:—

Set these out of account, and with them too put away ART,
Those ravishings of mind, those sensuous intelligences,
By whose grace the elect enjoy their sacred aloofness
From Life's meagre affairs, in beauty's règenerate youth
Reading immortality's sublime revelation, adoring
Their own heav'nly desire; nor alone in worship assist they,
But take, call'd of God, part aand pleasure in crèation
Of that beauty, the first of His first purposes extoll'd...
From 'Epistle I to L.M.: Wintry Delights'.
In this extract an accent is used to indicate a syllable Stone counted as long, and the verse requires it to be so pronounced, though Bridges considered it as short, or at least, as doubtful. The V is placed in the gap where a final syllable should be lengthened, or nor shortened by position, but lacks its consonantal support

In 1904, we find the family wintering in the Cotswolds, near the sanitorium where Margaret, a daughter with great musical gifts, is recovering from serious illness. The winter of 1904-5 was spent in Switzerland. Eventually, after other wanderings, he planned and oversaw the building of Chilswell House, at Boar's Hill, just outside Oxford, which, save for a period when it was renovated following a fire, became his home for the rest of his life.

The Oxford Historical Pageant was presented from 27th June to 3rd July 1907. It consisted of fifteen scenes and an interlude or masque, and of these sixteen parts, nine were dramatic scenes with words and the rest were visual presentations. The authors chosen were Laurence Housman, author of *Victoria Regina*, who contributed the scene on *Saint Frideswide;* Robert Bridges characterised *Theobaldus Stampensis* and also wrote an introductory *Invitation to the Pageant;* Laurence Binyon, most widely remembered today for his poem *For the Fallen,* devised a piece on *Henry II and Fair Rosamund;* Charles Oman, the Chichele Professor of Modern History and Chairman of the Pageant's Consultative Committee wrote the scene on *Friar Bacon;* A. D. Godley, then Fellow and Tutor of Magdalen College, tackled *Saint Scholastica's Day;* Walter Raleigh, the Professor of English Literature, penned a *Masque of the Mediaeval Curriculum;* J. B. Fagan wrote *Henry VIII and Wolsey, A. D. 1518,* and Elizabeth Wordsworth *James I, 1605;* Stanley Weyman scripted *Magdalen College and James II;* the finale, *The Secret of Oxford* was written by Arthur Quiller-Couch, who in 1900 had edited *The Oxford Book of English Verse.*

Theobaldus Stampensis belonged to the days before the University was founded. There were students, though, before there were universities, and they gathered especially in the great towns where life was full of interest and where charity was abundant. Whilst Oxford had suffered from the Norman Conquest, and the Domesday Book tells a sad story of *waste houses,* its prosperity returned with Robert D'Oilgi, its castle-builder turned saint and church-builder. To this revived and prosperous town came Theobald Stampensis, the first of its long line of teachers. This was the man Bridges sought to bring to life in a scene set in Oxford's main thoroughfare.

By 1909, Bridges was writing prosody without the absolute tyranny of Stone's rules. That year he made a line-by-line paraphrase of a part of Virgil's *Æned, Book VI.* In these English hexameters, he used and advocated the use of Miltonic elision. He placed a | in the text where he had purposely allowed a short syllable to sustain a long place.

> They wer' amid the shadows by night in loneliness obscure
> Walking forth i' the void and vasty dominyon of Ades;
> As by an uncertain moonray secretly illumin'd
> One goeth in the forest, when heav'n is gloomily clouded,
> And black night hath robb'd the colours and beauty from all things.
>   Here in Hell's very jaws, the threhold of darkening Orcus,
> Have the avenging Cares laid their steepless habitation,
> Wailing Grief, pallid Infections, & heart-stricken Old-age,
> Dismal Fear, unholy Famine, with low groveling Want,
> Forms of spectral horror, gaunt Toil and Death the devourer,
> And Death's drowsy brother, Torpor; with whom, an inane rout,
> All the Pleasures of Sin; there also the Furies in ambusht
> Chamber of iron, afore whose bars wild War bloodyhanded
> Raged, and mad Discord high brandisht her venomous locks.

This is his last book *Christianity at the Crossroads.* I can't usually read such books, but I find his analysis most lucid, and his thought profound and clear. It strikes me as if a vast heap of rubbish stones were being arranged in patterns on the ground. I like looking at his patterns, but whether, when I have seen a little more of them I shall kick all his stones back into the heap again, I cannot yet tell.

Robert Bridges: From a letter to Henry Bradley written on 11th June 1911 about a book by the Jesuit, George Tyrrell

By a Modernist, I mean a churchman, of any sort, who believes in the possibility of a synthesis between the essential truth of his religion and the essential truth of modernity...

...Modernists are not such utopian dreamers as to imagine that those, whose temporal interests are vested in existing Catholicism and its worst corruptions, will ever open their arms to welcome such a science. Which of the sciences have they not persecuted? Much more will they persecute that which deals with religion itself, their peculiar field of exploitation. The control of men's consciences, and, thereby, of their conduct and resources, is too valuable a weapon of aggrandisement not to be grasped at by the secular power, be it that of Czar or King or Republic; of papal monarchy or the bureaucracy that works for its restoration...

...It is the spirit of Christ that has again and again saved the Church from the hands of her worldly oppressors within and without; for where that spirit is, there is liberty...

George Tyrrell: Quotations from 'Christianity at the

The Christian churches will not leave the old ruts. The Pope still hankers after temporal power, and to get it would crown Tilgath-Pileser in St. Peter's, while our Protestant church still begins its morning devotions by singing of *God swearing in his wrath that his people should not enter into his rest.*

Now in the religion of Christ, which, whether we will it or not, whether we know it or not, is deeply ingrained in our heart's reverence, and the life of our souls, and is ever rebuking and overruling our conduct—in this world-conquering Christianity the essentials are love and unity and brotherhood. But look at the Protestant sects, all quarrelling about crude absurdities and ridiculous unessentials. And ask yourselves how the Church shall be purified and edified when those who should compose it remain outside of it.

> *Robert Bridges: From 'The Necessity of Poetry'*

Robert Bridges has just been in on the way down the hill. He is delightfully grumpy. He mentions thing after thing which is commonly believed and says that of course it's not so. He's always right. His intellect has been so completely self-indulged that it now can't understand rubbish. He has never obeyed anyone or adapted himself to anyone, so he's as clear as crystal, and can't do with fogs...

> *Walter Raleigh in a letter of 30th October 1912 to Lady Echo*

Midway, of all this tract, with secular arms an immense elm
Reareth a crowd of branches aneath whose leafy protection
Vain dreams thickly nestle, clinging unto the foliage on high:
And many strange creatures of monstrous form and features
Stable about th' entrance, Centaur and Scylla's abortion,
And hundred-handed Briareus, and Lerna's wildbeast
Roaring amain, and clothed in frightful flame the Chimæra,
Gorgons and Harpies, | and Pluto's three-bodied ogre.

> *Robert Bridges: The opening lines of 'Ibant Obscuri'*

In 1911 he was asked by the Church Music Society to write an article about the words of hymns. Here is part of his letter of response:

> It is a difficult subject, and I do not see my way to deal with it. It seems to me that the clergy are the responsible people. If they say that the hymns (words and music) which keep me away from church draw others thither, and excite useful religious emotions, then they must take the responsibility wholly on themselves. I would not choose for them. All I can urge is that they should have at least *one* service a week where people like myself can attend without being offended or moved to laughter. Any society for the improvement of church music, as it appears to me, can deal only with the worthier *music*—and it is for that reason that I have been unable to interest myself in the work of a hymn-committee. For, judging by the number of approved hymns, its aim is to exclude the *worst*, and to distinguish the *tolerable* things. But I suppose that the *worst* are often just those very vulgar things that the clergy find so useful. I have always advocated a division of hymns into two classes: (1) the worthiest (e.g. the old Church hymns); (2) the rest; and I think that a Church Musical Society should not meddle with the second class. It seems a pity that editors of recent hymn-books have not seen their way to adopt such division. They would have done better if they had divided their books into two sections, but it is of course difficult to draw the line, and it might be more satisfactory to make three classes.

> Now as to words merely, which is what you ask me to deal with. The words are in much the same confusion as the music. I could only approach the subject of words from the musical point of view—and then one of the proper questions that would first arise would be the relation of words to music; and here, how far the artistic form of the hymn-tunes renders the tunes independent of the grammar of the words; e.g. whether the accented notes in the tune require always a corresponding accent in the words. I think that the intelligent hymn-singer is getting much too squeamish on this head. I do not find that an occasional disagreement between accent of words and of music offends me in a hymn. A fine tune is an unalterable artistic form, which pleases in itself and for itself. The notion of its giving way to the words

is impossible. The words are better suited if they fit in with *all* the quantities and accents of the tune, but it is almost impossible and not necessary that they should. Their *mood* is what the tune must be true to; and the mood is the main thing. If the tune also incidentally reinforces important words or phrases, that is all the better, and where there are refrains, or repetitions of words the tune should be designed for them; but the enormous power that the tune has of enforcing or even of creating a mood is the one invaluable thing of magnitude, which overrides every other consideration.

For this reason the tune is more important than the words. It shocks the clergy to tell them this, but they all concede the premisses, viz. (1) that the best words can be rendered invalid or even ridiculous by bad music, and (2) that unworthy words can have a worthy sense imparted to them by good music. Whence of course it follows that (within reasonable limits) the tune is the more important. Whatever hymn the Apostles sang after the Last Supper, you cannot imagine a silly vulgar tune, but with a worthy solemn and pathetic tune almost any words. Put aside archaeology, and try the experiment in your imagination.

Music being the most ideal and supramundane of all the arts, it cannot be equated item for item with poetry. A melody is a whole and the notes which are its units retain none of their meaning when isolated. In the words of hymns the different words have meanings—and no one should expect that the units of the one can be equated with the units of the other.

Again, to suppose that the melody is intended for the *words* (rather than for the mood of them) introduces the critical judgement of their correspondence. How do they fit? Oh, very well, or pretty well, or not at all well—and since it is *impossible* that they should all fit very well, it is plainly wrong to raise an expectation which is bound to be often disappointed, and thus provoke a critical attitude incompatible with emotion. Since it is only good tunes that will justify themselves when they do not fit well with the words, it may very likely be the prevalence of bad tunes—sentimental rubbish—which has made people squeamish about the false accenting of the words.

These considerations do not of course apply to chanting, the essence of which is that it should follow the speech-rhythm; the absurdity of our Anglican chanting is due to the chant being treated as a hymn tune.

How far the general sense of the words of a hymn can be independent of their worthy verbal expression is another question.

A few of us were talking one afternoon in that home of leisurely conversation, the library of Chilswell...about the state of the English language and the dangers which seemed to be threatening it under modern conditions. How would it be possible...to safeguard our inherited form of speech from some at least of these dangers, to help defend its integrity and beauty, and make it, perhaps, into an even more adequate means of expression for modern ideas...?
...he would not have been Mr. Bridges if he had not found some slight element of gratification, and, if I may say so, a kind of school-boyish glee, in throwing stones at academic windows...
Logan Pearsall Smith describing how the Society for Pure English began in 1913

I object to *Anyone*. I think we must be selective so far as to exclude people who might swamp us. Also there is the danger that people might join us for their own credit and then discredit the Society by their practice. I wish we had discussed this point. The invitation must be so worded as to leave the Society the power of refusal. Moreover if we are going to send our circulars to all the members, it w'd be a great nuisance to have useless members...
Robert Bridges in a letter to Logan Smith about the Society for Pure English. Life was difficult for the secretary, who had the delicate task of interesting eminent persons in joining, some of whom Bridges might think should be refused membership

As regards his general attitude, he was at once conservative and democratic, aesthetic and rational. Besides fighting to preserve the traditional and characteristic beauties of our language from the dangers of slovenly and meaningless degradation, and from all confusion and ugliness, whether of thought or sound, he was at the same time a keen experimenter, and no one was more ready to appreciate and encourage all natural and healthy developments of the natural genius. It was indeed the strength of his desire to secure to that genius the right conditions for free growth along ideal lines, that moved him to lay the foundations of this Society.

Elizabeth Daryrush: 'Robert Bridges' Work on the English Language'. This paper about her father was commissioned and published after his death by the Society for Pure English

As the metre or scansion of this poem was publicly discussed and wrongly analysed by some who admired its effects, it may be well to explain that it and the three other poems...are strictly syllabic verse on the model left by Milton in *Samson Agonistes;* except that his system, which depended on exclusion of extra-metrical syllables (that is, syllables which did not admit of resolution by *elision* into a disyllabic scheme) from all places but the last, still admitted them in that place, thereby forbidding inversion of the last foot. It is natural to conclude that, had he pursued his inventions, his next step would have been to get rid of this anomaly; and if that is done, the result is the new rhythms that these poems exhibit. In this sort of prosody rhyme is admitted, like alliteration, as an ornament at will; it is not needed...

From Robert Bridges' note about 'Noel: Christmas Eve, 1913'

The people's choice for Poet Laureate in 1913 would almost certainly have been Rudyard Kipling. But it was Robert Bridges who was honoured with the appointment.

One of his twelve poems written that year was published in *The Times* on 24th December under the heading *Pax hominibus bonae voluntatis.*

A frosty Christmas Eve
   when the stars were shining
Fared I forth alone
   where westward falls the hill,
And from many a village
   in the water'd valley
Distant music reach'd me
   Peals of bells aringing:
The constellated sounds
   ran sprinkling on earth's floor
As the dark vault above
   with stars was spangled o'er.

Then sped my thought to keep
   that first Christmas of all
When the shepherds watching
   by their folds ere the dawn
Heard music in the fields
   and marveling could not tell
Whether it were angels
   or the bright stars singing.

Now blessed be the tow'rs
   that crown England so fair
That stand up strong in prayer
   unto God for our souls:
Blessed be their founders
   (said I) an' our country folk
Who are ringing for Christ
   in the belfries to-night
With arms lifted to clutch
   the rattling ropes that race
Into the dark above
   and the mad romping din.

But to me heard afar
   it was starry music
Angels' song, comforting
   as the comfort of Christ
When he spake tenderly
   to his sorrowful flock:
The old words came to me
   by the riches of time
Mellow'd and transfigured
   as I stood on the hill
Heark'ning in the aspcct
   of th' eternal silence.

Robert Bridges: 'Noel: Christmas Eve, 1913'

In 1915, Bridges prepared *The Spirit of Man*, an anthology in English and French from the philosophers and poets, dedicated to the King. In the acknowledgements, he decribes William Butler Yeats as a friend, and they had an extensive correspondence over the years.

The Poet Laureate was not a person to write poems to specific royal command but the composition of an ode for the tercentenary celebration of Shakepeare's death in April 1616 appealed to him.

> For God of His gifts pour'd on him a full measure,
> And gave him to know Nature and the ways of men:
> To dower with inexhaustible treasure
> A world-conquering speech,
> Which surg'd as a river high-descended
> That gathering tributaries of many lands
> Rolls through the plain a bounteous flood,
> Picturing towers and temples
> And ruin of bygone times,
> And floateth the ships deep-laden with merchandise
> Out on the windy seas to traffic in foreign climes.
>
> Thee SHAKESPEARE to-day we honour; and evermore,
> Since England bore thee, the master of human song,
> Thy folk are we, children of thee,
> Who knitting in one her realm
> And strengthening with pride her sea-borne clans,
> Scorn'st in the grave the bruize of death.
> All thy later-laurel'd choir
> Laud thee in thy world-shrine:
> London's laughter is thine;
> One with thee is our temper in melancholy or might,
> And in thy book Great-Britain's rule readeth her right.
>
> *Robert Bridges: Stanzas 3 and 4 of 'Ode on the Tercentenary*
> *Commemoration of Shakespeare, 1916'*

When Field-Marshall Kitchener was drowned while on his way to Russia in 1916, Bridges wrote a poem for publication in *The Times,* giving permission for it to be freely reproduced. He also had twenty copies printed privately.

In 1917, his house was severely damaged by fire, and for nearly two years during its renovations he and his wife lived in Oxford. In 1918, as the First World War continued to massacre many of the nations' youth, Bridges, who had prepared for the press editions of the poetry of several of his friends, was quietly doing so for the most gifted of them, Gerard Manley Hopkins, who also had died young.

Although the Society for Pure English was born in Bridges' library in 1913, and the initial membership was recruited before the First World War, it was not until 1920 that active steps were

Authors selected for inclusion in *The Spirit of Man*.

Lascelles Abercrombie
Henri-Frédéric Amiel
Aristotle
Matthew Arnold
Augustine of Hippo
Francis Bacon
Edwyn Bevan
William Blake
George Borrow
Francis Bourdillon
Robert Bridges
Emily Brontë
Rupert Brooke
Edmund Burke
Robert Burns
George Byron
Thomas Carlyle
Geoffrey Chaucer
André Chénier
Samuel Coleridge
William Collins
Abraham Cowley
Richard Crashaw
Ailes D'Alouette
George Darley
Jan Antoine De Baïf
Thomas Dekker
René Descartes
John De Tabley
Richard Dixon
Digby Dolben
John Donne
Charles D'Orleans
Fyodor Dostoievsky
Francis Doyle
Epictetus
Charles Fontaine
Thomas Gray
Gregory the Great
Julian Grenfell
William Hazlitt
George Herbert
José Hérédia
Robert Herrick
Homer
Gerard Manley Hopkins
William James
Francis Jammes
Jellaludin, Sufi poet of Islam
Kabir of North India
John Keats
Selma Lagerlöf
Charles Lamb
Andrew Lang
Sydney Lanier
Abraham Lincoln
James Lowell
Lucian of Samosata
Marcus Aurelius
Andrew Marvell
John Masefield

continued in margin overleaf

116

possible to implement the ideas. The other initiators were Henry Bradley, Logan Pearsall Smith, and Walter Raleigh. The 83 initial pre-war members included James Elroy Flecker, Walter de la Mare, Gilbert Murray, Henry Newbolt, Arthur Quiller-Couch and Hugh Walpole. Both Bridges and his wife played an active role, and it could be said to be his last hobby. It was essentially Bridges' brain child and he wanted it to grow. Equally he wanted to avoid its falling into academic hands. (Had not Bridges three decades earlier refused to be put forward as the next Professor of Poetry at Oxford?) Nevertheless, its membership grew to around 400 and it published a series of papers for circulation to its members. These included several which Bridges wrote or introduced with a preface, and one he and his wife contributed jointly under a pseudonym. Another was co-written with Henry Bradley, whose death in 1923 was greatly mourned. Bridges' subjects included: *On English Homophones*; *Dialectical Words in Blunden's Poems*; *Pictorial, Picturesque; Poetry in Schools*; and *The Society's Work*. Over twenty contributors tackled such varied subjects as *The Englishing of French Words*, *American Pronunciation*, *The Split Infinitive, English Idioms, English Handwriting* and *The Nature of Human Speech*.

> It is due also to *the poverty of our accidence* that, if we would secure the full force of our diction, we need great care to avoid any sequence of words which without special punctuation and apart from the context might be other parts of speech and so combine differently to make a different sense. Few writers are heedful of this, and it is a counsel of perfection: but even where the context so ensures the meaning and right reading that nothing else is suspected or consciously suggested, yet the lurking ambiguity will take the edge off the expression, because it unconsciously calls away some part of our attention.
>
> *Robert Bridges: From the Introduction to William Cuthbert Morton: 'The Language of Anatomy', one of the papers published by the Society for Pure English*

Meanwhile, also in 1920, Bridges wartime material and some other unpublished texts were issued under the title *October and Other Poems* in a volume dedicated to Jan Christiaan Smuts, appointed as Prime Minister of South Africa in 1919.

> April adance in play
>   met with his lover May
>   where she came garlanded.
> The blossoming boughs o'erhead
>   were thrill'd to bursting by
>   the dazzle from the sky
>   and the wild music there
>   that shook the odorous air.

Each moment some new birth
hasten'd to deck the earth
in the gay sunbeams.
Between their kisses dreams:
And dream and kiss were rife
with laughter of mortal life.

But this late day of golden fall
is still as a picture upon a wall
or a poem in a book lying open unread.
Or whatever else is shrined
when the Virgin hath vanishèd :
Footsteps of eternal Mind
on the path of the dead.

Robert Bridges: 'October'

Land, dear land, whose sea-built shore
Nurseth warriors evermore,
Land, whence Freedom far and lone
Round the earth her speech has thrown
Like a planet's luminous zone,—
In thy strength and calm defiance
Hold mankind in love's alliance!

Beauteous art thou, but the foes
Of thy beauty are not those
Who lie tangled and dismay'd
Fearless one, be yet afraid
Lest thyself thyself condemn
In the wrong that ruin'd them.

God, who chose thee and upraised
'Mong the folk (His name be praised!),
Proved thee then by chastisement
Worthy of His high intent,
Who, because thou could'st endure,
Saved thee free and purged thee pure,
Won thee thus His grace to win,
For thy love forgave thy sin,
For thy truth forgave thy pride;
Queen of seas and countries wide,—
He who led thee still will guide.

Robert Bridges: From 'Britannia Victrix'

Fount of creative Love
Mother of the Word eternal
Atoning man with God:
Who set thee apart as a garden enclosed
From Nature's all-producing wilds
To rear the richest fruit o' the Life
Ever continuing out from Him
Urgent since the beginning.

Robert Bridges: a stanza chosen from 'Our Lady'

Emily Daniel presided over war-work done in the Provost's lodgings at Worcester College, Oxford, during the last two years of the First World War. Fifty one of her fellow-workers presented her in April 1919 with a copy of William Blake's *Lyrical Poems* bound with a light-hearted piece of some 260 lines written by Bridges for the occasion.

As for the boys, tho' our *juventus*
Was not perhaps all as God meant
us,
Too eager in th' exploit of pastime,
Yet on our books we spent no less
time,
Pronouncing Latin quite as oddly
As A. C. Clark or A. D. Godley,
And sportively intent on getting
A first in Greats against the
betting:
For teachers know examination
To be the crown of education:
Since minds cannot like plants
be trusted
To keep their rootlets
well-adjusted,
They who would rear them
must examine 'em
To guage th' effect of what
they cram in 'em...

*Robert Bridges: Lines from 'To
Emily Daniel'*

118

> Love and the Muse have left their home, now bare
> Of memorable beauty, all is gone,
> The dedicated charm of Yattendon,
> Which thou wert apt, dear Hal, to build and share.
>   What noble shades are flitting, who while-ere
> Haunted the ivy'd walls, where time ran on
> In sanctities of joy by reverence won,
> Music and choral grace and studies fair!
>
>   These on some kindlier field may Fate restore,
> And may the old house prosper, dispossest
> Of her whose equal it can nevermore
>   Hold till it crumble: O nay! and the door
> Will moulder ere it open on a guest
> To match thee in thy wisdom and thy jest.
> Robert Bridges: 'To Harry Ellis Wooldridge'
>
> Folk alien to the Muse have hemm'd us round
> And fiends have suck'd our blood: our best delight
> Is poison'd, and the year's infective blight
> Hath made almost a silence of sweet sound.
>   But you, what fortune, Percy, have you found
> At Harrow? doth fair hope your toil requite?
> Doth beauty win her praise and truth her right,
> Or hath the good seed fal'n on stony ground?
>
>   Ply the art ever nobly, single soul'd
> Like Brahms, or as you ruled in Wells erewhile,
> —Nor yet the memory of that zeal is cold—
> Where lately I, who love the purer style,
> Enter'd, and felt your spirit as of old
> Beside me, listening in the chancel-aisle.
> Robert Bridges: 'To Percy Buck'

The volume also included poems addressed to two musicians. One was to Harry Wooldridge, who died in 1917. The poem was actually written in 1905, and gives also a portrait of days at Yattendon, where the musician and artist was a regular visitor. The second, written the previous year, was to Percy Buck, sometime organist at Wells Cathedral, at the time of writing Director of Music at Harrow School. His roles, besides those of writer and composer, included a spell as Musical Adviser to the Education Committee of London County Council. The decision to print them for the first time so long after they were written, emphasises just how fulfilling were the Yattendon years before the departure of Henry Beeching from the church there. *The Yattendon Hymnal* remains their memorial.

1921 was another productive year for the poet. There were seven poems using neo-Miltonic syllabics, which were woven together for publication in 1925 as *The Tapestry,* the title also of one of the individual poems. They included *Kate's Mother,* quoted earlier when decribing Bridges' childhood. In 1921, there were also two written in accentual measures and some in the old-style. These last included lines spoken by Johnston Forbes-Robertson at the opening of the Theatre of the Royal Academy of Dramatic Art by the Prince of Wales. Some of this writing appeared in the *London Mercury, The Queen, Cornhill Magazine* and the *Yale Review* in 1923 and 1924.

> While Northward the hot sun was sinking o'er the trees
> as we sat pleasantly talking in the meadow,
> the swell of a rich music suddenly on our ears
> gush'd thru' the wide-flung doors, where village-folk in church
> stood to their evening psalm praising God together—
> and when it came to cloze, paused, and broke forth anew.

A great Huguenot psalm it trod forth on the air
with full slow notes moving as a goddess stepping
through the responsive figures of a stately dance
conscious of beauty and of her fair-flowing array
in the severe perfection of an habitual grace,
then stooping to its cloze, paused to dance forth anew;

To unfold its bud of melody everlastingly
fresh as in springtime when, four centuries agone,
it wing'd the souls of martyrs on their way to heav'n
chain'd at the barbarous stake, mid the burning faggots
standing with tongues cut out, all singing in the flames—
O evermore, sweet Psalm, shalt thou break forth anew.

Robert Bridges: Opening stanzas of 'The Psalm'

Poetry being the most intimate expression of Man's Spirit, it is necsssary to education; since no man can be a worthy citizen of any earthly state unless he be first a citizen of the heavenly.

Robert Bridges opening the preface to 'The Chilswell Book of English Poetry' published in 1924 for schools

After that burst of poetry in 1921, it looked as if Bridges' canon was complete. Well into his seventies he busied himself with the affairs of his Society for Pure English. In 1923 he met Stanley Morrison, who had been born in Wanstead in 1889, the son of a commercial traveller and of a mother who was a dogmatic agnostic and believer in Thomas Paine. Stanley Morrison's passion was typefaces, by which Bridges had been fascinated since his first volume was printed. Morrison was entrusted with printing *The Tapestry*. Bridges and his wife spent three months in 1924 in America as the guests of the University of Michigan at Ann Arbor, where he was honoured as an honorary Doctor of Letters, a distinction also bestowed by the Universities of Harvard and Saint Andrews. His own university had awarded him the honorary degree of Doctor of Literature. His eightieth birthday was marked by the gift from his friends of a clavichord made by Arnold Dolmetsch. To acknowledge it, he had a letter in his own hand printed and sent with his photograph and that of the clavichord to all of the donors.

In 1926, the BBC formed a committee to seek expert advice on broadcast English. They invited Bridges to be its chairman: other members included the actor Johnston Forbes-Robinson, who had come to public notice through his casting in Jerome K. Jerome's *The Passing of the Third Floor Back*, and the renowned playwright, George Bernard Shaw.

Poetry, however, had not been silenced. In terms of wide acclaim, his most renowned work was still to be written. *The Testament of Beauty* received recognition from well beyond the group, still not large, that knew the rest of his poetry. By the outbreak of the Second World War, the complete poem had run through thirteen editions, eleven of them before the end of 1932. The poem is in four books, and the first of these was issued separately when it was completed in 1927. The first full edition co-incided with the poet's eighty-fifth birthday in 1929. Bridges

There were 219 poems and extracts in the anthology, Bridges rating the following worthy of more than one item:

William Shakespeare 23
Percy Bysshe Shelley 21
John Keats 14
William Wordsworth 13
John Milton 12
Alfred Tennyson 10
William Blake 9
Robert Burns 9
George Gordon Byron 8
Walter Scott 6
George Herbert 5
Alfred Housman 5
Samuel Taylor Coleridge 4
Richard Dixon 4
Alexander Pope 4
Robert Louis Stevenson 4
Lawrence Binyon 3
Walter de la Mare 3
Rudyard Kipling 3
Henry Newbolt 3
Thomas Campbell 2
William Cowper 2
Ben Jonson 2
Richard Lovelace 2
Thomas Moore 2
William Butler Yeats 2

120

*Words on the BBC list
beginning with C considered by
the Bridges' Committee*

wanted his poem to be as accurate in syllabic terms as possible, and secured the help of Robert Trevelyan, author of *The Bride of Dionysus*, in the tedious task of syllable counting.

Book 1, called simply Introduction, begins thus:

> Mortal Prudence, handmaid of divine Providence,
> hath inscrutable reckoning with Fate and Fortune:
> We sail a changeful sea through halcyon days and storm,
> and when the ship laboureth, our steadfast purpose
> trembles like as the compass in a binnacle.
> Our stability is but balance, and conduct lies
> in masterful administration of the unforeseen.

Almost 400 lines on, Bridges muses:

> So musing all my days with unceasing wonder
> and encountering many phases of many minds,
> thru' kindly environment of my disposition
> I grew, as all things grow, in the pattern of Self;
> til stumbling early upon the mysic words, whereby
> —in the Semetic matrix of my father's creed—
> Jahveh reveal'd his secret Being to the Jews,
> and conning those large letters I AM THAT I AM
> I wonder'd finding only my own thought of myself,
> and reading there that man was made in God's image
> knew not yet that God was made in the image of man;
> nor the profounder truth that both these truths are one,
> no quibbling scoff—for surely as mind in man groweth
> so with his manhood groweth his idea of God,
> wider ever and worthier, untill it may contain
> and reconcile in reason all wisdom passion and love,
> and bring at last (may God so grant) Christ's Peace on Earth.

The second book was entitled *Selfhood* and began:

> The vision of the seer who saw the Spirit of Man.
> A chariot he beheld speeding twixt earth and heaven
> drawn by wing'd horses, and the charioteer thereon
> upright with eyes upon the goal and mind alert
> controlling his strong steeds, that spurn'd the drifted cloud
> as now they sank now mounted in their heav'nward flight.

Book 3 is named *Breed* and begins:

> Having told of SELFHOOD, ere now I tell of BREED
> the younger of the two Arch-Instincts of man's nature,
> 'twer well here to remember how these pictured steeds
> are Ideas construed by the abstract Intellect.

Around 200 lines on we read:

> Breed then together with Selfhood steppeth in pair,
> for as Self grew thru' Reason from animal rage
> to vice of war and gluttony, but meanwhile uprose
> thru' motherly yearning to a profounder affection,

so Breed, from like degrading brutality at heart,
distilleth in the altruism of spiritual love
to be the sublimest passion of humanity,
with parallel corruption; in its supremacy
confess'd of all, since all in their degree hav felt
its divine exaltation and bestial abasement.
It hath sanctified fools and degraded heroes;
and tho' the warrior wil lightly leave his lady
to join in battle (so the weight of the elder horse
side-wrencheth at the yoke), he wil return to her
more gladly, and often rue his infidelity.

The year 1929 saw Bridges honoured with the Order of Merit.
In February he gave a broadcast talk, an experience he could
hardly have foreseen in his Victorian childhood, though the
occasion was marred by a heavy cold. Robert was feeling his age
and it was against the inclination of the body that he finally
completed the fourth book of *The Testament of Beauty* entitled
Ethick. Our story ends with the final lines of the poem as printed
below. He won a little victory with his publishers, who agreed
to use his manuscript spellings, which have been reproduced in
these extracts. The volume was published on his 85th birthday:
a few months later, his earthly wanderings ended at Chilswell
House in 1930. His mortal remains were laid to rest
appropriately at Yattendon.

I feel as if this year is my last lap
in the race, and I don't know that
I shall pull through—but I hope
now in a few days to be at work and
finish up with the poem.
Robert Bridges writing to
Robert Trevelyan on
16th March 1929

It will be a great pleasure to read
the poem as a completed whole,
undistracted by conscious
syllable-counting, and concerned
only with the ideas and the poetry.
Robert Trevelyan writing to
Robert Bridges on 27th October
1929

        This Indivualism is man's true Socialism.
This is the rife Idea whose spiritual beauty
multiplieth in communion to transcendant might.
This is thatt excelent way whereon if we wil walk
all things shall be added unto us—thatt Love which inspired
the wayward Visionary in his dóctrinal ode
to the three christian Graces, the Church's first hymn
and only deathless athanasian creed,—the which
    "except a man believe he cannot be savèd".
This is the endearing bond whereby Christ's company
yet holdeth together on the truth of his promise
that he spake of his great pity and trust in man's love,
Lo, I am with you always ev'n to the end of the world.
    Truly the Soul returneth the body's loving
where it hath won it...and God so loveth the world...
and in the fellowship of the friendship of Christ
God is seen as the very self-essence of love,
Creator and mover of all as activ Lover of all,
self-express'd in not-self, without which no self were.
In thought whereof is neither beginning nor end
nor space nor time; nor any fault nor gap therein
'twixt self and not-self, mind and body, mother and child,
'twixt lover and loved, God and man: but ONE ETERNAL
in the love of Beauty and in the selfhood of Love.
Robert Bridges: The closing lines of 'Ethick', the fourth and final book of
'The Testament of Beauty'

Himself a master of language and
a poet who by study and practice
had acquired a technique,
unrivalled since Milton, in the
handling of words and their
metrical arrangements...ling-
uistic experiments had always
possessed for Mr. Bridges a very
great interest...
Logan Pearsall Smith writing
about Robert Bridges after his
death for The Society for Pure
English

Frederick Pratt Green

Fred Pratt Green

Frederick Pratt Green was born in the year that Liverpool University received its charter and the year before work began on Liverpool's Anglican Cathedral, designed in the Gothic style by Giles Gilbert Scott. In 1903 Roby, his birthplace, was still a village rather than a suburb on the eastern side of the conurbation. Fred's father had come to Liverpool expecting to emigrate to the United States of America, but found work, settled, and married his 'Shropshire lass' in 1886.

By the time Fred was born, his father had built up a good business in leather goods. Fred's father had been a Wesleyan local preacher, but had resigned that office because he could not accept current teaching about eternal damnation for unbelievers. Fred was a late arrival in the family and his sister and brother were both

> Ever constant, thrifty, cheerful,
> Lov'd by all who knew thee best,
> May thy future, Hannah Greenwood
> Still be such, though *wood the less.*
> *Charles Green: From 'Verses to*
> *his Wife to be, Hannah Greenwood'*

in their teens by the time he was four. Fred's mother had grown up in the Church of England, and there being no nearby Wesleyan Church, Fred's early experience of Christian worship was in Childwall Parish Church where he became aware of something called *Ancient and Modern.* Sundays were kept as special days. Games were not allowed, but it was permitted to play hymn tunes on the piano. One Sunday, Fred managed to play *Aurelia* in 3/4 time and his mother, trying not to smile, protested gently that they did not dance on Sundays. Such restraints do not seem to have bothered Fred.

The family moved to Wallasey and on Sundays Fred attended Claremount Road Wesleyan Church. He was to recall in later life that they sang lots of hymns, most of them terribly long. Generally they made little impression on him, but one Sunday morning, after announcing *There's a light upon the mountains and the day is at the spring*, the minister waved his hand towards the crowded transept, adding to a stir of excitement, "We have the author of this hymn with us this morning. Will he please rise?" Henry Burton, a very old white-haired gentleman stood up for a moment. Little did Fred Pratt Green think that one day this might happen to him.

Fred's friendship with Eric Thomas, a fellow-pupil at Wallasey Grammar School, began in a curious way. One morning, the local cemetery was disturbed by a satchel fight between Fred and Eric, who received a cut lip. Consequently, Eric's parents complained to the school and the culprit was ordered to own up. Fred did and the result was an invitation to tea from Eric's parents. From that day Fred and Eric became fast friends.

Eric, destined to become an Anglican priest, and Fred, who would be ordained as a Methodist minister, worshipped

Trinity Sutton was what I sometimes call—half ironically and half affectionately—Gothic Wesleyan. We were one of the few churches remaining in Methodism with Morning Prayer every Sunday morning, with certain modifications: I did not have to intone, or sing the versicles and the choice of the Psalms was very selective. It seemed strange, at the end of my ministry, to be so vividly reminded of Sunday morning worship in the parish church of Childwall when I was a child.

Fred Pratt Green compares his final appointment in Methodist Circuit with his childhood

together in each other's churches on Sunday evenings. The key to Fred's eventual choice of Methodism was its open welcome at Holy Communion. Each Sunday between morning chapel and dinner, eaten of course at what the upper classes would have called lunchtime, there was Fred's ritual walk with his father to the promenade: their conversation did not always lead to communication. Fred's family background would be incomplete without mentioning the two grandmothers of childhood days, *one too buxom in black silk, one petite in white lace*!

Parents are a mixed blessing.
They are tied to us at birth,
in death do not cut adrift.

Either they love too little,
or much too much, rarely
in the correct proportion.

From my mother I inherited
a peace-loving disposition,
from father a quick temper;

from her I got sensitivity,
from him an eye to business;
from both respect for deity.

What in me seems original,
this attraction of opposites,
I never noticed in either.

Now they watch from so great
a distance, I cannot make out
if they are pleased or anxious.
Fred Pratt Green: 'Parents'
written in September 1979

Even as a child I noticed that though father laid down the law it was mother who got her own way. Her *Yes, dear* sounded submissive, but she it was who counted when it came to a crunch.
Fred Pratt Green recalls
his mother

It was expected of me, between chapel
and dinner, to walk with father.
Walking with father was a Sunday ritual,

like winding clocks, cream with the apple-
pasty, and the dead afternoon
waking to the tinkle of crown-derby

at five precisely. Our shoulders back,
we walked to the gusty promenade
by a golf-course where Sabbath-breakers

enjoyed themselves, by a cinder-track
edged with scented mayweed
where stones could be accidentally kicked.

Enoch walked with God, I with my father,
who talked as I scanned the sea
for Cunarders, of unspecified sins

I had given up guessing at. Rather
than listen, I filled my lungs,
as I was told, with life-giving ozone,

and day-dreamed. Our walk home took us
by fine houses where ship-owners
dined on salmon, by a small terminus

where trams stood or started with raucous
grindings and exciting sparks.
By now father was joking, poking me

with a gloved finger, pleased (I suspect,
looking back) at having got
my sins off his chest, and we arrived

in high spirits, *all present and correct*,
he would say, as we pushed open
the smell of dinner. After the grace,

my mother would ask, *How did you enjoy*
your walk? forgetting it was
the same walk, the same father, the same boy.
Fred Pratt Green: 'Walking with Father'

My grandmothers McCartney and Billington
ticked in our lives like the two clocks
we were proudest of in our Liverpool home.

The dining-room clock was of black marble,
bold-faced and pilastered, with a loud
tick and an imperiously metallic strike;

but the drawing-room clock was a confection
of whispering wheels in a glass case,
prettily gilded, with a silvery-soft voice.

What a contrast they made, my grandmothers
McCartney and Billington, one too buxom
in black silk, one petite in white lace!

My father's mother had been married thrice;
bossy in a house full of bric-a-brac,
she died, out shopping, at twelve o'clock.

My mother's mother had been married twice;
the beloved relict of a drunken lay-about,
she lived with us, mousily, for ten years,

and stealthily departed after sipping milk
laced with brandy. At times, when I stop
to ask myself what it is makes me tick,

I can hear the two clocks chiming together
in my carcase, detect the McCartney in me
playing at cat with the Billington mouse.

Fred Pratt Green: 'Grandmothers'

Hannah Green

Today, hearing of your death, I remember
how we slugged each other with satchels,
your cut lip sealing our friendship; how,
between games of bagatelle we slaughtered
tin soldiers, as flags moved backwards
on the sagging map towards disaster; how
we built sand-castles, and abandoned them
to the invading tide, like tired Romans
called home to defend nearer frontiers; how
we lazed in warm hollows among the sand-
dunes, screened by scratchy marron-grass,
furtively probing each other's defences
until we reached the perimeters of alarm,
and drew back; how life parted us, without
cutting the thread, so that for thirty years
we wrote at Christmas, yet without meeting,
until, time pressing, I crossed your path
(you were standing outside a shop, smiling,
clerically benign); how, paralysed by sadness
I drove on. I cannot believe you are dead.

Fred Pratt Green: 'In Memoriam: EWT'

Fred completed his schooldays at Rydal, the Methodist Boarding School at Colwyn Bay in North Wales. They were happy times, with a solid religious base that was never oppressive. He was there in the early days of a great headmaster, the Reverend A. J. Costain, who was to serve the school until his retirement in 1946. He was a keen sportsman and a fine schoolmaster.

In particular Fred was influenced by the master who taught English and History. A. G. Watt was a mildly eccentric teacher with a rare gift of making every lesson interesting. Fred's love of poetry springs from this master's exposition of John Milton's *Lycidas*, of all unlikely poems.

> I've eaten all my tuck but 1/2 of pot of Aprecot & your tin of pears. We have to share here. Boys have huge wooden tuckboxes here. We provide (out) our own jam etc at tea, & of course there is break & other odd times to feed in. Other boys took a huge store of jam.
>
> *Fred writes to 'Dearest Brother' from Rydal*

> At Rydal one hymn had a special significance. It was a tradition for the hymn *Jesus, still lead on* to be sung before the announcement of a whole holiday. Imagine our fury when some evil-disposed master had it on a perfectly ordinary day! Another tradition concerned the last hymn on the Sunday night before holidays: *The day Thou gavest, Lord, is ended,* which the school sang so fast and lustily we arrived at the *Amen* before the congregation. What was the use of anyone making a fuss—we were going home tomorrow!
>
> *Fred Pratt Green: From 'Myself and Hymns'*

You were eccentric, sir, and awfully bald.
Flapping about in front of a blackboard
You might have been an excitable blackbird
Defending its territory. So time crawled
Rarely for us, sir. We admired the way,
As you explained it, some obscure affray
Of the Roses had blossomed in red and yellow.
History, thanks to you, was never grey.

Fred Pratt Green: From 'Ballade of the coloured Chalks'

Where were ye, Nymphs, when the remorseless deep
Closed o'er the head of your loved Lycidas?
For neither were ye playing on the steep
Where your old bards, the famous Druids, lie,
Nor on the shaggy top of Mona high,
Nor yet where Deva spreads her wizard stream;
Ay me! I fondly dream—
Had ye been there—for what could that have done?
What could the Muse herself that Orpheus bore,
The Muse hereself, for her enchanting son,
Whom universal nature did lament,
When by the rout that made the hideous roar
His gory visage down the stream was sent,
Down the swift Hebrus to the Lesbian shore?

John Milton: From 'Lycidas'

Rydal School, Colwyn Bay

Fred's thoughts had been towards the profession of architect, but when he left school he went into his father's business. Fred's brother had unhappily parted company from their father and had set up a rival leather business; and Charles Green was delighted that his younger son had decided to join him. In the next four years, as he undertook different jobs, Fred gained business skills which he found invaluable in his eventual chosen profession.

> We boys went to work by the river-ferry,
> The gangways steep when the tide was low,
>> Leaning on the wind,
>> Dodging the spray,
> With the lyver-bird golden in the sky,
> And the rubbish blown out of a boy's mind.
>
> We came home at night by the river-ferry,
> The gangways flat when the tide was high,
>> Staring at the serpents
>> Of light in the water,
> With the lyver-bird leaden in the sky,
> And the rubbish blown out of a boy's mind.
>
> On days when the fog foxed the river-ferry
> We rushed for the lift to the Low-level,
>> Swaying on a strap,
>> Mouthing a fag,
> With only the draught from a black tunnel
> To blow the rubbish out of a boy's mind.
>> *Fred Pratt Green: 'Memory of Liverpool'*

Charles Green

128

O Christ who holds the open gate,
O Christ who drives the furrow straight,
O Christ, the plough, O Christ, the laughter
Of holy white birds flying after,
Lo, all my heart's field red and torn,
And Thou wilt bring the young green corn,
The young green corn divinely springing,
The young green corn for ever singing;
And when the field is fresh and fair,
Thy blessèd feet shall glitter there.
And we will walk the weeded field,
And tell the golden harvest's yield,
The corn that makes the holy bread
By which the soul of man is fed,
The holy bread, the food unpriced,
Thy everlasting mercy, Christ.

John Masefield: From 'The Everlasting Mercy'

During the pastorate of the Reverend William Rushby at Claremount Road Wesleyan Church, Fred made his commitment to Christ after hearing Rushby's sermon on John Masefield's *The Everlasting Mercy*. Here, Fred felt called to the Wesleyan Methodist ministry, a circumstance which at first angered his father, who eventually became reconciled to the decision in a rather unusual way. During his candidature for the ministry, Fred was allowed to lead worship at the Claremount Road Church, a rare honour for a local preacher. His father and mother were in their pew close to the pulpit. Fred seems to have come through the ordeal in a satisfactory manner, for his father, now bursting with pride, hurried to the door and shook hands with the outgoing congregation as if he were the minister. Fred put down his father's conversion to his son's success that day. Charles Green had made a success of *his* life and was prepared to believe that his son was capable of being successful too although in a different sphere. It is worth mentioning that he candidated for the Wesleyan Methodist ministry as Frederick P. Green, but was asked to let himself be known officially as F. Pratt Green because there was already a Frederick Green, a man of some distintion, in the ministry. The change seemed appropriate since he had been christened Pratt after a relative who had been a Methodist preacher.

In 1924 young Green was sent by the Wesleyan Methodist Conference to serve a year in the Severn Valley Circuit. In his poem *Backslider,* published in 1963, he paints a vivid word picture of the puritanical Welsh chapels he passed by.

I've seen so many chapels in Wales
Called by Bible names, beautiful names,
With their windows square as honesty,
Rounded as charity, clear as purity
I thought *He must have come back*;
But the deacons all walked with a tread
So solemn, I thought He was dead.

Why, I cried, are the holy chapels
Surrounded by spikes and spears,
And never a flower but the dandelion,
Which I love, mind you, and the singing
Oh beautiful singing but lugubrious,
And the deacons all dressed in black
As if He had never come back?

So I passed by the chapels of Wales
Respectfully, mind you, and walked
Where lambs sucked, chaffinches sang,
And lilies of the field were arrayed
Better than Solomon, and the thorn
Flowered, and my heart that had lack
Of Him flowered and put off black.

When I touch my cap to the deacons
They call me by bad names, Bible names,
Such as Backslider, and Son of Belial,
But I go to my own chapel, thank you,
Which has no railings, walls, or windows,
With the singing joyful, and my head
Laughing itself off He isn't dead.

Fred Pratt Green: 'Backslider'

Green spent three years at Didsbury Theological College from 1925 to 1928. During those years all denominations were having to face the challenge of Modernism. It was no longer possible to brush aside the revelations and insinuations of Biblical Criticism or to ignore the profoundly disturbing findings of the Freudian psychologists or the distressing accusations of Marxist sociology. Traditional religion was being relentlessly attacked from three quarters at least. Green's evangelical friends warned him that the colleges were centres of Modernism. 'What am I?', the student wondered: 'a Fundamentalist?'

Many years later, Green recalled with some surprise that despite these obvious threats to college life, the never-ending arguments between students on the major issues of religion, and the diversity of backgrounds and personalities, they managed to live together in an extremely happy community. Their tutors, certainly the two most important, were clearly modernists, but it so happened they were also men for whom the students had respect and affection. They were quite prepared to listen to students' arguments and be patient with their naïve claims to have the truth. In their Principal, T. E. Barratt, the students had someone who knew how to handle a generation, some of whom had fought in the First World War and were resentful of authority.

While at college Green won several essay prizes, including an award for a 30,000-word study on agnosticism. He also wrote his first published work, a play, *Farley Goes Out,* reflecting the view of foreign missions prevailing at that time. It was performed in many parts of the Methodist world during the 1930s. Green emerged from Didsbury convinced that Fundamentalism is a grave misinterpretation of the Bible, that Christian unity, though seemingly unattainable, is an important goal, and that the Church must involve itself in social concerns.

What shall our greeting be:
Sign of our unity?
Jesus is Lord!
May we no more defend
Barriers he died to end:
Give me your hand, my friend:
One Church, One Lord!

What is our mission here?
He makes his purpose clear:
One world, one Lord!
Spirit of truth descend,
All our confusions end:
Give me your hand, my friend:
Jesus is Lord!

He comes to save us now:
To serve him is to know
Life's true reward.
May he our lives amend,
All our betrayals end:
Give me your hand, my friend:
Jesus is Lord!

Fred Pratt Green: 'A Plea for Christian Unity', winning entry in a competition for ecumenical hymns in 1974. Sung to MOSCOW

It was the custom for the Principal to interview students about their first appointment as probationer ministers, and Green was offered the choice of missionary service in Africa or a chaplaincy at the newly founded Methodist Boarding School for Girls at Hunmanby Hall, Yorkshire. Green, dubious about teaching girls, chose to go to Africa; but the Principal brushed this aside with the comment that he would be dead within a year and sent him to Hunmanby.

A tradition, continued over the decades, of a candle-lighting ceremony on the first day of term was initiated at Hunmanby Hall. It was for this ceremony that Green wrote his first hymn, very many years before he wrote his second.

The school is set in beautiful rolling country with the North-Sea coast nearby. Besides his duties as chaplain, Green served the Filey Circuit with its holiday congregations and village chapels. Londoner Marjorie Dowsett taught French at the school; Frederick and Marjorie were married in 1931.

God lit a flame in Bethlehem,
O Light! O Living Way!
And every saint who held it high
Was faithful in his day.
And now the splendid torch is ours,
For youthful hands to hold,
That fires once lit in Galilee
May light an English wold.

Thus we would consecrate our hands
To the same shining task,
And call Thy Spirit down on us
And for Thy presence ask.
O may no unlit heart be here,
No feet that miss the Way:
O let no cherished hope be lost,
No bright love ember grey.

Lord! fan thine ancient Faith in us
The bearer of the Flame,
That every thought and deed may be
A hallowing of thy Name;
That in the yet unravelled years
Flamebearers still to be,
Taking the torch from us shall say;
'These Lord, were true to Thee!'
Fred Pratt Green: 'The Flamebearer'
sung to FOREST GREEN

The grace of life is theirs
Who on this wedding day
Delight to make their vows
And for each other pray.
May they, O Lord, together prove
The lasting joy of Christian love.

Where love is, God abides:
And God shall surely bless
A home where trust and care
Give birth to happiness.
May they, O Lord, together prove
The lasting joy of such a love.

How slow to take offence
Love is! How quick to heal!
How ready in distress
To know how others feel!
May they, O God, together prove
The lasting joy of such a love.

And when time lays its hand
On all we hold most dear,
And life, by life consumed,
Fulfils its purpose here:
May we, O Lord, together prove
The lasting joy of Christian love.
Fred Pratt Green: 'Christian Marriage', a wedding hymn written in 1970 for
Lawes' PSALM 47, also sung to LOVE UNKNOWN and SAINT
GODRIC

**A treasured postcard, bought by Fred and Marjorie
whilst on honeymoon in Venice**

Pratt Green's first circuit as an ordained minister provided the young couple with a house, at a time when accommodation was scarce: a pleasant newly-furnished manse at Pool-in-Wharfedale overlooking the river. The Otley Circuit was in many ways an ideal location for a young minister. It had a well supported town church in Otley, suburban churches in Menston and Burley, a church closely associated with a unit run by the National Children's Home, and a wide range of villages, some, from the point of view of Methodism, prospering and some very weak indeed. Fred had six societies in his pastoral care, all nominally village causes, but two at least of special interest, the Pool society being benevolently dominated by the Whiteleys, who owned the paper mill, and Huby, a village near enough to Harrogate to attract a distinctly different kind of congregation. He even had a village where the vicar was violently anti-Methodist. One of his causes was divided around two conflicting personalities, an experience happily never to be repeated in his later ministry. He was blessed with a superintendent minister who was a fine gentleman and a very good friend. With him the frock coat and silk hat finally went out of fashion.

The second appointment was to Girlington in the Bradford (Manningham) Circuit. In the morning social status decided where you sat in the chapel. It was a time when traditions were crumbling but it was still true that if one went up in the world, one went down in the chapel! In the evening the gallery was crowded with young people. In those days of deep economic depression, Pratt Green found the social differences between

Early in my ministry, on Methodist Union, we had a new hymn-book, the one in use for the following fifty years. It was severely criticised by many Wesleyans as having too many chorus-hymns, beloved by Primitives, and other 'inferior' material. This dislike lingered. Even as late as 1965, on moving to a London church which still had Morning Prayer, I was told by my organist, *We don't have chorus-hymns at Sutton Trinity.* Of course we did; and I must say the congregation seemed more amused than offended. Every new hymn-book is opposed. The fiercest radicals in every other walk of life are fiercely conservative when it comes to hymns and liturgies.

*Fred Pratt Green: From 'Myself
and Hymns'*

132

those living in comfortable circumstances and the families from the rows of back-to-back houses disturbing and distressing. The first Harvest Festival sermon he preached at Girlington was on a text proclaiming that God had provided the produce of the earth for everyone.

In 1935 Fred took the unusual step of attending the World Congress of Faiths, a conference inspired by the vision of General Younghusband. It afforded him a wonderful opportunity of getting to know more about the other great Faiths at first hand. The effect of the Congress was electrifying. There was so much in other religions with which he could identify, not only that mystical experience which is the root of all religions, but what seemed like a common ethic. There were passages in the *Gita* that reminded him of the Fourth Gospel; there were teachings in *The Way of Life* reputedly by Lao Tzu, centuries older than the New Testament, which anticipated the Sermon on the Mount; there appeared to be in Islam a sense of brotherhood lacking in Christianity. 'Is it not possible', Pratt Green wondered, 'to move towards a world religion which gathered up from all the great Faiths? Were the Bahais leading the way?'

Pratt Green came back from the congress deeply disturbed. His liberalism made him sympathetic to other Faiths. Without losing his liberalism, he came to an important conclusion: that what is unique in Christianity is the Cross. He began to study the other religions in the light of the Cross. Not even the unacceptability of the Doctrine of the Atonement, as interpreted in extreme Fundamentalism, could destroy his discovery that the Cross is immeasurably more moving, more compelling, and closer to the realities of human life, than any other religious fact or symbol. Like many others at the time, he read a pamphlet by Dr. Russell Maltby on the Cross and said to himself, *Yes, I can believe this!*

> Arms are an instrument of evil, no measure for thoughtful men, until there fail all other choice but sad acceptance of it...Triumph is not beautiful...Conduct your triumph as a funeral.

> When a man cares, he is unafraid, when he is fair he leaves enough for others, when he is humble, he can grow.

> At no time in the world will a man who is sane over-reach himself, over-spend himself, over-rate himself.
> *Sayings selected by Fred Pratt Green from 'The Way of Life', a translation of the 'Tao Teh Ching' by Witter Bynner*

> I seek the truth, which never yet hurt any man. What hurts is persisting in self-deceit and ignorance.
> *From 'The Meditations of Marcus Aurelius', one of Fred Pratt Green's bedside books*

Others lay claim to know him in the flesh;
I in the spirit. This is not to boast
A private and superior Pentecost—
Only that when a Voice spoke, in a flash
That blinded me, I counted all things loss
for Christ. Now I rejoice in him; become
A laughing stock, a sacrifice, if some
May learn from it the glory of his Cross.

They say that I, who never saw the Lord,
Who never breathed the air of Galilee,
Corrupt the Gospel. What is more absurd?
They bind the Gospel: I have set it free!
They preach messiah; I the God who died,
Yes, for us Jews—and all the world beside!
Fred Pratt Green: 'Seven Sonnets for Lent: Paul speaks' published in 1970.

When in the 1980s Bradford had become a multi-Faith city, Pratt Green was still reading the *Gita* and *The Way of Life* with appreciation. Moslems, Hindus, Sikhs and Buddhists, now Pratt Green's fellow-countrymen in considerable numbers, were no longer heathen as he had once been taught. They possess valuable spiritual insights worthy of respect. It would be a simplification, and untrue, to say that in later life Pratt Green came to terms with all the problems created by comparative religion. Yet his hymns witness to his conviction that in redemptive love, the central tenet of Christianity, rests the hope of our salvation.

Those Bradford years were overshadowed not only by economic depression but by the gathering clouds that were to lead to the Second World War. A.R.P., the shorthand for Air Raid Precautions entered the language. The abdication of King Edward VIII in 1936 was another shock to the stability of the nation as it moved towards the end of an era. Fred, as Chaplain to the Lord Mayor of Bradford, was presented to the new monarchs when they visited the city. The ceremony was carefully rehearsed and Fred later recalled the difficulty of walking backwards between rows of hydrangeas after shaking hands with their Majesties. Here and later in London and Norwich, Fred wrote plays on a variety of themes for drama groups, *The House at Arrow Ghyll*, written in Bradford, and *A Kind of Resurrection*, presented in Norwich, being the most ambitious.

Fred also experienced at Girlington a period of breakdown, the common lot of many sensitive and creative writers at some time of life. He was allowed three months off and sent on a cruise to recover.

Fred and Marjorie moved to the capital at the outbreak of the Second World War. Fred was in pastoral charge of a church at Gants Hill, a nondescript piece of London's suburbia in Methodism's Ilford Circuit in East London. In 1939 it had the largest Sunday School in Britain, comprising 800 children; and in the evening, the congregation queued up for admission to the Church. But on Fred's first Sunday, 3rd September, most of the children had been evacuated to safer parts of the country. About three miles from the Thames, it was not far from major industrial sites, and en route to the London Docks for German bombers flying up the Estuary. Fred combined his ministerial duties with those of Air Raid Warden, eventually being put in charge of a post manned by thirty wardens from many different walks of life. There were many painful moments in Fred's pastoral ministry during these war years, sharing times of bereavement, separation and injury. Yet it was a time too of

How great a mystery,
Lord, is your love for me;
I scarcely dare believe you walked
our human ways.

Jesus of History,
You came to die for me:
Jesus! Jesus! How can I sing your
praise?

Love never counts the cost,
Goes to the uttermost:
Love seeks to save us from the
judgement we deserve.

You gave yourself for us,
Love is your way with us:
Jesus! Jesus! Save us that we may
serve.

Fred Pratt Green: 'Love is a Mystery' set as an anthem by Martin Ellis and published within 'In the Beauty of Holiness'

Elizabeth Shepherd

remarkable rapport between all members of society, providing many opportunities for caring which do not normally come a minister's way.

At the same time, tragedy struck a family on the far side of the world. Two missionaries in Burma were fleeing from the Japanese. En route the Reverend Vincent Shepherd contracted leprosy, and was a hospital patient at Velore in South India for some years. The Shepherds had a daughter, Elizabeth, and the Greens, who had no children of their own, accepted responsibility for her guardianship. Elizabeth attended Boarding School during term time spending holidays at the Manse. It was Elizabeth's dream to go on the stage and she became a gifted and versatile actress, continuing to keep in touch with Marjorie and Fred down the years.

Pratt Green moved in 1944 to a church which had been completed just as war broke out. The Church in the Orchard at Grange Park in the Finsbury Park Circuit was at the centre of a cultured community most of whom were well-off. As neither the wealthy nor the cultured escape human spiritual need, Fred found here a continuing pastoral responsibility. Fred's life as a Methodist minister committed wholeheartedly to this role had left him little time for writing. A chance pastoral visit to the father of one of his Sunday School scholars led to an encounter that was to wake the dormant poetry within him.

Fallon Webb, a gentle agnostic, crippled by arthritis, was a competent poet. It came out in conversation that Fred had written a poem or two. Fallon suggested that they both write a poem and then meet to criticise each other's work. As these two friends kept their poetry compact for twenty years, until Fallon's death, Fred's corpus of poems grew. In twenty pieces entitled *One Minor Poet to Another*, we are allowed to drop in on the two friends. Stanza XIX describes Fallon against the background of the utility life-style of the country just after the war:

What news, Elizabeth, what good news!
The paper critics, whose fingers
unfroze to applaud you, were quick
to detect your poise, your artistry,
your sense of character. So pose
for cameras, O sophisticated woman
of nineteen, but inwardly
be ingenuous as a Christmas rose!
Fred Pratt Green: The opening stanza of 'To a young Actress'

You look the poet more than I;
a disadvantage, it may be,
when a poet might be any guy

from any Board or Ministry.
For us—Utility's the stuff;
but I would sell my soul to see

your beard repose on ruche or ruff:
Holbein should paint you, or Vandyck
(or is it Velasquez?)—enough!

You are what poets should be like.

In 1947, Pratt Green wrote his second hymn *How wonderful this world of Thine* in a garden at Clare for a tune by Handel known as FITZWILLIAM II, which his college friend, the Reverend Francis Westbrook, wanted to include in a new Sunday School Hymnbook. At the time, the Epworth Press argued against the scientific explanation of the origin of the earth mentioned in the second line. By the 1980s, the hymn seemed dated to Fred and he was very reluctant to agree to its inclusion with minor alterations in *Hymns and Psalms* (to the tune POLWHELE).

> How wonderful this world of Thine,
> A fragment of the fiery sun,
> How lovely and how small!
> Where all things serve Thy great design,
> Where life's adventure is begun
> In Thee, the life of all.

In 1947, Pratt Green was pulled out from Grange Park to be Superintendent Minister at the Dome Mission, Brighton, with the task of healing wounds inflicted on the church in recent difficulties there. The Sunday evening congregation was often upwards of 2,000 in this concert hall. The preacher had no audio aids to help his voice carry and, to be heard, he had to keep still, not turning even his head to the right or left. It was a congregation which assembled from up to fifteen miles away, swollen by visitors to the South Coast in the summer. Amongst the regular worshippers was the renowned English cricketer, Jack Hobbs. Fred's parents lived long enough to be present on one occasion at the Dome.

By no means all the congregation were Methodists. Jews and Roman Catholics were amongst those who chose to be present, as well as many casual worshippers. Some chose to come to the Dome because it provided the opportunity for anonymity. Preachers had to remember that every word was liable to be reported in the Press.

III

My verse, you write, *is thin and cold,
centred in self —* etcetera.
But he who stares too long at gold

cannot believe that it is rare,
too close at beauty sees a wart;
what you call *thin* to me is *spare*

(as athletes' bodies stript for sport),
your *cold* to me is *clarity*;
self-centred — I salute an art

centred in self's integrity.

IV

Our verse, I said in idle talk,
is different as chalk from cheese
(was mine the cheese and yours the chalk?)

since when I have been ill at ease,
confounded by comparisons
not calculated much to please!

Now as I stand on our South Downs,
more beautiful for lack of trees,
and curse the crude, encroaching towns—

I stand on chalk and nibble cheese!

X

I praised his skill, his charming use
of balanced words: *precise, profound.*
Nonsense, he said with a grimace,

they came along, I liked their sound!
As rain that drips from stone and bark,
our casual thoughts sink underground,

to meet and mingle in the dark
and feed the springs of Helicon.
We have two poets in us. Mark

his promptings, the Unconscious One.
*Fred Pratt Green:
Selected stanzas from
'One Minor Poet to Another'*

136

When I moved to Brighton in September 1947 I joined a Poetry Group. A moving spirit was Mrs Ramsey, wife of an important member of the national Poetry Society. Mrs Ramsey borrowed the manuscript of the poems I had written to that date and showed them to her husband, who showed them to Erica Marx, who was then editing and producing the *Poems in Pamphlet* series. To my great surprise, Erica asked to publish most of these early poems under the title *This Unlikely Earth* as No. 1 in her 1952 series. Erica's aim was to promote the work of poets who had not yet received recognition. The series was well received by the critics. Some of Erica's poets became famous —Thomas Blackburn and Michael Hamburger, for instance. I was very lucky to get this unexpected *break*—but perhaps unlucky in that some of this early poetry is plainly immature. But critics, on the whole, were encouraging; and John Betjeman, then Literary Editor of *Time and Tide*, was particularly appre--ciative and began to publish some of my new poems in this periodical, which then had a good reputation.

Fred Pratt Green in his Poetry Scrapbook

When the Assistant Minister preached at short notice one evening and described Brighton as a den of iniquity, the town's Watch Committee demanded details and a public apology. Sister Mary Randell, a deaconess appointed to work with Fred, became a long-standing friend, and later shared the Greens' retirement home for many years. Amongst the townsfolk were many people who had once been well off financially but now had difficulty in making ends meet. Once again there were many opportunities for pastoral caring.

By 1952, there was enough poetry of quality for the Hand and Flower Press to publish a collection entitled *This Unlikely Earth.* in its series *Poems in Pamphlet*. It cost one shilling, or five pence in to-day's currency units!

These two verses selected from *Tribute* remember his mother's dying days with great sensitivity:

> There were times when she went from us
> and only her hands lived, feeling the fire;
> there were times when she came back to us,
> her eyes protesting — 'I am still here!'

> More often she missed associations;
> like a worn clock chiming the wrong hour
> she greeted us, her children, as strangers.
> It was this we found difficult to bear.

Although Pratt Green's poems ask searching questions about nature red in tooth and claw and the tragic element in human life, he never loses his confidence in the existence of a creative and loving Deity.

The thrush taps out a snail
  On a convenient stone;
Life shrinks to a broken shell
  And a warm stain.

The sun dries out the stain
  And the thrush is gone;
Only these fragments tell
  Of death on a stone.

Earth shall receive the shell
  As air the stain,
The thrush be as the snail,
  Pity as stone.
Fred Pratt Green: 'Snail'

I asked the plum-tree: is there a purpose?
Weighed down by a crop heavy as grief,
It answered, 'The purpose is to be a tree.
What other purpose could there be?'
But I watched it sicken of silver-leaf.

I asked the willow-warbler: is there a purpose?
Young innocent in the thorny brake,
It answered, 'The purpose is to be a bird.
What other purpose could there be?'
But I saw no mercy in the eye of the snake.

I asked my blood-brother: is there a purpose?
Busy at his craft in the sun-washed room,
He answered, 'The purpose is to be a man.
What other purpose could there be?
When they called him to breakfast he did not come.

I asked the Hidden One: is there a purpose?
Dear and doomed in brother and bird and tree,
He answered, 'The purpose is creativity.
What other purpose could there be?
Am I not creating you—and you Me?'
Fred Pratt Green: 'Question and Answer'

Before the Dreamer tossed a casual spark
on tinder of flesh-to-be and lit the fire
that burns us, is beacon to us in the dark,
the world, my loved, was ignorant of desire.
Tethered to the skirts of the sun, it kept
within the Dream its unpretentious course;
nothing lusted or loved in it, nothing slept,
nothing cried out in rapture or remorse;
only the crack of ice-packs shook the air,
thunder in the mountains, tumultuous rain
pelting a waste of sea through millenia
barren of meaning, innocent of pain,
of the lion's rage, the lover's kiss.
Or did He know that world would father this?
Fred Pratt Green: 'That World and This'

John Betjeman

During this period he wrote one more hymn to please Francis Westbrook, but it must be said that hymns were not of special interest to Pratt Green throughout his circuit ministry. Finding himself a minister, and having to choose hymns, lots of them, for Sunday services, week-night meetings, and all sorts of occasions, Fred had awoken as a young minister to the existence of the *Methodist Hymn Book* — the 1903 edition. Over the years, how many hours he spent turning over its pages and those of its 1933 successor, searching for something relevant to sing, in a panic if he had left it to the last moment! Like others, he usually settled for the good old stand-bys, the hymns that congregations enjoyed singing. He was different only in the respect that he was deeply interested in music and was keen that the tune should be one the congregation would know or could quite easily learn.

In 1952, Fred and Marjorie moved to the southern outskirts of London, to Shirley's gentle hills, then a favourite dormitory area for London commuters. His ministry there was especially rewarding through the loyalty and responsiveness of his congregation. Throughout the decade and until Pratt Green's

In times of growing tension,
Of stubborn social ills,
As London spread still closer
To Shirley's gentle hills,
God's servants built a church here
To meet a people's needs
Whose names we justly honour,
Their foresight and their deeds.
Fred Pratt Green: Verse 2 of
'How right that we should offer'
written for the Golden Jubilee
of Shirley Methodist Church in
1981. For the tune
JUBILATE(Parry)

second poetry collection *The Skating Parson* was published in 1963, he submitted his poetry to various periodicals, with work appearing in *The Listener, The New Yorker, Time and Tide, The Poetry Review, English, Outposts, The Countryman, The Tablet, The Methodist Recorder* and *The Yorkshire Post.* His verse was chosen too for five major anthologies, *New Poems 1954, New Poems 1955, New Poems 1958, Guinness Book of Poetry IV* and *Best Poems of 1960.*

Fred Pratt Green as a child

When you are eight, and you are old enough
not to stare at a cripple, not to look back,
not to ask loud questions then and there,
we shall take you, they said, to see Jack,
poor Jack, they said, as they looked where
there was nothing to look at, and their lips
stopped talking shutting up like mousetraps
because I was not old enough, I was there.

So when I was eight, and I was old enough
to feed spiders with flies, to feel fear
prickle the back of my neck, nobody near,
we must take you, they said, to see Jack,
poor Jack, they said, but be sure not to stare
at his right hand, if he kisses you forget
who it is, if he speaks to you answer back
politely, say it is a fine day or a wet.

The day was fine, with thunder in the air,
as we drove from the door with a whip-crack,
gee-up, whoa-there! Now you are old enough
we are taking you, they said, to see Jack,
poor Jack, they said, who sits in a chair
all day, all year, watching her, or asleep
like a child, no use to her, and bringing
nothing in, doing nothing to earn his keep.

We walked to a cottage, down a rutted lane
hedged with holly, wicked with nettles, sure
of finding him in, they said, because Jack,
poor Jack, has a sickness nobody can cure,
and whatever you do, they said, don't stare
at his right hand, but if it holds it out
take it, shake it politely, it won't bite,
and accept nothing, only an apple or pear.

Where sunflowers glared at us over a fence
we are here, they said, stroking my hair
to comfort me, seeing Jack was asleep there
in the doorway, with his head lolling back,
and his right hand, small as a baby's, limp,
dangling, for a hand is nothing to fear
and more use, they had said, than a stump.
But you can't teach the heart not to stare.
Fred Pratt Green: 'You can't teach the heart not to stare'

Walking home afterwards, I am struck
by the lane's stillness in mid-December,
the muffled elms and ghostly hemlock.

Movement there is. A friendly mongrel
trots by with loose gait; a wood-pigeon
panics from a tree. This is rational;

and were the wind to blow its head off
in apple-orchards, scattering branches,
this, too, would be natural enough,

for nature does everything with ease,
even her worst. It is our humanity
begets the nightmare children, these

hostages to the uncontrollable flesh,
who risk themselves like lovable clowns
on their tight-rope lives with a rash

courage. Watching, who wouldn't confess
he moves here like a mole in daylight?
Are we not all children of darkness?—

As was Brueghel that day he painted
his group of moronic peg-leg cripples,
pity not being the effect he wanted.

Waving for the last time, I am shaken
by a wasteful and misdirected anger
against something which is itself broken.

Fred Pratt Green: 'Spastics'

In 1957, the Methodist Church, without changing the name, decided to change the system. Previously a Chairman had to carry the double responsibility of caring for his circuit as well as for the surrounding circuits which made up his particular District. It was a heavy burden. So it was decided to create larger Districts to be superintended by a minister without circuit responsibility. In other words, 'separated chairmen' were invented. The title, which was convenient and temporary, created a good deal of both hilarity and suspicion: hilarity, because it suggested separated milk, a commodity of the time, and suspicion because it was seen in some quarters as a dangerous step towards union with the Church of England and therefore the acceptance of the Doctrine of the Apostolic Succession. Pratt Green was appointed by the Methodist Conference to the newly-combined districts of York and Hull, both of which had other ideas as to who should be chairman. His skills as an administrator, a reconciler and a Father-in-God to the Methodist ministers were to be well tested. The Greens made their home in the historic city of York and despite Fred being a Lancastrian and his wife a Southerner, they came to love the Yorkshire countryside and people.

My hour is not come
said the dragon-fly nymph
said the blossom of pear
said the Son of Man

but when it is come
I shall mate in the air
I shall hang from the bough
I shall lie in the tomb

said the dragon-fly nymph
said the blossom of pear
said the Son of Man

and when it is gone
I shall die in my turn
I shall fall to the ground
I shall put on my crown

said the dragon-fly nymph
said the blossom of pear
said the Son of Man

I shall comfort my own
said the Son of Man

*Fred Pratt Green: 'My
Hour is not come'*

140

Father of all mankind,
Our Ground of Unity,
Be Thou the glory of this House
We dedicate to Thee.

Here shall the stranger test
The truth of brotherhood;
Here find in all that alienates
The reconciling good.

O break the barriers down
That keep Thy sons apart
And may this very House declare
That Love is what thou art.

Then let the word be peace
To all who come or go;
And let the Master's will be
                            done—
Better than servants know.
Fred Pratt Green: 'Break down
the barriers' , written for the
opening of Hull International
House in 1961. The opening
line of Pratt Green's only
hymn whilst Chairman has
since been amended to 'Father
of every race'. Sung to
FRANCONIA

Since Mister Wong opened *The Lucky Star*
Between the Minster and St. Enoch's Square
The exotic has become our daily fare,
And even Vicars Choral stoop to stare
At unburnt joss-sticks in a porcelain jar,
If, my dear Cantor, that is what they are.

Behind venetian slats of duck-egg blue,
A brass Buddha, and eucalyptus plants,
The Archdeacon orders from a pink menu
Beaten-egg soup, and several Africans,
Enjoying life like playful elephants,
Eat their chop-suey with enormous hands.

Over their heads a tasselled lantern turns
From gold to silver with a silken sound
As bowing Mister Wong, whose brother burns
Cash to buy off the demons, with profound
Non-attachment lodges an English pound
In his deep till, computing what he earns.

He earns our gratitude, or perhaps not,
For setting up his Chinese melting-pot
Here in our gothic city, where he watches
Cantonese waiters glide from serving-hatches,
Like him cosmopolite and polyglot,
Turning silver to gold in all he touches.

Only an imperial dragon shows surprise
As foreign devils catch the savoury pork
With chopsticks, celestials with knife-and-fork;
That nobody bothers if it's right or wise
To scorn the Analects and fraternise
With crude barbarians in a cloud of talk,

Obscuring principles the Ancients made
Politely clear. For vital frontiers fade
When Mister Wong places a piece of jade
In a small alcove next to the same sauce
They serve in snack-bars on the West Parade
In any of the Hundred-and-one Resorts.

This odd encounter with the coloured races
Causes the Archdeacon seriously to ask
If crossing cultures everywhere produces
Merely the incongruously picturesque,
Not knowing the most perfect time and place is
When Madame Wong sings lieder in the dusk.

Upstreet an aerial cuts the moon in half,
And the warm echo of an international laugh,
Born in Kowloon or Kano, bids us meet
Strangers half-way. Let rice be the staff
Of life, my dear Cantor, noodles a treat!
As late as this, there's nowhere else to eat.
Fred Pratt Green: 'Chinese Restaurant'

The Old Couple, Pratt Green's best-known poem, was first published in *The Listener* in August 1964. Among many anthologies, it has won a place in *The Oxford Book of Twentieth Century Verse* and *Everyman's Book of English Love Poetry.*

The old couple in the brand-new bungalow,
Drugged with the milk of municipal kindness,
Fumble their way to bed. Oldness at odds
With newness, they nag each other to show
Nothing is altered, despite the strangeness
Of being divorced in sleep by twin-beds,
Side by side like the Departed, above them
The grass-green of candlewick bedspreads.

In a dead neighbourhood, where it is rare
For hooligans to shout or dogs to bark,
A footfall in the quiet air is crisper
Than home-made bread; and the budgerigar
Bats an eyelid, as sensitive to disturbance
As a distant needle is to an earthquake
In the Great Deep, then balances in sleep.
It is silence keeps the old couple awake.

Too old for loving now, but not for love,
The old couple lie, several feet apart,
Their chesty breathing like a muted duet
On wind instruments, trying to think of
Things to hang on to, such as the tinkle
That a budgerigar makes when it shifts
Its feather weight from one leg to another,
The way, on windy nights, linoleum lifts.

Fred Pratt Green : 'The Old Couple'

Dannie Abse recommended Fred Pratt Green for the 1964 Greenwood Prize for his long poem *Head and Shoulders*. He deplored, though, the standard of the several thousand entries that year but wrote of the winning entry that, despite its too prosaic tone, and occasional banalities, it was far superior, and altogether more firmly handled than any other poem submitted. Pratt Green adds in his scrapbook that he was never happy about this ambitious piece—and he revised it in 1989.

Although Pratt Green greatly enjoyed his new responsibilities, Fred wanted to end his Circuit Ministry at the grass roots. There were many ex-Primitive Methodist churches in the District who

Now you must paint me in
This gown, which identifies
My function, my profession.

It never struck me before
How much the things we wear
determine what we are.

In this black silken gown
I assume a self-importance
I would otherwise disown.

In it I am pedagogue
And puritan, a type
Of the Genevan holy man.

Yet something in me loaths
My reverential image.
I itch under my clothes.

Perhaps we are more ourselves
In a state of undress.
Perhaps truth is nakedness.

Or is our aching flesh
A garment which qualifies
The quintessential self?

If so, what I truly am
Is a problem without solution.
Or waits my dissolution.

Fred Pratt Green: 'Fifth Sitting'
from 'Head and Shoulders (in
Six Sittings)'

Rashly I ask: down episcopal fingers
   travels what grace
And authority? Is this magic? or the
   Unfailing Source
Channelling Himself to us through swamp
   and desert? Or nothing worse,
Or better, than the dressing-up in cope
   and mitre a commonplace
Process? Or is it true, as the Dissenter
   in me contends,
That each of us is a priest on whom God
   has laid His hands?

Consider Cranmer; how trapped between
   Tudor patronage
And the Bloody Tower, he framed these
   liturgies for an age
When words were the deadly swords men
   fenced with. Without the least
Doubt he ordains you, in this rite, both
   minister and priest—
A Genevan minister, a Roman priest,
   which of us knows
So well he cultivated his hybrid Anglican
   rose.

¤   ¤   ¤   ¤   ¤

A truce, then to controversy. It is
   prayer spans the abyss
Of our separation, is the deep therapy
   that must cure this
Sickness of Christ's Body. Freed from
   entanglement of words,
I pray for all who dispense Word and
   Sacrament in the Lord's
Church; for all who seek out His sheep
   that are dispersed abroad;
For all who, not following with us, serve
   compassion's Lord.

¤   ¤   ¤   ¤   ¤

Yet surely this is a time to rejoice in, not
   to bemoan!
Even in York, where masons are renewing,
   stone by stone,
The great Church of Saint Peter, where
   gargoyles keep their grimaces,
An unpredictable future boldly and
   brashly replaces
The past. A new age beckons from
   inter-stellar spaces.
And shall not the Eternal God claim this
   age as His own?

*Fred Pratt Green: Stanzas from 'Poem for Ralph
Lawrence on his Ordination to the Priesthood' The
poem, written for an Anglican friend, is a gentle protest
against the disunity of Christians as it was in 1965.*

feared that the forthcoming vote on union with the Church of England would lead to the imposition of bishops, and when Pratt Green told the District he was leaving, he joked it would help him to get episcopacy out of his system. So in 1964 he returned to London's southern outskirts as superintendent minister of the Sutton Circuit in pastoral charge of Sutton Trinity.

Here Pratt Green found in his congregation many professional people and those prominent in commerce and industry. The caretaker, there called the Curator, proved to be exceptionally helpful and became a valued friend. It is not every minister who can say that his last charge was his happiest. Of all the churches in which Pratt Green served, Sutton Trinity was the most united, the most free of cliques and divisions that make the work of a minister difficult; though in some ways extremely demanding, it was free from the stresses and strains that can break a minister's heart or sour his mind with cynicism. Only two clouds darkened the horizon. The 1960s were difficult for traditional churches. This was the beginning of the generation gap and the rise of the Youth culture; of the Beatles' Age, by no means to be lightly decried or dismissed; of the intrusion of guitars into worship, of the alienation of youth from the Church, about which Christians agonised, sometimes blaming themselves, sometimes youth. It was the decade when the Church was being most vigorously attacked for its inwardness, its refusal to leave the pew and go out into the world, the age when it was becoming fashionable to talk of a Churchless Christianity. The second cloud is familiar to Londoners: the ceaseless movement of the population, or rather of the more affluent, away from the old centres to new suburbs. Even Sutton was becoming less fashionable, more cosmopolitan, and would soon suffer development. Fred left the Circuit ministry before these and pressures from ageing buildings became a real cause for anxiety.

So be it, Lord; Thy throne shall never,
Like earth's proud empires, pass away;
Thy kingdom stands, and grows for ever,
Till all Thy creatures own Thy sway.
John Ellerton: The final verse of "The day Thou gavest, Lord, is ended'

Open, Lord, my inward ear,
And bid my heart rejoice;
Bid my quiet spirit hear
Thy comfortable voice;
Never in the whirlwind found,
Or where earthquakes rock the place,
Still and silent is the sound,
The whisper of Thy grace.

From the world of sin, and noise,
And hurry I withdraw;
For the small and inward voice
I wait with humble awe;
Silent am I now and still,
Dare not in Thy presence move;
To my waiting soul reveal
The secret of Thy love.
Charles Wesley: The first two verses of the hymn

Rise, Lord, judge Thou the earth in might,
This longing earth redress;
For Thou art He who shall by right
The nations all possess.

The nations all whom Thou hast made
Shall come, and all shall frame
To bow them low before Thee, Lord,
And glorify Thy name.
John Milton: Verses from 'The Lord will come, and not be slow'
These texts are taken from the 1933 'Methodist Hymn Book'

In 1967 Fred Pratt Green was co-opted to a working party appointed to prepare a supplement to the 1933 edition of the *Methodist Hymn Book*. It was felt he would be competent to advise on the literary merit of new material. The most significant other member of that group, from the point of view of our story, was John Wilson, a former Director of Music at Charterhouse who was then on the teaching staff of the Royal College of Music. In Pratt Green, this leading scholar in the field of hymnody found a craftsman with words with the particular ability to write significant texts for the music he was given.

Occasionally, over the years, I had yielded to pressure and written a hymn for some special occasion. But even as late as 1965 I refused a request from a West Midlands District. They wanted a hymn for a big rally. I made it plain that I had no desire to write hymns. Why this unhelpful attitude? After all, I was politely known as *the Methodist poet*. In 1963 the Epworth Press had actually published a small volume of my poems under the ironic title *The Skating Parson*. Other poets had written hymns, why not F.P.G.?

I try now to analyse my obstinacy. In the first place, I was not a hymn lover. I had never given any serious thought to the place of hymns in worship. I had made no study whatsoever of hymnody. In the second place, I had the notion that hymns are an inferior form of poetry, better described as verse, and all too often amateurishly weak and sentimental. The hymns I liked best were nearly all poems by reputable poets which the Church had adopted. I was prepared to concede that Isaac Watts and Charles Wesley towered above all other hymn writers and that both, in their own way, were genuine poets. If I may put it this way: I had been converted by Masefield's *The Everlasting Mercy* and not by *And can it be that I should gain*. Perhaps I am exaggerating my coolness towards hymns and dislike of sessions given up entirely to hymn singing. I can remember being carried away by the singing of the last verse of *The day Thou gavest, Lord, is ended*; and by the mystical appeal of Charles Wesley's *Open, Lord, my inward ear*; and by the strength of Milton's *The Lord will come and not be slow*. So let us just say that in 1967, I was surprised to be asked to join the Working Party appointed by the Methodist Conference to prepare a supplement to the Methodist Hymnbook of 1933.

Fred Pratt Green: From 'Myself and Hymns'

It was very much a Working Party rather than a committee that had been appointed by the Methodist Conference. The first tune thrown at Pratt Green was CHRISTE SANCTORUM. It calls for the Sapphic verse form, which, however excellent in Latin, is not well-suited to the English language owing to its weak feminine line endings. To avoid this problem, Pratt Green wrote words which fit the tune but are not strictly in the 11 11 11 5 Sapphic metre. Instead, in *Christ is the world's Light, he and none other,* Pratt Green adopted the metre 10 11 11 6. This hymn, which has been translated into several languages, is also sung to ISTE CONFESSOR (ROUEN: POITIERS). Another tune presented to Pratt Green was John Gardner's ILFRACOMBE. It called for a triple Alleluia at the end of each line, which meant that every line must express a sentiment to which *Alleluia* is an appropriate response. This challenge resulted in *Glorious the day when Christ was born,* which again uses the imagery of Light in the final verse. It may also be sung to TRURO if the Alleluias are omitted.

> Christ is the world's Light, he and none other;
> Born in our darkness, he became our Brother.
> If we have seen him, we have seen the Father:
> Glory to God on high.
>
> *Fred Pratt Green: Opening Verse*

> Glorious the day when Christ fulfils, *Alleluia*!
> What man rejects yet feebly wills; *Alleluia*!
> When that strong Light puts out the sun, *Alleluia*!
> And all is ended, all begun. *Alleluia*!
>
> *Fred Pratt Green: Final verse of*
> *'Glorious the day when Christ was born'*

The third of Pratt Green's texts in this Methodist Supplement *Hymns and Songs* came to be written during a residential working weekend. The text *Life and health are in the Name* by J. R. Darbyshire sung to WYTHAM or AMSTERDAM had already been chosen but the Working Party, nearing the completion of their task, felt there was a whole sphere of mental healing not covered by that text. So Pratt Green was urged to write something to fill the gap. He spent most of the night, while in bed, struggling with the theme and produced the first draft by breakfast. During the day improvements were introduced. Brian Frost helped the author with the last line of the third verse; Pratt Green has never been happy about *shelves* on literary grounds though it perfectly expresses a psychological truth. The hymn was chosen by the Ipswich St. Raphael Club for handicapped persons as their own. Another theme Fred was asked to tackle was a hymn on the Lord's Day expressing the difference between that Day and the Sabbath as experienced by the first generation of Christians. This was a text that Fred later revised.

In *This joyful Easteride*, Pratt Green's inexperience led him to use the same first line as G. R. Woodward's lively translation of the Dutch Carol already established to the tune of VREUTCHEN. The first line is of special significance because the hymn will be indexed and known by it.

The Working Party, as a matter of policy, decided to include a song section in the Supplement, so as to make possible the inclusion of texts of a more experimental type and in particular the folk-style song then popular, Sydney Carter's *Lord of the Dance* being the best known. Pratt Green's hymn *Life has many rhythms, every heart its beat* was written for the tune JONATHAN by Robin Sheldon, which the Working Party wanted to include. The text was experimental in the sense that *it argues rather than states* a Christian view of life. Its official title is *Dialogue* but its author called it his *Hymn for Hippies*, who were then very much in the news. There were those on the Working Party who objected, in vain, to the inclusion of Sydney Carter's *Lord of the Dance* in the Supplement. Pratt Green's *Dialogue* did at least help to get dancing established. Sadly, neither title found its way into British Methodism's *Hymns and Psalms* in the 1980s.

How strong, O Lord, are our desires,
How weak our knowledge of ourselves!
Release in us those healing truths
Unconscious pride resists or shelves.

In conflicts that destroy our health
We diagnose the world's disease;
Our common life declares our ills:
Is there no cure, O Christ, for these?

Fred Pratt Green: Second and Third Verses of 'O Christ the healer, we have come' sung to BRESLAU (ACH GOTT WIE MANCHES HERZLIED; HERR JESU CHRIST (Leipzig) and INVITATION (Lampe)

Each day throughout the week
As on the Lord's own day,
They walked in newfound liberty
His true and living way.

So on this joyful day
From needless burdens freed,
We keep the feast he made for us
To fit our inmost need.

Fred Pratt Green: Third and Fourth Verses of the definitive version of 'The first day of the week' sung to GARELOCHSIDE, SAINT THOMAS (Williams) and DAY OF PRAISE

Come, share our Easter joy
That death cannot imprison
Nor any power destroy
Our Christ, who is arisen.

Fred Pratt Green: The chorus of 'This joyful Eastertide'

Life has many rhythms, every heart its beat;
Everywhere we hear the sound of dancing feet
Life is this world's secret: Lord of life, forgive,
If we never asked you what it means to live.

Fred Pratt Green: Opening Verse of 'Dialogue'

Sydney Carter

...it was the arrival of Sydney Carter, with *Lord of the Dance*, unlike anything that English congregations had been asked to sing, which dramatically opened up the way for experiment.

Fred Pratt Green: From 'Speaking Personally' in 'The Hymns and Ballads of Fred Pratt Green'

Pratt Green had written one hymn for use at Sutton Trinity before he joined the Working Party. *When the Church of Jesus* deliberately tried to express some of the thinking of the sixties that the Church was over bothered with its own life and needed to be more involved in the world's concern. Unable to find a tune for it, he wrote the melody of SUTTON TRINITY himself. It has also been sung to KING'S WESTON. Although Pratt Green thought his work was over-represented in *Hymns and Psalms*, he was disappointed that this particular text did not find a place.

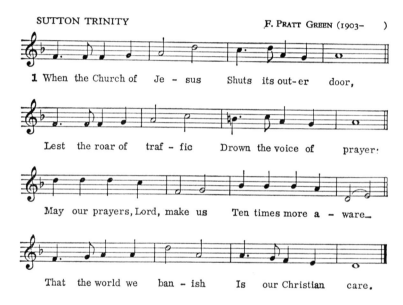

SUTTON TRINITY   F. PRATT GREEN (1903–)

1 When the Church of Je - sus   Shuts its out-er door,

Lest the roar of traf - fic   Drown the voice of prayer:

May our prayers, Lord, make us   Ten times more a - ware

That the world we ban - ish   Is our Christian care.

The Church in the World

WHEN the Church of Jesus
  Shuts its outer door,
Lest the roar of traffic
  Drown the voice of prayer:
May our prayers, Lord, make us
  Ten times more aware
That the world we banish
  Is our Christian care.

2
If our hearts are lifted
  Where devotion soars
High above this hungry
  Suffering world of ours:
Lest our hymns should drug us
  To forget its needs,
Forge our Christian worship
  Into Christian deeds.

3
Lest the gifts we offer,
  Money, talents, time,
Serve to salve our conscience
  To our secret shame:
Lord, reprove, inspire us
  By the way you give;
Teach us, dying Saviour,
  How true Christians live.

F. Pratt Green (1903–)

Pratt Green's birth as a fluent hymnwriter began just as he was about to retire and move to the outskirts of the beautiful East Anglian city of Norwich.

Here, beyond the boat-yard,
Where the sailing dinghies
Are put to bed until Easter,
I often come in winter-time
To watch the mallards take off
Noisily, as the wind whistles
In tags of metal and turns
Tarpaulin into thunder-sheets,
And the sad-faced anglers,
Shielded by green umbrellas,
Stare at the whipped waters
Of the slow-moving Yare.
How different it is now—
Now the dead staithes echo
To laughter as loving hands
Repair the ravages of winter,
And the boys, the lucky-ones,
Shout in the sun, shaking a
Sail out, and dinghies take
To water, graceful as swans.
Fred Pratt Green: 'By the River Yare'. The river runs through Norwich

The Greens shared their Norwich retirement home with two cats, Jespah and Smoke, for twelve years. They won a place in a series of light-hearted *Cat Poems.*

Is he shut in the garage
Or under the bed?
Or stretched in the warmth
Of the potting shed?
Or gone for a walk?
Run over and dead?

Is he blackmailing neighbours
Into giving him food?
Or sleeping it off
In the depths of the wood?
There's no end to the things
He couldn't or could!

Have animal snatchers
Whisked him off, God knows
                         where?
An absence so long
Is breeding despair—
Oh, he's just come in,
His tail in the air?
*Fred Pratt Green: 'Where is our
Jespah?'*

Pratt Green joined a movement already in full swing, although those participating in the English Hymnwriting Renaissance did not perceive at that time just what was happening. It had begun perhaps in the late 1940s when the Congregationalist minister, the Reverend Albert Bayly, quietly beavered away at hymns which welcomed science as part of the miracle of God's creation rather than a hostile discipline which was the enemy of religion; and translated Biblical images into contemporary terms.

Sydney Carter certainly did not seek to break the mould of English hymnody. His folk-carols danced with both faith and doubt—*which is which*, he would ask us , as he identified with a generation desparately seeking spiritual expression in thought-forms with which it could identify with integrity. Essentially though, Sydney Carter's questing songs seemed out of place in a liturgy interspersed with Victorian hymnody; it was the soap-opera writers who chose *Lord of the Dance* as the hymn of the day when featuring an episode in church; whilst some regular members of congregations found the whole concept of the song obnoxious. The compilers of the *New English Hymnal,* though, chose it as one of a comparatively few new texts in their 1980s' revision, seeing its appropriateness to that drama which is at the heart of all Christian Liturgy.

Lord of the boundless curves of space
And time's deep mystery,
To your creative might we trace
All nature's energy.

Your mind conceived the galaxy,
Each atom's secret planned,
And every age of history
Your purpose Lord, has spanned.

> Albert Bayly: the opening verses. Sung to SAN
> ROCCO and LONDON NEW

I danced in the morning when the world was begun,
And I danced in the moon and the stars and the sun,
And I came down from heaven and I danced on the
earth,
At Bethlehem I had my birth.
Dance then wherever you may be
I am the Lord of the Dance, said he.
And I'll lead you all wherever you may be
I'll lead you all in the dance, said he.

I danced on a Friday when the sky turned black,
It's hard to dance with the devil on your back.
They buried my body and they thought I'd gone;
But I am the dance and I still go on.
Chorus.

> Sydney Carter: Verses 1 and 4 of 'Lord of the Dance'
> sung to SHAKER TUNE

Hope of the world, Mary's child,
You're coming soon to reign;
King of the earth, Mary's child,
Walk in our streets again.

> Geoffrey Ainger: Last verse of 'Born in the night' sung
> to MARY'S CHILD

'Moses, I know you're the man,' the Lord said.
'You're going to work out my plan,' the Lord said.
'Lead all the Israelites out of slavery,
And I shall make them a wandering race
Called the People of God.'
So every day we're on our way,
For we're a travelling, wandering race,
We're the People of God.

'Look at the birds of the air,' the Lord said,
'They fly unhampered by care,' the Lord said,
'You will move easier if you're travelling light,
For you're a wandering, vagabond race,
You're the People of God.'
Chorus

> Estelle White: Verses 1 and 4 sung to THE PEOPLE
> OF GOD

Sydney Carter's output was numerically greater than most of his contemporaries in this genre; a group meeting in London's Notting Hill included the Reverend Geoffrey Ainger whose *Mary's Child* has become widely established. The Reverend Peter Smith, then a Methodist Minister in Sheffield, caught the mood of the moment with his folk anthology *Faith Folk and Clarity* linking songs of faith and worship with songs of community concerns. Estelle White wrote folk material which was used in many Roman Catholic circles.

At Scottish Churches House in Dunblane, a remarkable group came together for residential writing sessions. The team included Congregationalist Reverend Erik Rouley, the Anglican Reverend Alan Luff, and the then Warden of the ecumenical house, the Reverend Ian Fraser. The result was two booklets called *Dunblane Praises* later published more widely as *New Songs for the Church*. Canticles as well as hymns were included. Meanwhile, down in Plymouth, a Dutchman who had taken English nationality served as a Congregationalist Minister at Pilgrim Church. He produced a whole hymnbook of texts to match his weekly sermons. Fred Kaan published his work as *Pilgrim Praise*. The Reverend Timothy Dudley-Smith edited *Youth Praise* whilst the Twentieth Century Church Light Music Group was promoting new tunes and occasional new words. The Reverend Brian Wren was emerging as a talented writer of the younger generation.

Albert Bayly

Fred Kaan

All who love and serve your city,
All who bear its daily stress,
All who cry for peace and justice,
All who curse and all who bless.

In your day of loss and sorrow,
In your day of helpless strife,
Honour, peace and love retreating,
Seek the Lord, who is your life.

Erik Routley: Opening verses sung to BIRABUS,
MARCHING and CITY

Forgive our careless use
Of water, ore and soil—
The plenty we abuse
Supplied by others' toil:
Save us from making self our creed;
Turn us towards our neighbour's need.

Ian Fraser: Verse 2 of 'Lord, bring the day to pass' sung
to NEW EARTH, CREATION, GOSPAL and
CROFT'S 136TH

All that kills abundant living,
Let it from the earth be banned;
Pride of status, race, or schooling,
Dogmas that obscure your plan.
In our common quest for justice
May he hallow life's brief span.

Fred Kaan: The third verse of 'For the healing of the
nations' sung to GRAFTON, RHUDDLAN, ,
MANNHEIM, ALLELUIA, DULCE CARMEN
(TANTUM ERGO) AND PICARDY

Tell out, my soul, the greatness of the Lord:
Unnumbered blessings, give my spirit voice;
Tender to me the promise of his word;
In God my Saviour shall my heart rejoice.

Timothy Dudley-Smith: The opening verse of
'Magnificat' sung to WOODLANDS

Praise God for the harvest that comes from
the ground,
By drill or by mineshaft, by opencast mound;
For oil and for iron, for copper and coal,
Praise God, who inlove has provided them all.

Praise God for the harvest of science and skill,
The urge to discover, create and fulfil;
For all new inventions that promise a gain,
A future more hopeful, a world more humane.

Brian Wren: Verses 3 and 4 of 'Praise God for the
harvest of farm and of field' sung to MINIVER

Visits by the Greens over the years to the Western Highlands inspired two poems which reveal a different kind of religious emphasis.

A heron, its neck long as a sermon,
fished in the loch this Sabbath morning,
and seals, trailing seaweed, surfaced.

One of the seals was like somebody;
but when I searched memory for the face
all I could see were the silhouettes

of Rum and Eigg, those misty islands
we ought to visit. This Sabbath morning,
yielding to the conventional rhythms

of godliness, we fluttered our hands
at the kirk door, but nobody shook them,
and the elders didn't ask who we were.

We feel there's a theological reason
for this; as if, in a manner of speaking,
we had called upon the wrong Person.

So we sit rigidly, stand uprightly,
and deny ourselves the gross pleasure
of singing in parts. In sermon-time,

as the minister gives a modern twist
to pre-exilic prophecy, I enjoy
a private revelation. It was Bacchus,

bald-headed, festooned with flowers,
who surfaced in a sea of debauchery
beside the kirk this Sabbath morning!
            Fred Pratt Green: 'Sabbath Morning in the Western Highlands'

Smoke is in Jespah's chair,
Curled up, in full possession,
With a very smug expression.
Now why should Smoke be *there*?
She knows perfectly well
Which chair is hers. Well,

The truth is, Smoke is that
Odd creature—a Copy Cat.
If he changes his habitat,
Elects to sleep on a mat,
She too must sleep on a mat,
Not any mat, just that mat.

But Jespah is too well-bred
To argue with ladies. Instead
He squats on the window-sill,
Eyeing his favourite chair
With a slightly outraged stare,
And thoughts I expect would kill.
    Fred Pratt Green: 'Copy Cat'

A hooded crow on the Wee-Free roof
is cleaning his feathers. This is a day
for a short walk in a waterproof.

Out of the rain, psalm-singing Christians
clear their consciences, never posing
the bleak and unanswerable questions.

This is the day for listening to the lark
singing in the leaden sky of a summer
cold as Christmas, for watching the dark

waters of the sea-loch slipping away
from the seaweed, the sea-gulls sailing
in long glissandos. This is a day

of dulled vision. In dripping woodlands
primroses rot and the rhododendrons
shake the rain off with hidden hands.

Listen to the crow croaking his psalm
on the Wee-Free roof! This is a day
when we need religion to keep us warm

in the dark kirk where the People of God
witness, with compulsive holiness,
to the strength of His arm and His rod.
Fred Pratt Green: 'Another Sabbath in the Western Highlands'

For two decades, Pratt Green was to respond to his new calling as hymnwriter, providing a corpus of nearly three hundred hymns and Christian songs. They have been collected in two volumes, *The Hymns and Ballads of Fred Pratt Green* published in 1982 and in *Later Hymns and Ballads and Fifty Poems* issued in 1989. The work is remarkably well documented because Pratt Green backed up his retirement 'hobby' with a series of scrapbooks. Little did he think when he pasted in his first cuttings that there would be fifty-one of these, with two more for poetry. The books contain drafts of texts, correspondence, comments and printed versions of texts, with material which interested their compiler about the hymnody scene in general. On his death, they will be lodged in the Pitts Theology Library at the University of Emory in Atlanta, with a copied set available in the United Kingdom alongside the Pratt Green Collection in the Library of the University of Durham.

For the harvests of his Spirit,
Thanks be to God:
For the good we all inherit,
Thanks be to God;
For the wonders that astound us,
For the truths that still confound us,
Most of all that love has found us,
Thanks be to God.
Fred Pratt Green: Verse 3 of 'Harvest Hymn',
which begins 'For the fruit of all creation'.
As well as EAST ACKLAM it is sung to
AR HYD Y NOS and SAINT BARBARA

Rejoice with us in God, the Trinity,
The Three for ever One, forever Three,
Fountain of Love, Giver of Unity!

How long and earnestly the Fathers strove
To frame in words a faith we cannot prove;
But O how dead our creeds
Unless they live in Christ-like aims and deeds!
Fred Pratt Green: Antiphon and Verse 2 of 'A
Hymn in Honour of the Holy and Undivided
Trinity' of which the first verse begins 'We would
rejoice again, and yet again'

John Wilson's influential position in the Hymn Society of Great Britain and Ireland, his involvement with *Come and Sing* sessions in Westminster Abbey, and his contacts in musical and religious life, both nationally and locally in Guildford, all played an important part in making Pratt Green's early texts known. John Wilson came up with neglected tunes for which he sought fresh words to give them a new lease of life; and a rapport grew between the two men so that they communicated about the drafts of new texts by constructive correspondence; and Wilson became Pratt Green's trusted and respected mentor. The tunes suggested by Wilson produced a rich harvest. To name a few, EAST ACKLAM provided *For the fruits of all creation,* now to be found in books across the continents; TRINITAS encouraged *Rejoice with us in God, the Trinity,* a hymn with a second verse declared by Erik Routley to express what no other hymn on the Trinity managed to say;

An upper room did our Lord prepare
For those he loved until the end:
And his disciples still gather there
To celebrate their Risen Friend.

A lasting gift Jesus gave his own:
To share his bread, his loving cup.
Whatever burdens may bow us down,
He by his Cross shall lift us up.

And after Supper he washed their feet
For service, too, is sacrament.
In him our joy shall be made complete—
Sent out to serve, as he was sent.

No end there is! We depart in peace;
He loves beyond the uttermost:
In every room in our Father's house
He will be there, as Lord and Host.

*Fred Pratt Green: 'An Upper Room', a Methodist hymn
sung by Roman Catholics*

How fierce the torrents that divide
    The citizens of this unhappy state!
Build us a bridge, we cried,
    To span these centuries of hate.
Before the statesmen could decide
    How best to give democracy full sway
Build us a bridge, we cried
    The flood has swept your words away!

As politicians vainly tried
    To frame the formula that turns the tide,
Build us a bridge, we cried,
    Above our passions and our pride!
Still violent men of either side
    Darkened the waters with each other's blood
Build us a bridge, we cried
    Or all will perish in the flood!

We turned to Him, the Crucified,
    Betrayed by those who glory in His name:
You are the Bridge, we cried
    And hid our heads for very shame.
O let us come from either side,
    And on that Bridge be reconciled at last!
Who but the Crucified
    Can teach us to redeem the past?

*Fred Pratt Green: 'The Bridge', a poem requested
by Northern Ireland Methodists. This text was
recently rediscovered by the author, and with its
sister poem 'The Dove of Peace' is omitted from
the definitive list of Pratt Green's poetry in 'Later
Hymns and Ballads and Fifty Poems'*

O WALY WALY led to *An Upper Room
did our Lord prepare*, which, sweeping
across denominational boundaries, was
sung at a Papal Mass in Tasmania;
ENGLEBERG produced *When, in our
music, God is glorified*, which in its turn,
produced several anthem settings besides
its wide use as a hymn; HERMON
produced the strongly Biblical *What
Adam's disobedience cost*;   and
THEODORIC motivated the Advent
Song *Long ago prophets knew.*

For services in Guildford Cathedral, Pratt
Green provided *Man cannot live by bread
alone* for a Feed the Minds service; *One
in Christ, we meet together*, from which the
Bishop quoted in a farewell statement on
his translation to Salisbury; and *Lord of
every art and science,* for a service for
journalists, artists and broadcasters.

Lord of every art and science;
Source of all creative skill,
Help us use all kinds of media
For the doing of your will

Whatsoever's just and loving,
Whatsoever's true and pure:
Only to our smooth evasions
Is your simple word obscure;

So may those who mould opinion
Help us get our values right,
And the artist's private vision
Sharpen our defective sight.

All the lines are open to us,
All resources we require:
May the world of our creation
Be the one that you inspire.

*Fred Pratt Green: 'A Hymn for Communicators' in
its original form. Verse 2 is normally omitted. Tunes
include LAUS DEO (Redhead), DRAKES
BROUGHTON and HALTON HALGATE
(BOYCE; SHARON [Boyce])*

In the early 1970s Erik Routley was
editing the new edition of *Cantate
Domino*, the hymnbook of the World
Council of Churches. Here the challenge

was to write English paraphrases which could be sung to the same tune chosen for the text in its mother tongue.

Pratt Green was provided with literal translations of words by French writers Edmund Budry, Dominique Ombrie, Didier Rimaud and Claude Rozier; by German writers Christian Gottlob Barth, Christian David, Jochen Klepper, Christian Nehring, Kurt Rummel, Paulus Stein and Dieter Trautwein; and by the Uraguyan writer Frederico J. Pagura. Routley also provided several assignments based on tunes, remarking at the time how good Pratt Green was with unusual metres. For WAS IST, DAS MICH BETRUBT, the text *A new day bids us wake* was provided in 6.7.6.7.6 6. Wilson had not been satisfied with Pratt Green's offering for CHILSWELL (Holst's tune for Robert Bridges' *Gird on thy sword, O man, thy strength endue*), but Routley chose *God is our Song, and every sinner blest* for *Westminster Praise*, a supplement issued in 1976 for the use of Westminster Choir College at Princeton. Routley also played a significant role in making Pratt Green's work and name known in the United States.

The Greens became involved with the local life of their retirement city and county, with Fred joining a Writers' Circle and Marjorie becoming a cathedral guide. Texts were provided over the years for a number of local groups including an ecumenical healing and counselling centre in Norwich, the 11th Norwich Guide Company, the Christian Aid Commission of Norwich Council of Churches, The Life for the World Trust for the rehabilitation of drug addicts (to be sung in one of the chapels of Norwich Cathedral), to honour Saint Withburger, Virgin, who founded a great church and nunnery in the eighth century at Dereham, to honour Saint Giles, to

---

God is our Song, and every singer blest
Who, praising him, finds energy and rest.
All who praise God with unaffected joy
Give back to us the wisdom we destroy.

God is our Song, for Jesus comes to save;
While praising him we offer all we have.
New songs we sing, in ventures new unite,
When Jesus leads us upward into light.

This is the Song no conflict ever drowns;
Who praises God the wrath of man disowns.
Love knows what rich complexities of sound
God builds upon a simple, common ground.

God is our Silence when no songs are sung,
When ectasy or sorrow stills the tongue.
Glorious the faith which silently obeys
Until we find again the voice of praise.
Fred Pratt Green: 'God is our Song'

By the Wood which sings a song of nuptial
gladness,
Of God who takes for his bride our human race:
Jesus Christ, we thank and bless you!
By the Wood which raises up in his full vigour
The Son of Man who draws all men by his grace:
Jesus Christ, we glorify you!
By the Wood where he perfects his royal
priesthood
In one High Priest who for sin is sacrifice:
Conquering God, we your people proclaim you!
Fred Pratt Green: From 'Images of the Cross'
from the French of Didier Rimaud for music by
Josef Gelineau. The first line is 'By the Cross
which did to death our only Saviour'

Once upon a time they went,
King and page together,
On a deed of kindness bent,
In the winter weather.
Every legend has its truth,
May this one remind us
Where a neighbour is in need
Christ expects to find us.

Victims of injustice cry:
On your own confession
Charity is not enough,
We must end oppression.
Yet, in such a world as this,
Daily we are proving
There are evils none can cure
Without deeds of loving.
Fred Pratt Green: Verses 1 and 2 of 'Christian
Aid' sung to TEMPUS ADEST FLORIDUM, the
tune of 'Good King Wenceslas'

The candle she lit
Six centuries gone,
By darkness beset
Shines quietly on.
Her cell is no prison,
Though narrow and dim,
For Jesus is risen,
And she lives in him.

How bright is her cell
The showings of God!
No writings could tell
What love understood.
She suffers his Passion,
She grieves over sin;
She knows his compassion
Has made us all kin.

How courteous is God!
All love and all light!
In God's Motherhood
She finds her delight.
She pleads for the sinner,
She wrestles with Hell;
God answers: *All manner
Of things shall be well!*
*Fred Pratt Green: Verses 2 to 4 of 'In Commem-
oration of Julian of Norwich' sung to LAUDATE
DOMINUM[Gauntlett] (GAUNTLETT)*

Rejoice in God's saints, today and all days!
A world without saints forgets how to praise.
Their faith in acquiring the habit of prayer,
Their depth of adoring, Lord, help us to share.

Some march with events to turn them God's way;
Some need to withdraw, the better to pray;
Some carry the gospel through fire and through
flood:
Our world is their parish: their purpose is God.

Rejoice in those saints, unpraised and unknown,
Who bear someone's cross, or shoulder their
own:
They share our complaining, our comforts, our
cares:
What patience in caring, what courage, is theirs!

Rejoice in God's saints, today and all days!
A world without saints forgets how to praise,
In loving, in living, they prove it is true:
Their way of self-giving, Lord, leads us to you.
*Fred Pratt Green: 'In Celebration of Saints', an
adaptation of the second Mother Julian text for
wider use. Sung to OLD 104TH*

whom an Anglo-Catholic church in Norwich is dedicated, the Norfolk Battalion of the Boys' Brigade, the blessing of a civil marriage of a local Anglican friend, and Bowthorpe School on a new estate on the outskirts of Norwich.

In the Methodist Church, Pratt Green provided a text for Midnight Communion on Christmas Eve at Thorpe Road Methodist Church in Norwich, a hymn for a Festival of Praise at Downham Market arranged by the East Anglia District, a song for another District occasion to express purposefulness, jollity, and a general air of celebration, and words to fit a tune written by Matthew Evan-Jones, a fifteen-year old member of Heartsease Lane Methodist Church in Norwich. The winning entry for a competition in 1974 for ecumenical hymns sponsored by Queen's College, Birmingham, was sung in Norwich Cathedral in 1981 when the Methodist Conference visited the city.

Alan Webster, then Dean, invited Pratt Green to contribute texts for special occasions in Norwich Cathedral, including two hymns for an ecumenical eucharist in May 1973 to celebrate the six hundredth anniversary of Mother Julian's *Revelations of Divine Love*; for a civic service in 1974; a text for an Act of Thanksgiving attended by the Queen on completion of works of restoration in April 1975; and a hymn for the Queen's Silver Jubilee in 1977.

A phone call from Lambeth Palace led to the inclusion of this last hymn in the Offical Order of Service for celebration of the Queen's Jubilee. It was sung throughout the country and the Commonwealth. Harry Eskew, then editor of *The Hymn*, suggested that with minor changes it was relevant for America and appropriate amendments were made. The music chosen was

VISION, John Wilson's arrangement of a tune by his late uncle, Walford Davies, one-time Master of the King's Music and music teacher to the young Princess Elizabeth.

John Wilson

It is God who hold the nations in the hollow of his hand;
It is God whose light is shining in the darkness of the land;
It is God who builds his City on the Rock and not on sand;
May the living God be praised!

It is God whose purpose summons us to use the present hour;
Who recalls us to our senses when a nation's life turns sour;
In the discipline of freedom we shall know his saving power:
May the living God be praised!

When a thankful nation, looking back, unites to celebrate
Those who reign in our affection by their service to the state;
When self-giving is a measure of the greatness of the great:
May the living God be praised!

He reminds us every sunrise that the world is ours on lease—
For the sake of life tomorrow, may our love for it increase;
May all races live together, share its riches, be at peace:
May the living God be praised!

Fred Pratt Green: 'A Hymn for the Nation'

The alternative opening to verse 3 for wider use reads:

When a thankful nation, looking back, has cause to celebrate
Those who win our admiration by their service to the state...

Marjorie Green's association with Norwich Cathedral produced a very different kind of hymn when a tourist enquired about texts for Christingle services, a tradition originating in Central Europe.

O round as the world is the orange you give us!
And happy are they who to Jesus belong:
So let the world know, as we join in Christingle,
That Jesus, the Hope of the World, is our song.

O bright is the flame of the candle you give us!
And happy are they who to Jesus belong:
So let the world know, as we join in Christingle,
That Jesus, the Light of the World, is our song.

Go northward or southward, go eastward or westward,
How happy are they who to Jesus belong!
So let the world know, as they join in Christingle,
That Jesus, the Peace of the World, is our song.

When homeward we go, we must take Jesus with us,
For happy are they who to Jesus belong:
So let the world know, as we join in Christingle,
That Jesus, the Saviour of all, is our song.

Fred Pratt Green: 'Carol for a Christingle Service' set to a traditional Czech tune, now christened CHRISTINGLE, to be found in 'The Galliard Book of Carols'.

Do we have a cat-door?
　Oh, yes!
Do they know what it's for?
　Oh, yes!
Can they go in and out?
　Oh, yes!

If their slaves are about
Do they use the cat door?
　You guess!
Have they got it worked out
What we humans are for?
　You guess!

Do we hurry downstairs?
　Oh, yes!
Or wake from a nap?
　Oh, yes!
To lift up the flap?
　You guess!

Fred Pratt Green: 'Cat Door'

Though love is greatest of the three,
And Faith one step behind,
It's Hope completes the trilogy,
Lest Faith and Love be blind:
For hopeless Love is blind with tears,
And hopeless Faith with rage,
But Hope has seen beyond our fears
God's juster, kindlier age.

God does not ask our faithful Love,
Then leave us in despair,
When life's misfortunes seen to prove
There is no God to care:
But gives us Hope to steady Faith,
And in our grief restore
Love's confidence that even death
Is but an opening door.

God give us hope, if Hope we lack
Of these three gifts to man,
That faith may never turn its back
On all that Love began,
But strive against outrageous odds,
Our new destructive powers,
To build a world more truly God's,
And therefore truly ours.

Fred Pratt Green: 'Hope completes the Trilogy'.
The tune is SAINT MATTHEW

God in his love for us lent us this planet,
Gave it a purpose in time and in space:
Small as a spark in the fire of creation,
Cradle of life and the home of our race.

Thanks be to God for its bounty and beauty,
Life that sustains us in body and mind:
Plenty for all, if we learn how to share it,
Riches undreamed of to fathom and find.

Long have our human wars ruined its harvest;
Long has earth bowed to the terror of force;
Long have we wasted what others have need of,
Poisoned the fountain of life at its source.

Earth is the Lord's: it is ours to enjoy it,
Ours, as his stewards to farm and defend.
From its pollution, misuse, and destruction,
Good Lord, deliver us, world without end!

Fred Pratt Green: The definitive version with
some changes from the original competition entry
of 'The Stewardship of the Earth'. Sung to
STEWARDSHIP, QUEDLINGBURG,
LIEBSTER I[E]MMANUEL (EMMANUEL),
LIME STREET and CONSERVATION

In the 1970s, Pratt Green entered hymnwriting competitions arranged by the Hymn Society of America. *Though Love is greatest of the three* was printed in 1971 with six other texts on the theology of hope. *God in his love for us lent us this planet* won a place in *Sixteen Hymns on the Stewardship of the Environment* published in 1973. He tried his hand with *Now praise the hidden God of Love* in a competition for a hymn which could be sung both by Christians and non-Christians believing in a living God. His first American commission came from Russell Schulz-Widmar at University United Methodist Church, at Austin in Texas. It was to be sung at the closing service of an eight-month long festival concerned with worship, music and the arts, and to involve the dedication of new church furniture and a rededication of God's people there. The tune was specified: Schulz-Widmar wanted to introduce ABBOT'S LEIGH to the congregation. The result was *God is here! As we his people.*

Lee Hastings Bristol, Jnr., a member of the Episcopal Church of America, commissioned Pratt Green to write texts for his radio work and special preaching appointments. Most of these were story-texts or short ballads. Seven centred round women of the Gospels: besides Mary Magdalene and Martha and Mary, the subjects were the woman who touched the hem of Christ's garment, the woman taken in adultery, the widow who added her mite to the Temple offering, the Samaritan at the well, and the woman who anointed Christ with costly oil. These were followed by a group of ballads featuring Zacchaeus, Pilate, the penitent thief on the Cross, the rich young ruler, the man at the Pool of Bethesda, the brothers seeking arbitration from Jesus about their inheritance, and the man born blind. Two scripts looked at feasting and fasting and the call to true discipleship.

The final group covered cities: Bethlehem, Jerusalem, Damascus, Caesarea Maritima and a typical city of our own time. Sadly, Lee Bristol died before further assignments were proposed.

In the 1970s Pratt Green attended the Annual Conferences of the Hymn Society of Great Britain and Ireland and of the Methodist Church Music Society and a hymn of his was often included in the Hymn Society's annual Act of Praise. Alan Luff, Secretary and later Chairman of the Hymn Society, also made a series of requests over the years. The first came from this Welsh-speaking Englishman when he was a priest in the Bangor diocese, whose Music Committee was planning a book of Welsh carols. His request was for English words, catching perhaps the theme of the Welsh, but essentially following the elaborate rhyme structure, including the original rhyming of the originals. *Look! the sun awakes the sky* was the response to a request for an Easter text: it was probably first sung by Catholic and Protestant voices lustily in unison at a service led by Methodist minister, Alan Dale, author of the Bible paraphrases *New World* and *Winding Quest*. Later, as Precentor of Westminster Abbey, Luff commissioned a hymn for a Festival there involving the National Association of Flower Arrangement Societies of Great Britain. Pratt Green's very last British commission came from Luff. English words, to be sung simultaneously with the Welsh text were needed for a hymn by the most famous of Welsh hymnwriters, William Williams for a celebration in 1988 of the four-hundredth anniversary of the translation of the Bible into Welsh. *Lord, I know your Word will lead me* is set to the tune GROSEWEN by the nineteenth century Welsh composer John A. Lloyd.

Lord of all, of Church and Kingdom,
In an age of change and doubt,
Keep us faithful to the gospel,
Help us work your purpose out.
Here, in this day's dedication,
All we have to give, receive:
We, who cannot live without you,
We adore you! we believe!

> *Fred Pratt Green: the final verse of 'The Church of Christ' of which the first line is 'God is here! As we his people'. Besides ABBOT'S LEIGH, it is sung to BLAENWERN and BETHANY (Smart)*

Pray for our cities! Grown too fast,
How many lives they crush or break!
Their golden nets too widely cast,
They gather more than they can take.
How many seeking gold find dross!
Who can assess the gain and loss?

Look kindly on each nameless face,
All who make up the motley throng:
The immigrant of alien race;
The lonely old, the rootless young;
The ones who rise, the ones who fall;
The rich, the poor: pray for them all!

What sins the great apostle saw
In Corinth, Athens, Ephesus!
What breaking of the moral law!
How these same problems stare at us,
From sordid sex to double-talk
In modern London or New York.

But Christ, who teaches us to care,
Who loved the city David planned,
Who wept for it, and suffered there;
Who builds on rock and not on sand:
He shares with us each urban task,
And gives new life to all who ask.

> *Fred Pratt Green: 'The Contemporary City'*

Long before God gave us birth—
We or any creature—
Flowers adorned the naked earth,
Changed the face of nature.
Tended now by hands of ours,
See how they are thriving!
Deck the Abbey Church with flowers:
They are our thanksgiving.

> *Fred Pratt Green: Verse 2 of 'For a Flower Festival in Westminster Abbey' of which the first line is 'Praise the Lord for all delights' for the tune TEMPUS ADEST FLORIDUM*

continued in opposite margin

Among the composers with whom Pratt Green was in touch in the 1970s were David McCarthy, now Second Master at Woodhouse Grove School in Yorkshire; Michael Dawney, a free-lance Roman Catholic composer; the late Francis Westbrook , British Methodism's 'Mr. Music', with whom Pratt Green had been at college; the late Stanley Fuller, a Norwich organist; Ida Prins-Buttle, a leading member of the Methodist Church Music Society; Martin Ellis, now Head of Music at Reigate Grammar School and in charge of music at Dorking Parish Church; Pam Barton, a teacher of physically handicapped children in Liverpool; Philip Hill, Director of Music at Seaford College; Walter Webber; Brian Coleman, a fellow-minister in the Methodist Church; and Valerie Ruddle of Sevenoaks Methodist Church.

It was for David McCarthy's tune NEW MALDEN that Pratt Green wrote a hymn which many have found helpful when their Christian faith has been sorely tested:

> When our confidence is shaken
> In beliefs we thought secure;
> When the spirit in its sickness
> Seeks but cannot find a cure:
> God is active in the tensions
> Of a faith not yet mature.
>
> Solar systems, void of meaning,
> Freeze the spirit into stone;
> Always our researches lead us
> To the ultimate Unknown:
> Faith must die, or come full circle
> To its source in God alone.
>
> In the discipline of praying,
> When it's hardest to believe;
> In the drudgery of caring,
> When it's not enough to grieve:
> Faith maturing, learns acceptance
> Of the insights we receive.
>
> God is love; and he redeems us
> In the Christ we crucify:
> This is God's eternal answer
> To the world's eternal why;
> May we in this faith maturing
> Be content to live and die.
>> *Fred Pratt Green: 'A Mature Faith'. Sung also to* RHUDDLAN

In 1977, Fred Pratt Green and Bernard Braley were thrown together by their appointment as joint editors of an ecumenical book *Partners in Praise*. Helped by an ecumenical team of advisers, the book was to be a supplement to main denominational books of texts appropriate for occasions when old and young worship together. The beginning of the Joint Editors' Preface reads:

> This book tackles a dilemma of all who lead such services. How do we prepare so that the event is not an occasion for adults with children looking on, or for children with adults on the sideline?
>
> A major part of a full diet of hymnody comes from the rich heritage it is the privilege of present-day Christians to enjoy. There are, however, difficulties where words have changed their meanings or where imagery used is now outside common experience. But usually these drawbacks are outweighed by the experience that we are part of a worshipping community at one with Christians of every age and place. Insights given to Christian believers over many centuries are a necessary balance to be set alongside the theological emphasis of a particular time and place.
>
> None the less, our role is to serve the present age. To omit from our worship the insights and creativity of recent writing would be to deprive worshippers of the chance of enjoying a rich harvest of words and music in praise of God. Some hymns and songs will not survive the limited life-span of this book. Others will be passed on to future generations as the particular insights of our times. The Joint Editors hope too that the book will encourage contemporary writers to put into hymn or song what the theologians are discerning may be the special contribution of this last part of the twentieth century.
>
> The General Editors have encouraged the Music Editors to use music of many styles in this collection...

Several thousand items were considered before 177 texts were finally chosen. 178 older texts were listed as being especially suitable for all-age worship and appropriate for use side by side with the new material. Over seventy different authors' work was chosen, and more than one hymn or song was included from the writing of Geoffrey Ainger, Bernard Braley, Basil Bridge, Sydney Carter, Emily Chisholm, Timothy Dudley-Smith, Ian Fraser, Anders Frostenson (in translation), Fred Pratt Green, Cyril Hambly, Rosamond Herklots, Michael Hewlett, Richard Jones, Fred Kaan, David Mowbray, Chris Rogers, Peter D.Smith, Cecily Taylor, John Tearnan and Brian Wren.

In 1979, Pratt Green was invited to provide both secular and sacred words for a group of carol tunes editors wished to include in *The Galliard Book of Carols* where the existing words were dated or mundane. Besides texts for the Christian year, Pratt Green's contributions included items on concert-going, mistletoe and a love song. In *A Herb Carol* Pratt Green has made rue a bad thing, noting that it has long had a double reputation, both as the herb of grace and an instrument of Satan.

continued from opposite margin

TREGWYN
UNE JEUNE PUCELLE
VREUTCHEN
WAS IST, DAS MICH BETRUBT
WIGAN
WINSON
YR HEN DDARBI

When God created herbs
He gave them work to do:
Sweet Marjoram has flavour,
Bergamot has fragrance,
Rosemary cures headaches
(And these are but a few);
Then Satan planted Rue.
When God created herbs,
Then Satan planted Rue,
The sad, mysterious Rue.

So Eve made use of herbs
That in her garden grew:
Sweet Marjoram for flavour,
Bergamot for fragrance,
Rosemary for headaches
(And these were but a few)
But she was piercèd through.
So Eve made use of herbs,
But she was piercèd through
When Adam plucked the Rue.

Our Lady loved the herbs
That in her garden grew:
Sweet Marjoram for flavour,
Bergamot for fragrance,
Rosemary for headaches
(And these are but a few):
But she was piercèd through.
Our Lady loved the herbs,
But she was piercèd through
When Jesus plucked the Rue.

All you who dote on herbs
And praise the good they do;
Sweet Marjoram for flavour,
Bergamot for fragrance,
Rosemary for headaches
(And these are but a few);
Lest you be piercèd through,
All you who dote on herbs,
Lest you be piercèd through,
Let none you love touch Rue.
Fred Pratt Green: 'A Herb Carol'
for the tune of John Dowland's
lutesong 'Now cease my
wandering eyes'

Here's a donkey you may trust;
While you can, escape you must!
When the baby had been fed:
Time to go, the donkey said.
Hey, Sir Donkey, hey!

Every day they lived in dread,
Little Saviour, make no sound:
Wicked men are prowling round!
Watch your step, the donkey said–
Hey, Sir Donkey, hey!

Out of Egypt, Israel fled;
Back to Egypt they must go.
Soft the sand, the going slow:
Take your time, the donkey said–
Hey, Sir Donkey, hey!

When the donkey disobeyed,
Joseph raised his stick in wrath.
There is danger in our path–
Think of Balaam, Mary said–
Hey, Sir Donkey, hey!

Where's the manna, magic bread?
Where's the water Moses struck,
For the thirsty, out of rock?
Trust in God, the donkey said–
Hey, Sir Donkey, hey!

Look, a city shines ahead!
Look at all the houses there!
Will they vanish into air?
Time will show, the donkey said–
Hey, Sir Donkey, hey!

Safe they are, with bed and board;
Safe and sound, our little Lord.
Till at last, King Herod dead:
Home we go, the donkey said:
Hey, Sir Donkey, hey!

Fred Pratt Green: 'The Donkey's Carol'. Written for the tune ORIENTIS PARTIBUS in the 'Galliard Book of Carols'. This melody was used as a pilgrim's song on the route to Compostela, and later in Medieval France at the annual Festival of the Donkey, commemorating the flight into Egypt of the Holy Family.

At the International Hymnody Conference in Oxford in 1981 Pratt Green met several of his American correspondents for the first time. He also met Pastor Friedrich Hofmann of Roth, West Germany, who has since done much to commend Pratt Green's work in that country and has translated a dozen texts into German. Pratt Green was delighted to meet him again in 1987, when he came to Norwich with a German choir.

The question of sexist language, which had become a major issue in the United States, had hardly touched Oxford before 1981, save perhaps through the views of the Revd. Brian Wren. Pratt Green, whilst sensitive to some of the arguments, to which he has since responded in his work, finds his respect for Biblical tradition leaves him unsympathetic to those who would carry these changes too far in what may be a merely passing fashion.

How can we sing the praise of Him
　Who is no longer He?
With bated breath we wait to know
　The sex of Deity.

Our Father is our Mother now,
　And Cousin too, no doubt.
Must worship wait for hymnodists
　To get things sorted out?

O rise not up, you men of God!
　The Church must learn to wait
Till Brotherhood is sisterised,
　And Mankind out-of-date.

O may the You-know-who forgive
　Our stunned ambivalence,
And in our sexist anguishings
　Preserve our common-sense.

Fred Pratt Green: 'A Hymn for the Nineteen-Eighties' written for the International Hymnody Conference, Oxford, 1981

In 1982, as guests of the Hymn Society of America and the Hope Publishing Company, the Greens set foot on American soil for the first time. The University of Emory conferred upon Pratt Green an honorary doctorate in Humane Letters in recognition of his hymnwriting. He was also appointed as a Fellow of the Hymn Society of America—at home, he is a Vice-President of the Hymn Society of Great Britain and Ireland and an honorary Associate of the Royal School of Church Music.

Atlanta was the scene where many new friendships were begun: much of Pratt Green's writing in the next six years was to be in response to American commissions. Several American denominations published new hymn-books in the 1980s. Pratt Green is well represented and in the new book of the United Methodists, more of Pratt Green's texts were chosen than from the work of any other living author. Pratt Green chose to use his formal lecture at the Hymn Society Convention to comment on the way hymn-book committee members often wished to rewrite texts. Whilst Pratt Green has always been ready to change texts for valid theological reasons, he is less tolerant of amateur committee poets! That is not to say that he does not welcome criticism while a hymn is in the making. Most of his texts written to commission have been the subject of several drafts sent for consideration and comment. Bernard Braley's commentary on each text in *The Hymns and Ballads of Fred Pratt Green*, published to coincide with the Convention, shows how this refining process has led to the final version of many texts.

From Atlanta, the Greens went to Savannah, strong in its Wesley associations, to stay with fellow hymnwriter Reverend F. Bland Tucker, then in his extreme old age. They also accepted an invitation to Austin in Texas, where Fred was to preach, and during their stay found new friends several of whom have since visited Norwich to see them. Most significant perhaps was musician Russell Schulz-Widmar. Schulz-Widmar later served on a committee revising the *Yale University Hymnal* and asked Pratt Green to tackle a hymn which more truthfully expressed contemporary feelings at a War Memorial service than J. S. Arkwright's *O valiant hearts, who to your glory came.*

We Methodists are extremely fortunate that our own hymn-writer, Charles Wesley, was a fine poet. The quality of the Wesley hymns, allowing for the fact that he was an XVIIIth century stylist, is beyond question. We are foolish to tamper with them; except where sense is in question, however awkward we may find some of his polysyllabic words.
Fred Pratt Green: From 'On Amending Hymn Texts'

There are those, of course, who will complain that we come to sing hymns to the glory of God, not about conservation, or the problems of urban life, or world hunger. May it not be that they have too restricted a view of how we glorify God as well as of what constitutes a hymn?
Fred Pratt Green: From 'The teaching Ministry of Hymns' in 'Journal of Church Music' November 1981

God of the nations, God of all who live,
How many gave us all they had to give!
Now, in remembrance of our nation's dead,
In honesty and pride let prayers be said.

Some died sustained by promise of success,
Some in defeat's despair and bitterness;
Some died the victims of incompetence:
Through years of peril they were our defence.

'When you remember us,' we hear them cry,
'Take greater care how you let others die;
Whatever God you worship, or if none,
Pray that the nations learn to live as one.'

We lay our wreaths, perform the simple rite,
Anxious that we may see in clearer light,
As those for whom a nation's blood was shed,
How best to serve the living and the dead.

God of the nations, God of friend and foe,
Under whose judgement all must come and go,
In your compassion show us how to end
Fear of our foes and make of each a friend.
Fred Pratt Green: 'At a War Memorial'. Tunes include FARLEY CASTLE, HARRIS, VALIANT HEARTS and VALOR

We grow to trust Fred Pratt Green because he is trustworthy. His works are central and germaine; they exhibit a wide and charitable perspective and come from a steady hand; they are influenced and they influence; they indulge in characteristic hymnic diction, but they never become either too ambitious or too trendy. Often he strikes truth for us in a captivating and compelling way, and then—and here's the ultimate test—he is able to hold up in the face of it. In other words, he trusts his art, and he is very good at it.
Russell Schulz-Widmar : From a review of 'The Hymns and Ballads of Fred Pratt Green'

Another request for the same book was for a hymn that Christians and Jews could use when they worshipped together.

> Be it the Seventh Day or First
> We cherish and observe,
> As those who hunger still and thirst,
> And humbly seek to serve,
> God help us keep and use with care
> The precious heritage we share.
>
> *Fred Pratt Green: Verse 4 of 'A Hymn on the Sabbath' which begins 'God rested on the seventh Day'. The tune is O JESU*

...hymn singing has its dangers. A melody may drown the text; singing biblical truth may become a substitute for living it. It may become a drug. This explains the Puritan opposition to the arts, and to music in particular.

Fred Pratt Green in advice on a course of study on 'The Bible and Hymnody'

The Greens and Schulz-Widmars kept in touch, and when Russell and his wife Suzanne brought the sixty-five voices of the University United Methodist Choir to England in 1986 to sing in Westminster Abbey and at Wesley's Chapel in London, they travelled to perform in Norwich, too. When the Pratt Green Trust to assist hymnody was established, the choir sent an early donation with a greeting signed by all the members. Their donation was used to purchase a rare book for the Pratt Green Collection in the Library of the University of Durham.

The death of Erik Routley in 1982 was a blow to all lovers of hymnody.

> He was, of all of us, the most alive.
> He lived his life *allegro*, let us say,
> Even *con brio*; yet he could contrive,
> In his untiring and warm-hearted way,
> To play it *con amore*. To each friend
> He was most loyal, lovable, and kind;
> As author, teacher, his exciting mind
> Instructed us how wit and wisdom blend.
>
> His many gifts made debtors of us all:
> His love of hymnody, his dedication.
> But, as God's servant, was he apt to be,
> In giving of himself, too prodigal?
> Be sure of this: he needs no threnody;
> What he deserves of us is celebration.
>
> *Fred Pratt Green: 'In Memory of Erik Routley'*

Erik Routley

With Fred there's never a dull moment, and his concept of the hymn writer working with the potential user has been uniquely fruitful.

John Wilson interviewed by 'The Hymn', October 1982

Pratt Green, along with Fred Kaan and Brian Wren, were contributors to a memorial volume.

In his hymnwriting career, Fred has accepted numerous invitations to write texts for local occasions on both sides of the Atlantic. Besides those already mentioned, anniversaries of churches and institutions have been celebrated at Arlington Heights, Chicago (Illinois), Bristol New Room (Avon), Camelford (Cornwall), Denver (Colorado), Didsbury (Greater Manchester), La Porte (Indiana), New Orleans (Louisiana), Norfolk (Virginia), Princeton Theological Seminary (New Jersey), Sutton (London), and Walsall (West Midlands).

Saints celebrated include Boniface, the missionary to Germany when the 1300th anniversary of his birth was celebrated at Crediton, James the Great (for a church so dedicated in East Malling, Kent), Mark (for a patronal festival in South Norwood, London), Mary Magdalene, Ninian, (whose Priory church is at Whithorn on Scotland's Galloway coast,) and Peter the Apostle. Hannah Ball, an early pioneer in Sunday School work, should also be mentioned here.

Texts for use when church buildings, musical instruments and furnishings have been dedicated were especially written for use at Bowes Park (London), Bristol, East Finchley (London), and Richmond (Virginia). Fred gained a special affection for the Methodist Church at East Finchley, which he attended when visiting Bernard and Joan Braley; and its translation by Methodist architect Alan Bristow from Victorian church to flexible worship-centre appealed to his imagination. The text he wrote for the re-opening provided an interesting example of a hymn written for one specific purpose being used for another, when *What joy it is to worship here* was chosen for the American *Seventh Day Adventist Hymnbook*.

I have remained *a liberal Christian all my life*, though unhappy with all the labels, such as Christian Humanism, that would appear to cut one off from the acceptance of the great tradition. This is what I mean when I do adopt one label, with hestitation, and say that religiously I am *left of centre*...and at other times as *right of centre*. I have a strong feeling of belonging to the whole Church of Christ—and this surely has helped me to write hymns that ignore divides and stress Christian Unity and are sung by diverse denominations.

Fred Pratt Green

What joy it is to worship here,
And find ourselves at home,
Where God, who uses every gift,
Has room for all who come!
Yet are no two of us alike
Of all the human race,
And we must seek a common ground
If we would share his grace.

In partnership with all who work
To cure our social ills,
We bring to this community
Our own distinctive skills.
Though now we shut the city out,
Its tensions and despairs,
We, like our Master, care for it
And hold it in our prayers.

So God, each generation, gives
New meaning to his love:
His changing image changes us
And keeps us on the move
Towards the only kingdom where
All truths, all cultures, meet
And our unlikeness is his way
Of making heaven complete.

Fred Pratt Green: 'Partners' sung to TYROL (TYROLESE)

Mr & Mrs Schulz-Widmar

On each Thanksgiving Day
We name the name,
Our thoughts in disarray:
Thankful for what? we sadly say.

How often have we wept:
And yet, and yet
Through trials we have kept
Our hopes alive and have not
                              slept.

We follow One who wears
The crown of thorns,
Yet in his spirit bears
Our outward scars, our inward
                              fears.

Shake off despondency!
The past is past;
The present holds the key
To what, God blessing us, shall be.

No more need we defend
The dreams they dreamed
Who lived and died to end
The wrongs that shame our native
                              land.

On this Thanksgiving Day
We name the name
With honest hearts and pray
That right shall triumph, come
                              what may.

*Fred Pratt Green: 'Good shall
overcome: A Hymn for
Thanksgiving Day'. Pratt Green
was reaching towards a hymn
that could be sung not just by
American Indians but by all
Americans*

The year of Fred Pratt Green's eightieth birthday coincided with the publication of a new Hymn-Book for the Methodist Church entitled *Hymns and Psalms*. Twenty-seven of the author's texts were chosen. The 1980s indeed found his texts in use by Anglicans, Baptists, members of the Christian Reformed Church, the Church of Christ and the Church of Scotland, Congregationalists, Episcopalians, Lutherans, Mennonites, Mormons, Presbyterians, Roman Catholics, Seventh Day Adventists and members of the United Reformed Church. Besides Great Britain they have been printed, sometimes in translation, for use in Australia, Canada, Denmark, Finland, Hong Kong, New Zealand, Norway, South Africa, Sweden, Switzerland, the United States of America, and West Germany.

Most hymnwriters receive only small sums by way of royalties on their work. Because so many of Pratt Green's texts have been chosen for so wide a range of books, a few printing in hundreds of thousands, his potential income in this field is exceptional. Consequently he set up the Pratt Green Trust for the benefit of hymnody and church music, which will receive all the royalty income from his hymns for the duration of their copyright. The present trustees are the Reverend Alan Luff, the Reverend Brian Hoare, Methodist minister and hymnwriter, who provided the words and music of *Born in song!*, Mrs Carol Wakefield, Joint Managing Director of Stainer & Bell Limited, and Bernard Braley. Its funds have provided academic assistance by the establishment of the Pratt Green Collection of books on hymnody in the Library of the University of Durham and by enabling the library of the Methodist Church Music Society Library at Wesley College, Bristol, to be catalogued. Support has been given to the British Methodist Youth Choir, whose international tours have including a visit to the United States for which Pratt Green wrote *Praise the Lord for all pioneers* for the tune SONG OF PRAISE, originally written by T. Brian Coleman, one of the Music Editors of *Partners in Praise* for Pratt Green's opening text in that book, *There are songs for us all to sing*. The Trust has also provided bursaries towards the costs of attending workshops and conferences, funds towards the publication of the Bulletin of the Hymn Society of Great Britain and Ireland, easy to understand material about copyright for local churches and pump-priming funds to enable some publishing projects, difficult to justify in commercial terms, to get off the ground.

An unusual request to Pratt Green was for a hymn to overcome the difficulties American Indians have of singing traditional material on Thanksgiving Day. In view of their history and deprivation, for what are they to be thankful? Pratt Green replied that it was inappropriate for an Englishman to be asked for such a hymn, only to be reminded that it was the English who began the deprivation.

The Committee for the *United Methodist Hymnal* in America, besides selecting numerous Pratt Green texts for their book, also sought his help with scripts. They needed a metrical hymn translating or paraphrasing *Isaiah 55, 6-13*, a request not easily satisfied, and one which involved drafts passing backwards and forwards between the author and the committee. Pratt Green saw the final verse of *Seek the Lord who now is present* as a coda, which he prefers to be printed in italic type. They also sought two additional verses to be added to a single verse by John Troutbeck (from the German of Johann Rist), *Break forth, O pure celestial light*. The original seventeeth-century German hymn had eleven stanzas, and with the help of Friedrich Hofmann, Pratt Green obtained a literal translation which suggested the script for his supplement.

Another text included in the *United Methodist Hymnal* is a new paraphrase by Pratt Green of Joachim Neander's hymn, *All my hope is firmly grounded*. When John Wilson first suggested this task, Pratt Green wondered what was wrong with Robert Bridges' noble hymn *All my hope on God is founded*. When Pratt Green read a literal translation of the German, he discovered that Bridges' text should more properly be descibed as inspired by the author's original, rather than translated from it. Bridges' fine hymn, well worth singing in its own right, has a special emphasis on Beauty, one of his obsessions, whilst the original is concerned with God's providence.

In 1983 Maurice Checker, who had been a member of Pratt Green's congregation at Shirley, challenged him to provide new words for Claude Debussy's setting of *Noel des enfants qui n'ont plus de maisons* to replace its biting anti-German text. *Carol of the Homeless Children* rejects the notion of revenge for a better way.

Seek the Lord who now is present,
Pray to One who is at hand;
Let the wicked cease from sinning,
Evil-doers change their mind.

On the sinful God has pity;
Those returning he forgives.
That is what the Lord is saying
To a world that disbelieves:

'Judge me not by human standards!
As the vault of heaven soars
High above the earth, so higher
Are my thoughts and ways than yours.

See how rain and snow from heaven
Make earth blossom and bear fruit,
Giving you, before returning
Seed for sowing, bread to eat:

So my word returns not fruitless;
Does not from its labours cease
Till it has achieved my purpose
In a world of joy and peace.'

God is love! How close the prophet
To that vital gospel word!
In Isaiah's inspiration
It is Jesus we have heard!

All my hope is firmly grounded
  In our great and living Lord;
Who, whenever I most need him,
  Never fails to keep his word.
    Him I must
    Wholly trust,
God the ever good and just.

Tell me, who can trust our nature,
  Human, weak and insecure?
Which of all the airy castles
  Can the hurricane endure?
    Built on sand,
    Nought can stand,
By our eartly wisdom planned.

But in every time and season,
  Out of love's abundant store,
God sustains his whole creation,
  Fount of life for evermore.
    We who share
    Earth and air
Count on his unfailing care.

Thank, O thank, our great Creator,
  Through his only Son this day;
He alone, the heavenly Potter,
  Made us out of earth and clay.
    Quick to heed,
    Strong the deed,
He shall all his people feed.

Revenge? No! not revenge!
Hate cannot heal.
Noel! Noel!
Teach us your better way:
Help us to build a new world of justice and peace.

He was homeless when he came,
Born that night in Mary's womb:
Jesus! Jesus!
Born for us in Bethlehem.
To what a world he came, this little harmless boy!
Heavy the tramp of soldiers' feet, the beat of drum!
In search of him,
How many babes they would destroy!

Jesus, listen to us!
Is it true a Child shall lead the way?
O be our Prince of Peace, be our Lord of Glory!
Fred Pratt Green: Closing lines from 'Carol of the Homeless Children'

Tasting his salty sweat, he cries 'I thirst!'
His blood is spilt like wasted wine.
Who dies this way, they cry, *must be accursed*!

Forgive us, Lord, the times we do not heed
The simplest cry that springs from human need:
And by your dying teach us how to live.

    †   †   †   †   †   †

He hangs above the ultimate abyss,
For our sakes plunges into it.
Love makes no greater sacrifice than this.

Forgive us, Lord, our unredeemed despairs;
Forgive us if we doubted that God cares:
And by your dying teach us how to live.

    †   †   †   †   †   †

As pains kills pain, his tortured limbs are still;
A silence falls upon the hill.
He has accomplished all his Father's will.

Forgive us, Lord, what we have badly done;
That what you finished we have scarce begun:
And by your dying, teach us how to live.
Fred Pratt Green: Words inspired by the fourth, fifth and sixth sayings from the Cross in 'The Seven Words'

The following year Pratt Green's text based on Christ's sayings from the Cross was set by the talented American composer, John Carter, as a short cantata entitled *The Seven Words,* which quickly sold several thousand copies.

A significant impetus was given to Pratt Green's creativity when he was contacted by Ronald Watson, a Norwich Lecturer in Construction Management, who also was organist of a local Anglo-Catholic church, and a choral conductor. They quickly discovered a rapport and met regularly to work together. After experimenting with *A Sequence of Songs in Honour of Saint Valentine*, they worked on a sequence of eight hymns from Advent to Pentecost, of which the last verses are quoted:

These Advent days, with loving care
And childlike joy, let us prepare
Our waiting churches, hearts and homes,
To make him welcome when he comes.
He comes, our Saviour comes!
Fred Pratt Green: From 'Advent' of which the first line is 'How long, the prophets cried, how long?'. For KNARESBOROUGH'

On this Christmastide recall,
Shepherds, Wise Men, Christians all,
How we sought and found him, sought
                  him, found him,
Jesus Christ, the Lord of all.
Fred Pratt Green: From 'Christmas' of which the first line is 'Who is running up the street'. For THE THORNABY CAROL

Then Simeon sang *Nunc Dimittis*
And blessed our infant Lord;
And Anna spoke to all of this,
Of how God keeps his word
In him, the Prince of Peace.
Fred Pratt Green: From 'Epiphany' of which the first line is 'Now Simeon was an agéd man'. For BLYTH

Show us, Lord, by your example,
How to test the cunning pleas
By which Satan cannot trick us,
If we face him on our knees.
Fred Pratt Green: From 'Lent' of which the first line is 'Forty years the Chosen People'. For KIRKOSWALD

What to believe? We watch, we listen;
Blinded by love, we see
The inexplicable is simple—
You died for me!
Fred Pratt Green: From 'Good Friday' of which the first line is 'What have
you done to die in anguish'. For DRAYTON

Lord, we believe, like seeds that farmers sow,
Your peaceful Kingdom in the dark shall grow,
However hard the frost or deep the snow.
Then let us wake the world with praise
On these, our Easter days!
Fred Pratt Green: From 'Easter' of which the first line is 'Lord, we believe
for us you lived and died'. For PENWORTHAM

Lord, prosper the work you have given us to do,
For dark is the midnight the Light must shine through.
This day of Ascension Lord Christ lift us up,
Confirm our intention and strengthen our hope.
Fred Pratt Green: From 'Ascension' of which the first line is 'Three years
they had known him as Master and Lord'. For RESTORATION

Never must we forget
Each day is Pentecost,
When we, his Church, in faith proclaim
Salvation is in his Name.
Fred Pratt Green: From 'Pentecost' of which the first line is 'Never shall we
forget'. For ROSEBERRY

These two decades of hymnwriting left Pratt Green writing much less poetry. Two items appearing for the first time in the anthology *The Old Couple* published in 1976 were *Portrait of a Stoic* and *Accident* :

When grief shared the front page of his life
With an emergency meeting of the Directors
And the swarming of his bees, he took the bees,
Went up for the meeting, and buried his wife.

His directors put it down to a cold streak
In his nature, or to investments at stake,
Or an unhappy marriage. Actually, without
Intending to, he had acquired a technique.

How cool can you be? How hard can you get?
But the dust on the brim of his bowler-hat,
And a copy of *The Times* carelessly folded,
Betrayed that in fact he was very much upset.

Not being a clubman, and having few friends,
He took the train as usual to Leatherhead,
His face a mask. Only his bees detected,
In his handling of them, that a life ends

When a wife dies. Tomorrow his bowler-hat
Will be well-brushed, his copy of *The Times*
Folded immaculately. The noble Epictetus
Would not have asked more of him that that.
Fred Pratt Green: 'Portrait of a Stoic'

FOR RONALD WATSON'S
TUNE 'ROBY'

As darkness turns to light,
How shall we praise aright
The Sun of Righteousness,
Who ends our night?—

Who gives us one more day,
To stop, to think, to pray,
And, tired of wandering, find
In Christ the Way.

He teaches us to claim
Forgiveness in his name;
To make his way of life
Our daily aim.

To us, who have despaired,
It is as though he shared
That breakfast on the shore
Our Lord prepared.

All things are for our sake;
In Christ to give and take;
In Christ to live and die;
To sleep and wake.
Fred Pratt Green: 'A Hymn for
Laud'

As evening turns to night
Work done, we now unite
To worship One who is
Himself the Light.

So ends another day;
And even, as we pray
To God's eternal Son
Time will not stay.

Ashamed, we would confess
This day's unfaithfulness:
Time wasted, time misspent
Beyond redress:

And thankfully recall
Each known prevented fall;
How love has held us fast,
And shines through all.

All things are for our sake;
In Christ to give and take;
In Christ to live and die;
To sleep and wake.
Fred Pratt Green: 'A Hymn for
Compline'. Both items first
published in 'Hymns and
Congregational Songs', a peri-
odic publication of new texts

168

The clamour about sexist and racist language presents a different problem. Here we are dealing with more than linguistic changes. We are facing important issues of the Twentieth Century. While I think congregations have enough sense to know that *mankind* means *humanity* and *man* includes *woman*, I have to concede that sexist and racist prejudices exist within the Church. Here, it may be, we are in disagreement, as—coming clean—I cannot understand why women are excluded from the ministry of the Church today. I know the issue has shaken, if not split, the Episcopal Church; and is causing distress in the Church of England. To my own denomination it presents no problem at all.

Fred Pratt Green in a letter to David Pizarro in New York written in December 1986

May I say that it is hard for a poet—if I may claim to be this—to be a theologian. The theologian, rightly seeking to define as far as possible, even when backed with revelation, the indefinable, makes a bad partner with the poet, who trusts to intuition and the element of creativity in human experience.

Fred Pratt Green in a letter to S. Paul Schilling, American author of 'The Faith we sing'

The crash was so impersonal
It took crushed metal
To prove the human element
Fallible and mortal.

What was most incongruous
In the shock of crisis
Was that lights change colour
Though nothing crosses.

As slowly as the shaken town
Steadied, disappointed
Witnesses of a confrontation
Went off unwanted.

The rest was simply routine.
While a posse of police
Measured guilt and innocence
Without trace of malice,

We swapped names and addresses
For the usual purposes,
Thankful it wasn't a case
For coffins and hearses.

Fred Pratt Green: 'Accident'

The Poet and the Musician was first published in 1989. Described by Pratt Green as pastiche, it certainly shows a different view from that of Bridges on the relationship between author and composer. Here are the last four verses of twenty-one:

The Queen arose, a woman versed
In all the arts, her thin lips pursed
        To make offenders smart.
'Let us not bandy wasteful words—
Music or Poetry, my lords:
Which is the greater Art?

When so-called experts disagree,
You all, my lords, expect of me
        A firm and just decision.
Let Poetry and Music share
The world of beauty, as a pair
        And not in competition.

Go you, Musician, write a tune
To fit the Poet's words by noon
        Tomorrow—or by all
My ancestors I'll have you beat
From London Bridge to Watling Street!
        Make it a madrigal!

And let my choir be here to sing
At sundown what these artists bring
        To purge their jealousy.
Until that hour, let us be gone!
Music and Poetry are one—
        As all my folk must be!'

Fred Pratt Green: Closing Stanzas from 'The Poet and the Musician'

Poets in their later years are often called on to write party pieces for their friends and for societies to which they belong. Pratt Green wrote odes for the eightieth birthday of John Wilson, for the retirement of Reverend Brian Greet as Secretary of the Methodist Conference, and for the Golden Jubilees of the Methodist Church Music Society and the Hymn Society of Great Britain and Ireland. Perhaps the most delightful of these party pieces is an address to the members of the Hymns Subcommittee of the Hymnal Revision Committee of the United Methodist Church. It was carried by John Wilson to their meeting in Birmingham, Alabama, on 14th August 1985.

The Lord have mercy on you, gentlemen
(And you, dear ladies, I make haste to add):
For what's a Hymn? Come, tell us, why and when.
Some say a Hymn must be addressed to God.
Which means it must not be *about* him: so
Mine eyes have seen the glory has to go!
Cantate Domino!

How quickly language changes meaning, dates:
So Wesley's *motions* are a proper gaff!
Jehovah on his shining seat creates
In schoolboy circles an excuse to laugh;
Even *behest* is obsolescent: so,
The day Thou gavest, Lord, will have to go!
Cantate Domino!

From sexist language, Lord, deliver us;
As from the wrath of Woman when she's vexed;
To us, mere males, it matters not a cuss.
Let no one maul a long-accepted text.
A pity Whittier knew no better; so,
Dear Lord and Father of mankind must go
Cantate Domino!

Emotional excess must be avoided;
It turns religion, we are told, to dope;
Beware its side-effects as Marx and Freud did,
Preferring solid fact to sloppy hope.
Sentiment, yes! the sentimental, no!
Tell me the old, old story has to go!
Cantate Domino!

When choosing tunes a chill runs down the spine
(It's music makes nice people much less nice):
'Either AURELIA's out, or I resign!'
Printing too many tunes puts up the price;
Best keep the peace and leave the hymn out: so,
The Church's one foundation has to go!
Cantate Domino!

I do not doubt that a strong case has been made for the elimination of terms like *mankind* and *man*...But the objectors want to go much further than this. They are offended by *He* and *His* when used of God and by all those titles of Deity which presume his maleness, like *King*, *Lord*, and *Shepherd* and, most importantly of *Father*. I have already met these objections from an American editor, who suggests tortuous ways of getting rid of *He*, etc!
I wonder if the objectors realise that they will have to rewrite not only hymns but the Bible itself, and in particular the teaching of Jesus, for whom God is essentially *Father*. It may be that this attack on traditional ideas of God, together with other dissatis- factions about institutional religion, may lead to the final revolution which gives us, in whatever guise, a new religion. Such a new religion, sympathetic to non-Christian cultures, such as Buddhism, and philosophies, such as Vedanta, may be what the modern world needs. It would certainly mean the abandonment of the salvationist interpretation of the Gospel, to which Brian Wren would seem to cling!
At eighty I have ceased to be headstrong! I have seen so much abandoned in my lifetime that was once held to be sacred, or at least wise, in the end to no good purpose, rather to loss, I am reluctant to join the reformers, lest they prove themselves to be iconoclasts.

Fred Pratt Green, writing in his scrapbook, after pasting in an article by Brian Wren

When all is done, the critics will complain
You've left out all the hymns they wanted in;
And those who never go to church will rain
Abuse upon you, making such a din
Appreciation will be silenced: so
Why not let other suckers have a go?
Cantate Domino!

Fred Pratt Green: 'For Editors and Committees of a New Hymn Book'

It is the task and privilege of contemporary hymn-writers...to express for us new insights which prove ours is a living faith, a developing faith, a faith for to-day and tomorrow.

Fred Pratt Green in an article contributed to the 'Journal of Church Music'

Pratt Green was asked by the Chairman of the Lincoln District of the Methodist Church, the Reverend Alan Davies to write a text for an event in Lincoln Cathedral to mark the 250th anniversary of the conversion of John Wesley. It was later chosen for use throughout the British Connexion. The closing stanzas of the ballad are:

His Aldersgate experience
Assured him of salvation;
　　It set him free
　　In Christ to be
Apostle to our nation.
Unmoved by opposition,
Intent that none should perish
　　Through fire and flood,
　　For love of God,
He made the world his parish.

Met here, to do him honour,
We own the name he won us.
　　Our faith restored
　　We bless the Lord,
And feel his hand upon us.
Shall we, in times as urgent,
Rest easy with survival?
　　Bring us, though late,
　　To Aldersgate,
Renewed, Lord, for revival!

Fred Pratt Green: Closing stanzas of 'Aldersgate' which begins 'This day may God inspire us'. Sung to DELIVERANCE

...hymn writing has been more than a literary pursuit; it has been a very moving experience, a strengthening of faith, and a broadening of one's love for the People of God...There is no room in such an experience for pride—only for amazement and gratitude to the One who leads us where we do not want to go and to do the things we least expected.

From a letter from Fred Pratt Green to Harry Eskew, Professor of Music History and Hymnology, New Orleans Baptist Theological Seminary in December 1985

The singing of a text—any text—can be a magical experience ...

Fred Pratt Green in advice on a course of study on 'The Bible and Hymnody'

What a wonderful retirement it has been, not only in the work we enjoyed doing, but in touring holidays in Cornwall, the Lake District and Yorkshire, and even to the far north of Scotland. And all through these years my work as a hymn writer steadily developed and made ever greater demands upon me, until, except for holidays, I had little time for anything else.

Fred Pratt Green: 'On Retirement'

For Frederick Pratt Green, the world has unexpectedly become his retirement parish, with his ministry of hymnody reaching more persons than he ever reached in his busy and effective Circuit ministry. On Sunday, 6th November 1988, he pasted his last sheet in his fifty-first scrap-book. It ends:

It is time now, I feel, to finish the work I was given to do. This determination has grown stronger in recent months, as I have become more conscious of old age.

I am deeply grateful to all who have helped with with my writing; and most of all that in trying to express the truths of our Christian faith, I have found my own faith simplified, clarified, and confirmed.

It was not quite the end of Pratt Green's hymnwriting. Friends of Russell Schulz-Widmar asked him for a text with which to surprise Russell on a special occasion. Fred could not resist this invitation, and finding an old text on *The Sons of Asaph* he had discarded, was sparked off again to rewrite it and send it to Texas. Then in the spring of 1990, he was moved to respond to a request from a ministerial colleague to write a hymn for a memorial service for a baby entitled *So briefly in our Care* and beginning *Lord, Jesus, take this child*, to be sung to FRANCONIA.

Alongside Pratt Green's *Aldersgate* hymn, the British Methodists chose another of his texts to include in the Wesley celebrations. It reflects the theological emphasis evident at the time he began his hymwriting; yet, twenty years on, looks forward appropriately to the future of Christ's servant Church in the twenty-first and every century.

> The Church of Christ in every age
> Beset by change but Spirit led,
> Must claim and test its heritage
> And keep on rising from the dead.
>
> Across the world, across the street,
> The victims of injustice cry
> For shelter and for bread to eat,
> And never live until they die.
>
> Then let the servant Church arise,
> A caring Church that longs to be
> A partner in Christ's sacrifice,
> And clothed in Christ's humanity.
>
> For he alone, whose blood was shed,
> Can cure the fever in our blood,
> And teach us how to share our bread
> And feed the starving multitude.
>
> We have no mission but to serve
> In full obedience to our Lord:
> To care for all, without reserve,
> And spread the liberating Word.
> *Fred Pratt Green: 'The Caring Church'. Sung to HERONGATE and*
> *WAREHAM*

Late in 1990, the Greens moved to Cromwell House, and sought security in a Home for the Aged in Norwich. Very soon he felt that urge to write again which he thought he had lost for ever. Out of his new surroundings, *The Last Lap*, a sequence of verse on the theme of old age was born. Deservedly, it was quickly accepted for publication in 1991. The final item *A Death in the House* ends:

> A silence may say more than ritual words;
> a sense of gratitude may transcend grief,
> In death, as in life, we are the Lord's.

Lord Jesus, take this child,
So briefly in our care,
Into your own eternal world,
To breathe its purer air.

And as you shared their grief
Who mourned for Lazarus,
In our own time of sudden loss
Comfort and strengthen us.

Bless those who seek to heal
All kinds of human pain;
And grant we may not lose our
                              faith
Though mysteries remain.

As praying turns to praise,
Together we adore
The God who wipes away our
                              tears
And bids us grieve no more.
Fred Pratt Green:'So briefly in
our Care'

I suppose all hymn writers are interested in what happens to their hymns. They are like children who grow up and leave home and live their own lives.
Fred Pratt Green in a letter to Catherine Salika of G. I. A. Publications, Inc. in December 1985

I suppose the next generation even more than the present one, will realize what we owe to you.
Cyril Taylor on his 1982 Christmas card to Fred Pratt Green

INDEX OF PERSONS

The symbols I and II refer you to entries in the indexes of *Hymnwriters 1* and *Hymnwriters 2* respectively

INDEX OF PLACE NAMES

The symbols I and II refer you to entries in *Hymnwriters 1* and *Hymnwriters 2* respectively

GENERAL INDEX

The symbols I and II refer to entries in the indexes of *Hymnwriters 1* and *Hymnwriters 2* respectively

INDEX OF TUNES

This index lists tunes in the text; it does not claim to be a comprehensive list of all the tunes which particular words have been set. The symbols I and II indicate that the tune is also to be found in the corresponding index in *Hymnwriters 1* and *Hymnwriters 2* respectively